THE CRAFT OF CRIME

THE
CRAFT
OF
CRIME

Conversations with Crime Writers

JOHN C. CARR

Houghton Mifflin Company Boston
1983

Library of Congress Cataloging in Publication Data

Carr, John C., date
The craft of crime.

1. Authors—20th century—Interviews. 2. Detective
and mystery stories—Miscellanea. I. Title.
PN452.C29   1983   809.3′872 [B]   83-133
ISBN 0-395-33120-X
ISBN 0-395-33121-8 (pbk.)

Printed in the United States of America

S   10 9 8 7 6 5 4 3 2 1

THIS BOOK

is

dedicated

to

Patricia G. Sims

Barnes A. Carr

and to the memory of

James Legendre

Ignaramque manum spiritus intus agit.

—Andrew Marvell

ACKNOWLEDGMENTS

A book involving research and travel is impossible without all sorts of moral and logistical support. I want to thank Tom Hart and Laura Nash at Houghton Mifflin, Ivy Fischer-Stone at Fifi Oscard, Christian Garrison (whom I've known and loved for more than twenty years and who is beginning a brilliant career in detective fiction) and Aralee Strange (no slouch of a writer herself) — who gave me a base in New York — and George and Susan Garrett, whose praises I've sung in other places and who made everything north of Boston possible. What serious thinking I've done about detective fiction (and much more is left to be done) began during the old Wednesday Club meetings in the Garden District of New Orleans, where those of us who had no links with academe talked literature and drank gin. The presiding genius of those sessions was Jimmy Legendre, who I wish could have lived to read this book. My wife ran the kennel when I was gone and provided a great deal of the moral support, to say nothing of typing. And last but not least, this book would have remained merely a suggestion on an agent's desk if it had not been for the courtesy and patience of those who were interviewed and of their no doubt long-suffering families. They welcomed me into their kitchens and dining rooms, and porches and dens, or met me very early or very late at various spots in London, New York, or Boston. Many thanks to all.

CONTENTS

PREFACE

This book brings together conversations with thirteen practitioners — eight male and five female ("Emma Lathen" is, of course, the pen name of two women), seven American, four English, one South African, and one Dutch — of the novels of detection and pursuit, mystery, and police procedure. They are not formula writers, though they adhere to a form that has been in honorable use for a century. They are serious writers, and have been recognized as such by their peers, by reviewers, and by the large public that keeps their work in demand. Their subject matter — murder, corruption, and the subversion of the human heart — is serious indeed. They are serious writers because with them the people come first; in banks or in squad rooms, on houseboats in Amsterdam or on racecourses in England, people and their inner workings are always central.

What does the detective novel mean to those who write it? What are its conventions? How does it feel to work in this form and what are its rewards? The people interviewed here discuss these topics and others with clarity and passion, and talk about their lives with more than a little wisdom and modesty. I'll take clarity, passion, wisdom, and modesty any day.

ED McBAIN

To say that Ed McBain is a giant among popular writers is like saying the Colossus of Rhodes was a pretty fair piece of municipal sculpture. McBain (in real life, Evan Hunter, born Lombardino) has written about seventy-five novels and seven collections of short stories, three screenplays (including *The Birds*, for Alfred Hitchcock), three plays, and six juvenile books, and the well has not been capped yet. The books were published as by Evan Hunter, Ed McBain, Curt Cannon, Hunt Collins, Ezra Hannon, and Richard Marsten. McBain has been a cherished fixture of the detective fiction scene since the publication of *Cop Hater*, the first 87th Precinct mystery, in 1956. Movies have been based on his 87th Precinct novels and on *The Blackboard Jungle* (based on his experiences as a teacher), *Buddwing, Last Summer*, and *Strangers When We Meet*, for which he did the screenplay.

McBain, a hard-charging, amusing, sanguine man, was born in Manhattan on October 15, 1926, and was educated at Cooper Union, from 1943 to 1944, and at Hunter College, where he was elected to Phi Beta Kappa and received a B.A. in 1950. During the hiatus in his college career he served in the navy.

James McClure writes of the McBain novels in *Murder Ink*, in an essay entitled "Carella of the 87th," that some writers would not have known how to handle "cop corn," but that McBain "accepts things as they are; if the field that engrosses him is knee-high in clichés, so be it. In he goes, as eager and uncompromising as a child, to grasp the thistle that grows between the rows." The characters of the 87th Precinct, Steve Carella, Meyer Meyer (his father decided he would not have a "Christian" name), Cotton Hawes, Bert Kling, and Andy Parker, are memorable and original and, what's more important, they feel as comfy as old shoes.

McBain writes memorable fiction under the name Hunter, too, of course: *Love, Dad,* for instance, was one of the best novels of any genre of its year. *Streets of Gold,* told from the viewpoint of a blind man, is about the immigrants who came to America expecting to find streets paved with gold and in many ways found that the place was as advertised, if only metaphorically. *Last Summer* is an extremely sympathetic and arresting novel about kids growing up, and the movie made from it is an American classic.

Nor should one forget the Ed McBain novels written from the viewpoint of the criminal. *Guns* is mesmerizing: the central character is a pitch-perfect poem of amorality and yet touching in his own way.

Calypso centers around the detectives' attempt to solve the disappearance of a musician many years ago, the murder of another, and the enslavement of one human being by another. *Ghosts* is McBain's venture into the police supernatural. *Blood Relatives* opens with violence and confusion: a girl is slashed mercilessly in front of her cousin. But who did it? The cousin is also hurt. She couldn't have done it. Could she?

To say that McBain invented the police procedural is only technically inaccurate. There were others before him (after all, Sherlock himself is a sort of honorary copper), but the modern police procedural began with McBain, and its present practitioners can now be found not only in the United States and Great Britain but also in France, Scandinavia,

Japan, and, of course, South Africa. But his books have not been so successful and have not endured for so long merely because McBain is at the park every day, taking his turn at bat. His style is really the reason.

The young writer could do a lot worse than to study how extremely well tuned McBain's ear is and how dead right the tone always is. And McBain's language is, within the form of the police procedural, near poetic in the range of effects it is capable of achieving.

The world of the 87th Precinct is fascinating. Don't look for maps. Just hit the streets.

ED McBAIN: I was born right here on 120th Street, between First and Second avenues, October 15, 1926, on the kitchen table. My aunt Jennie was a midwife and she delivered me and referred to me for the rest of her life as "my baby." It wasn't a rough neighborhood. It was a ghetto, but there were no street gangs in those days as such. It was a very comfortable area to grow up in. We were poor, but it was very nice, and everybody was poor, so it didn't make any difference. Then I joined the navy, in 1944, just before my eighteenth birthday, to get out of going into the army. Anyone at that time who was drafted was being sent to Italy, to get their asses shot off. I was a radar man, striker, seaman first class radar instructor. I was in from November '44 to July '46. I got to see quite a bit of the United States and the Orient. We were in Pearl Harbor and then Japan. I saw a lot of Japan.

CARR: Did you like Japan?

McB: Oh, I loved it. And when I got out, I went to Hunter College. I had pretty much decided by the time I entered college that I wanted to be a writer, and I plunged ahead in that direction and took every writing course they had to offer. I started on the Bronx campus of Hunter, and I guess it was in my junior year when I went downtown to the building on Sixty-eighth Street — the Thousand-Window Bakery, we used to call it. I had a lot of writing instructors. The two who were most helpful to me were Compton Mendel and Professor Freeman. Mendel was just teaching a regular lit. course, an introductory course to something or other, but he got interested in my writing and would read a lot of my stories and criticize them. Then Professor Freeman at night taught a creative writing course. I was a day student, but I used to hang around at night and wait and catch him between class breaks — before and after his class — to talk to him.

C: Had you wanted even as a boy to write?

McB: No, I wanted to be a cartoonist. I went to art school. Before I went into the navy, I got a scholarship to the Art Students' League here in New York, and then I went to Cooper Union for a year. I was determined I wanted to do something in art. I started writing in the navy, really. I wrote one story — a detective story really, a madman story — about a guy who commits a murder, and it was sort of poetic and all of that. In fact, I'm getting together a collection of stories now, to be called *The McBain Brief*, and my typist just brought back five hundred pages or so of it today and she said that there was one story she really didn't like and it was that one, the first story I ever wrote, called "Chalk." But I wrote everything and just sent them off from the South Pacific, thinking they would take pity on a poor serviceman adrift. But they didn't. They didn't buy anything. But it was lively and interesting, and there was a guy aboard ship who'd been a philosophy instructor at the University of Wisconsin and he took an interest in my work and would criticize it: there's not much to do on a ship. Plus the war had ended and we were just playing games.

C: Then you taught high school.

McB: Very briefly.

C: And *The Blackboard Jungle* came out of that. The movie version was one of the first modern youth movies. Were you pleased with that?

McB: It was a pretty good movie. I don't think there was a line of dialogue in the movie that came from the book. But he stuck to the spirit of it, not the letter, and I thought it was a good movie. It still seems to hold up today, or at least when you see it on late night television.

The first 87th Precinct book was published in 1956. I'd done a couple of other mysteries before that, one published under the name Evan Hunter (*Don't Crowd Me*) about an honest citizen involved in a murder — murder piling down around him everywhere — and I did a lot of so-called procedurals for the then existing magazine *Manhunt*. So after *The Blackboard Jungle* was published, a man named Herb Alexander was the editor of Pocket Books and my agent submitted to him a mystery novel I had written. He submitted it under a pseudonym, but the editor caught something in the style and called my agent and said, "Is this our friend Hunter?" My agent said it was, and the editor said, "I didn't know he wrote mysteries" [laughs] and my agent said, "Yeah, he's written quite a few of them." I'd had a lot of short stories published, all types of short stories — mysteries, men-on-the-run, women-in-jeopardy, private-eye, suspense — you name it, I'd tried it. And so I had lunch with him one day, and the gist of the conversation was that Erle Stanley Gardner was getting old and Gardner was the mainstay of Pocket Books at that time. They just kept bringing them out, bringing out old ones with new jackets, and they sold constantly. They were looking for a replacement. They asked me if I had any ideas for a series character and I came up with a notion that I think was unique. There had been police novels written before, but I don't think there had ever been a police novel where there was a conglomerate lead character, where the entire squad room was the lead character, in fact. And the editor said, "Great. Let's go with it." They gave me a contract for three books. He said, "We'll see how it does," and it did well.

C: Did you get the Mystery Writers of America award in 1957?

McB: No. I never got an Edgar for anything; that's another piece of misinformation. As Hitchcock said when I was in his office one day, looking at all his framed awards on the wall — when I was writing *The Birds* for him — "Always a bridesmaid, never a bride." Because he never got the Academy Award, you know, and I think it was a sore point all his life. But no; I never got an Edgar. A lot of runner-up awards, though — scrolls, they call them. And you know what you do after you roll up a scroll . . .

C: You must have published a hundred books.

McB: Books? No; that can't be.

C: You've done two or three a year since you started out.

McB: Now, there are two McBains a year. No; I'm positive there are not — There are thirty-seven or so 87th Precinct mysteries and perhaps another dozen that are not 87th Precinct. And there are sixteen or seventeen Hunter novels. So that's sixty books, something like that.

C: That's a lot.

McB: Well, I work hard. I really do. Oh, not on weekends, but — I work from nine in the morning to five at night, sometimes six, sometimes seven.

C: Where do you get the emotional and physical stamina to do that?

McB: I enjoy it. I really do. Time just flies by. I look up and the day will be gone. My wife will sometimes call — she's a writer as well. She'll leave the office at three or four in the afternoon and she'll call over from the house at six, six-thirty, and she'll say, "Are you about to wind up there? Because I want to put dinner on." So I really just enjoy it so much and I can't imagine anything I would want to do more than write.

C: How did you choose the name McBain?

McB: When I finished the first of what would become the 87th Precinct series (it was called *Cop Hater*), I just walked out of there — I was living on Long Island at the time and I was working out of the bedroom of a very small development house — and I went into the kitchen. My former wife was feeding the twins or something, and I said, "How do you like McBain?" She said, "It sounds good." I said, "Ed McBain." And she said, "Good; that's good." It was really out of the blue. I think there may have been some unconscious association with poison: *bane*. But it sounded to me like the kind of name that would be associated with someone writing about cops; it sounds like a former cop or a police reporter. It just felt right to me.

C: One of the things people like about your work is that it is a series and there is a narrow focus, which is the 87th Precinct detective squad within this rather circumscribed area of the world's greatest city. But you've constantly done variations; you've never allowed it to go stale. It's never gotten entirely predictable, and there are books, like *Ghosts*, that come along that one couldn't have predicted would be found in the series.

McB: I don't know why I did that one.

C: It's great, though. I have it here, and this, I think, is one of the keys to what a great job you're doing: "They might have been ghosts themselves — the detectives who stood in the falling snow around the body of the woman on the sidewalk." In another place you compare a tree to someone "standing like a Napoleonic sentinel outside Moscow." There are echoes in your style that help it transcend what Americans have come to think of as "tough guy" writing.

McB: I think of myself as a softy. I think the 87th Precinct novels are very sentimental and the cops are idealistic guys still, although they're getting a little crotchety as time goes on and as the job wears on them. But I like to keep it fresh for myself, otherwise you're just typing. You're dealing with the same characters all the time in the same mythical city. To keep it fresh for me, I'll try things. I really don't care about mystery writing rules; I just don't. I learned them a long, long time ago and I feel I've earned the right to forget them if I want to. When I worked for Scott Meredith Literary Agency, we handled a lot of mystery writers and I knew what they were writing and what was selling. I talked to a great many editors every day of the week and I learned the rules. And then I wrote so many of them myself, trying different types of stories.

If I may interrupt myself, the reason I chose cops when they came to me to do the series is that there is always a suspension of disbelief involved when anyone but a bona fide cop is investigating a murder. Even in the Matthew Holt series I have to justify why there's a lawyer involved. It seems to me that the only valid people to deal with crime are policemen: you don't have to suspend your disbelief. In reality, if private eyes find a body, they'll call the cops. Private eyes are chasing after errant husbands. Insurance investigators rarely get involved in murder. Certainly little old ladies sitting in some British country house never get involved with murder. So there's always that stretch of the imagination, that leap you have to make to justify why anyone but a cop is involved in a murder.

But to get back to what I was saying earlier, to keep my own working day enjoyable I like to try other things and take certain risks. I know when I'm coming into a comic scene that I can write that with one hand behind my back. I always figure if it makes me laugh, it's going to make the reader laugh. I may be wrong, but ... So I like to take other risks where the writing won't be that sure, where I won't be that certain of myself as I go into it, and try to do something that will amuse me, make me happy.

C: You have the only ongoing villain since Conan Doyle's Professor Moriarty — the Deaf Man.

McB: He's very hard to write about, which is why he puts in appearances only every so often. When he appears, the police invariably behave like Keystone Kops, running all over the lot. He's only been in three: *The Heckler, Let's Hear It for the Deaf Man,* and *Fuzz.*

C: Which was an hysterical movie.

McB: Yeah, it wasn't bad. They took a lot of liberties with it. They concentrated more on the humor than on the story underneath it. And there were several scenes that worked. That interrogation when they're both in nuns' habits — that worked. It wasn't a bad movie, I guess. I always tend to be more critical of my own work than others are. I didn't even like *The Birds,* you know. I wrote the screenplay for *Fuzz* and *The Birds* and I didn't like either movie.

C: *The Birds* is still terrifying. In the scene in the bar a character says, or words to this effect, "Well, they're getting back at us for what we've done to them." That right there makes it intelligent.

McB: That's the best scene in the movie in terms of well-constructed dramatic scenes. You know you can always bring a bird in and scare somebody, but that was a very well constructed dramatic scene. That scene at the Tides Restaurant was almost like a one-act play.

C: How did you like working with Hitchcock?

McB: I loved it. I learned a lot from him.

C: Did he work from story boards or just get out there every day and figure it out?

McB: We would talk over the screenplay every day. When he called me, he said he wanted to get rid of the Daphne du Maurier novella entirely, except for the notion of birds for no reason turning on people. So we sat down. I had some ideas. He had some ideas. We got rid of all those in the first two days and then we started from scratch. We would talk it over all day — no notes or anything, just talk it. We'd go out at the end of the day and tell Peggy Robinson, his assistant, what we had done, as if we were going home to Mom after school. The next day we'd come in and I'd summarize where we were to date. I'd just tell the story from the beginning and then we'd go from there onto the next thing. And when we finished our discussions, we wrote the screenplay.

In a lot of the screenplays you do nowadays you don't call any shots, especially when you're working for television, where you have to get in and get out of a scene very rapidly. In three pages you're in and out; you haven't got time to do all your angles and your shots, but Hitch wanted every shot in the movie called.

It was on the page. Then a story board came in. After that the art director would do the story board. But he had a lot of trouble with *The Birds*. He didn't know what he was bargaining for with this movie because he had a lot of trouble with the birds. Some of them were real, some were animated, some were puppets. One of the scariest scenes in the film is when Rod Taylor is trying to board up one of the windows and a bird comes in and starts pecking at his hand. That was a puppet, a hand puppet. The scene that no one ever asks about — they just take it for granted, I guess — is the scene where the gas station is burning and you see a flock of gulls up there, and all of a sudden they start peeling off like fighter planes, as if someone had said, "Now, go." No one ever asked about that scene. I guess they thought Hitch was up there in a helicopter saying, "All right, now." But that whole thing was animated. They had a shot of the thing burning and the animators put in the birds swooping down from the sky. And that's the only scene in the movie that lets you attribute some sort of intelligence to the birds, as if they had knowledge of what they were doing. That made it scary, because they're just flying above and then they peel off and dive.

C: I saw an interview with you years ago and if I'm not mistaken you said you read more nonfiction now than fiction.

McB: No, I've never really liked to read nonfiction. I read nonfiction only for research. I don't normally read nonfiction for pleasure.

C: Do you read fiction for pleasure?

McB: I read fiction, but not mysteries.

C: Who do you like to read?

McB: John Fowles, William Styron, Dick Francis, Joseph

Wambaugh, Irwin Shaw. I try to read whatever is around that is getting some interest. *The White Hotel*, by D. M. Thomas, I read recently and loved it. I try to see what other guys are doing and sometimes I can learn from them, but more often not. I get bored and just put it aside.

C: Is there a kind of constant learning process on your part, even though you're a master of your craft and have all these books behind you?

McB: I know that when I get excited by something, it inspires me then to move on. It can be a play or a book or a movie. If I get excited by it, it then inspires me to go home and write something. If I get fifty pages into a novel by somebody and I know the guy is just fumbling around and doesn't know what he's doing, then I'll just put it aside. My wife will read anything she opens from cover to cover, and I can't understand how she does that, but she does it.

C: I'm sort of puritanical about that too, although I picked up a detective novel recently and the first scene showed the cops exhuming a skeleton from a hidden and anonymous grave, meaning there'd been a murder et cetera. As they lifted the fibula and tibia out, the author described these as "the calf," which is a part of the body corporeal, or a muscle. I just put it down.

McB: So you know there is a right way of doing things and a wrong way. You either know what you're doing or you don't.

C: What do you look for among people who don't know what they're doing? What would indicate a person really doesn't know how to write a novel?

McB: When you start reading a novel and from page 1 you know the lead character is unsympathetic, and he's not *deliberately* unsympathetic, and you think, "Why am I going to spend four hundred pages with this guy?" There are novels, like *King Rat,* for example, where the guy is deliberately unsympathetic. But this character is not deliberately unsympathetic; the writer is just sitting down and writing a character who is unsympathetic, maybe because he as a man, or whoever is writing the book, is himself unsympathetic, I don't know. Or you see where the writer himself has had second thoughts about what he's forcing his characters to do and will begin commenting on it, with something like " 'Oh, what a silly thing that was to say,' Jane said." So then you know that the writer thought it was a silly thing for her to say and he shouldn't have had her say it. He should've stricken it out. In so many you can see a plot development coming in from forty pages ahead. You know the guy is just handling it clumsily and you figure, "Well, what am I bothering with this for?"

C: Do some of these guys get better? Have you followed the careers of other writers who have kind of gotten better as they've gotten older?

McB: Some of them know instinctively what they're doing from the start, like Wambaugh, who knew what he was doing from go. I reviewed his first novel, *The New Centurions*, for *Life* magazine years ago, and it was crude and he was unpolished, but he knew what he was doing. He had an instinctive sense for where he was going and how he was developing characters, which has evolved into a very polished sort of art. The characters still sound crude, but there's a very polished style there now; it's the real development of a writer. You know, he started as a cop who writes, but now he's a writer who happens to write about cops. He's really good, and there's your case of a man who's developed over the years.

C: Your preference, though, is for realism in that you say the police should handle crime rather than someone's granny.

McB: When I was doing private eye stuff years and years ago, it was obligatory in the genre to have the private eye in conflict with the cops. The cops were always getting in the way of the private eye solving the case, instead of his being in their way. It was kind of reversed. And it was obligatory.

C: Isn't that convention still around?

McB: In private eye novels. I don't read private eye novels anymore.

C: You prefer police procedurals?

McB: Yeah. But I don't read police procedurals either, because, immodestly, I feel that there is no other writer of police procedurals in the world from whom I can learn anything, and in fact they all learn a lot from me.

C: Some of them have said that.

McB: So there's no real sense in reading them. That's like Michelangelo watching an apprentice paint in the white of an eye. I hate to sound that way, but it's true.

C: Did you actually hang around, or at least visit, some NYPD precinct rooms when you first started?

McB: In New York? Oh sure, yeah, everything, the courts, the labs, the line-ups. They used to have line-ups here in New York City years ago — not for identification, just roll call kinds of things for the guys they had nabbed during the night, the felony offenders. They used to parade them before all the detectives. You drew line-up duty as a routine thing once every two weeks, something like that. Cops from all over the city would come in to headquarters. I went to those and talked to parole officers. I tried to get a whole overview of the entire setup, from riding with the cops in the street, from the minute the arrest is made, to the mugging and booking. They don't do that anymore; then, the mugging and booking and printing would be done the next morning and then they would go into court. I tried to follow the whole process and then, coincidentally, because I began to be known as someone who wrote about cops, whenever a cop thing or a crime-related thing came along for television or something, they would offer it to me. I spent time at San Quentin for a prison series that never got off the ground. I spent time in Houston, with the Houston police, for a series about them that never got off the ground — tough cops; tough city, too. Then I was doing a half-hour television series, called "Emergency 911," about the cops in New York, so I read the emergency cops and I keep getting input all the time.

C: You've visited the Houston and New Orleans and New York police departments. Are they different?

McB: They're essentially the same. Their communication systems are the same. They're all on the SPRINT computer. They all have a central dispatcher and the radio calls will differ only slightly. In New Orleans, the radio calls are by the number of the felony in the criminal code. It's different in New York and other cities. I think in Houston they just call out what it is — robbery or homicide. So the radio calls would differ, but the system is pretty much the same. The cop mentality is the same in most cities.

C: Although I might say the New York Police Department has a better reputation than most. Did they tell you in New Orleans about the Algiers shootings?

McB: Yeah, that was a big thing. But New York has had its shakedowns too — the French Connection theft and the Serpico affair. The thing about cops everywhere is that they're overworked and underpaid and usually understaffed. In New Orleans their full complement should be fifteen hundred cops and they've got nine hundred. The salary for a detective there is twelve hundred bucks a month.

C: From the viewpoint of an extremely well informed layman, has police work changed in the last thirty-five years?

McB: Only in that the scientific techniques are greater, and, of course, communication is greater and record keeping is greater because it's all computerized now. If they get a call from Twelfth and Broadway or whatever, they just flash that and they do a twenty-four-hour scan on the computer, a six-hour scan, and a four-hour scan, and they know if it's been reported before, if it's been cleared, if it's a new incident, and they can dispatch cars immediately. You used to have to call your local station house and they would get on the pipe and see who was busy. Now they know exactly where every car is at every minute, so the response is quicker.

C: How do you react to the criticism that the cops in the 87th Precinct are a little too humane and liberal?

McB: There are rotten cops in there. Andy Parker is a rotten cop. Genero is a stupid cop. Cotton is a man about town.

C: Falling into bed with material witnesses, et cetera.

McB: And there's Fat Ollie Weeks; he's not in the 87th, but he's spent a lot of time there and he's a real bigot. And he smells bad. No, I think there's a good mix. I once killed off a bad apple in the precinct — Roger Haviland. I killed him off and I recognized almost at once that I had to resurrect him, and I did, in the guise of Andy Parker.

C: When people talk about serious novels versus genre novels, does that make you mad?

McB: I consider the 87th Precinct novels very serious stuff.

C: What would your definition of "serious" be: that it was seriously done and/or seriously perceived?

McB: "Serious" means well intentioned. When critics say that such-and-such is a serious novel, they mean something with an important theme, I would guess.

C: One of the great important themes?

McB: Yes.

C: But wouldn't it be truer to say — I'm not trying to put words in your mouth — that if you do it seriously and do it hard and write it as well as you can, that it's just as serious as it can be?

McB: Yes. I've written comic novels that I thought were very serious. Dealing with comedy is a very serious job. But I consider the 87th Precinct a continuing novel about crime and punishment in our times, and each separate novel is like a chapter in a long, long novel and I'll finish when I die. What can be more serious than dealing with life and death? You know, any serious, any good novel should be a mystery. You should consider what is going to happen next and how this is going to unravel, or whether it's going to unravel, and whether that makes it a serious novel or not, I really don't know. I write what they consider serious novels as Evan

Hunter, so I don't have to worry about the reception of the 87th Precinct novels. It's a great relief, as a matter of fact, to come home to the 87th Precinct every time. You don't *have* to be serious.

C: You don't have to introduce Great Themes of Western Man?

McB: No. There's enough of a theme going when you find a guy dead on the floor with an ax in his head.

C: What, in your opinion, are the ingredients for a successful popular detective or police procedural novel? What have you found works for you? There must be some 87th Precinct novels that don't do as well commercially as others. What were you able to surmise about that?

McB: I really don't know. I think from the letters I get from readers, they are really more involved with the characters than with the mystery aspects. They expect there will be a crime and that it will be solved, and the crime is usually a murder. I've dealt with arson, armed robbery, bank holdups where murder comes in as a side element, but it's usually a dead body. And they expect that that part of it will be correct — that you know how to write a mystery and that all the clues will fall into place and everything will be right if they want to go back and check it later on. But they're more interested in the people in the books. They have — with the 87th Precinct, anyway — identified very strongly with these cops and their home lives and their problems. I'll get letters from women saying, "Will that poor boy, Bert Kling, ever find happiness?" With a woman, or I certainly hope so. When they read *Ghosts* I got some letters saying, "Hmm, a likely story. Didn't know whether she was real or not in his room that night and he *did* kiss her and I hope that's the end of that. No more of that from Steve Carella; let common whores do that sort of fooling around."

C: And he *was* fooling around at the moment.

McB: He was, as a matter of fact. But they really get involved with these characters. They behave almost as if they're real. And it's strange.

C: I just finished *Love, Dad*, which I liked a lot.

McB: Thank you.

C: What was a major theme in *Love, Dad*, and treated as the thing that mattered most — the man's struggle to leave his wife *and* keep his child, who calls his mistress-then-wife Goldilocks — is treated in a minor key in *Goldilocks*.

McB: Very often I'll explore something in one way and then the other. I'll sometimes explore it in a mystery and then it will seem to me a theme that requires larger treatment, so I'll do it in a straight novel, or sometimes the reverse will happen. I wrote a book called *Buddwing*, which is a so-called serious novel, whatever that may be, and then I wrote the criminal side of *Buddwing* in *He Who Hesitates*, an 87th Precinct where the guy is wandering the city: variations on a theme, like a five-finger exercise, warming up for the difficult ones.

C: One of the themes that comes up in your work a lot is leaving your wife or having that relationship threatened.

McB: Only recently. Only since I left my wife. Only since 1970. Up until then, people didn't leave their wives in my books; they were unfaithful to their wives, they were arguing with their wives, but they didn't leave them. But that's a major American theme these days — divorce.

C: I have heard it said that the four great American themes are leaving your wife, making money, sex, and violence.

McB: Who was it who said — some woman writer — there are only two things worth writing about: love and money?

C: I hate to keep throwing up the term "popular fiction" — I really can't justify that term — but is it true that in popular fiction you rely a great deal on archetypes? Carella is the honest man and Cotton Hawes is the libidinous man and Meyer the theological man.

McB: In a series, I think so. When I started out to write this, I conceived of the squad as a conglomerate hero; so instead of giving one man all these traits, I put the traits in a group of men so that when they come together they form one man. A friend of mine and I once had an idea for a comedy series for television (nothing to do with cops), and we contacted Mel Brooks to see if he would want to write the pilot because he's had more experience, obviously, with comedy than I've had. He said something about a successful continuing series on television that might apply to a successful series of novels. He said that any successful series is about a family in a house. He said the house can be a real house with a real family in it, or it can be a hospital and the family is then the doctors and nurses, or it can be a police station. You think of the lieutenant as the father and Carella as the older brother and Kling as the younger brother and Fat Ollie Weeks coming in as a visiting cousin, the black sheep.

C: How have detective novels grown and developed since you've been writing?

McB: I think in depth of characterization; although if you look back at Raymond Chandler, his characters certainly had a lot of depth. The way it has evolved from the pulp fiction it used to be dictates that the mystery must be there and must be solved, but I think there's a greater depth of characterization and I think the characters are emerging more as well-rounded human beings, moving more toward "Qual. Lit." Very often in qual. lit. the characters are all there, but there's no story. But detective fiction is moving more toward that and away from the puzzle type mystery that Agatha Christie used to write, where all the characters are just ciphers to move around. They really had no depth at all except for the lead, perhaps.

C: English novels were very plotty. John Dickson Carr, although his father was a Pennsylvania congressman and he went to Hill School about the time John O'Hara was growing up a block or two away, was of that school and he could always think of a zowie plot.

McB: He was very good.

C: What's the difference *now* between English and American mystery writing?

McB: I don't know. John Creasey was writing police procedurals, the Inspector Gideon series. They were all set in London and in Scotland Yard, but they had a distinctly American flair to them, I thought. I don't know; I'm really not an expert on mystery stories.

C: Did you learn anything from Hammett and Chandler?

McB: Sure. I read all of theirs before I started writing. I also read Ngaio Marsh and Agatha Christie when I was first beginning, but I decided that was not the kind of mystery I would choose to write. I don't think I would know how.

C: Had anyone done police procedurals before you?

McB: There were some before, and there were some books that had all the documents in them. I found those fascinating. I still use documents. I think the reader likes to see those and I like to do them. One of the first editors who worked on this series said that the thing he liked about the 87th Precinct was that it had a tone of clinical verity. That doesn't mean reality; it means a semblance of reality, an illusion of reality. If you can get that illusion in, that there are really cops and this is the way cops really work and this is what it's like, folks, then I think you've accomplished something.

C: Hasn't it been true since Defoe that people read novels to find out how the world is? Even from the beginning there was the didactic element. Mary McCarthy says somewhere that in *Anna Karenina* there is at least the part that teaches you how to make strawberry jam.

McB: The novel is sort of a running commentary on our times, an attempt to illuminate those times, to filter it through your sensibility and imagination and illuminate it for someone else, if you're successful. For me what's important is that things be the way they really are when I'm writing about them, or at least the way they are in the mythical city I write about. That's the way it is. And I've been in enough cities with enough cops to know that's the way it is, although slightly askew to suit my needs. I don't know how much importance that has for the reader, who doesn't know how cops work, and for all he knows I may be lying. So I don't know how important it is, except that in the context of the books I think they have to trust that this is real, or they won't believe anything. They've got to believe this is the way it is, that when there's a body on the sidewalk, this is how the cops handle it.

C: And look at it.

McB: And talk about it and take pictures of it; this is the way we do it.

C: This may be a niggling point, but I've always wondered about it. Why Isola instead of New York?

McB: When I started writing the first book, I found I was on the phone with the cops every ten minutes to check something. I knew I had to write three books and I thought, "This is going to be a real headache; I'm going to be spending more time talking to the cops than writing the books." And I said, "I'm going to make this an imaginary city," which I felt was also a unique contribution to police fiction.

C: Is Isola just New York tilted east and west?

McB: Not really. I invent communities that don't exist and historical facts about those communities.

C: I love the historical facts, which are all obviously manufactured.

McB: They're all baloney, but I have so much fun doing those — figuring out how communities got their names, where the British were in the Revolution — and they're all lies.

C: What would you tell a young person today who —

McB: Tell him to practice his forehand and his backhand.

C: No, not that.

McB: Forget about writing.

C: Suppose they were just crazy and wanted to do it anyway. What would you tell them? Especially if they wanted to write mysteries and not particularly police procedurals?

McB: First, I would tell him or her to read what's been written so that they know the field and what they're up against and how a mystery has to be constructed, because there are rules and you can't abandon the rules until you know them. That's the same with anything. And then I would tell them to put themselves in the chair and put their hands on the typewriter keys and begin writing.

C: Do you think the field is overcrowded now?

McB: I don't think so. I think there'll always be mysteries as long as there are people who read books. I don't know what will happen with the Western genre. It's gone now; whether it will come back, I really don't know. I don't know what will happen with science fiction. We live more and more in a science-fiction world, so that may disappear from the stands entirely. But our world is becoming increasingly violent. We're historically a violent nation. I think people think a lot about death and crime and I think they derive some sort of satisfaction in reading a book in which, at the end, everything is set in order again and you can relax for a while.

C: The detective novel in that sense serves an almost theological function.

McB: I think it reconfirms our faith that a society of laws can work.

C: Joan Kahn said once in an interview in *Publishers Weekly* that it was only the industrial Western nations and Japan who write and read detective fiction.

McB: The 87th Precinct books are very popular in Japan. In fact, they made a television series, twenty-six hours of it, based on four or five 87th Precinct novels. One of the best films ever made of the 87th Precinct books was made by Kurosawa, based on *King's Ransom*. It was called *High and Low* and starred Japanese actors, including Toshiro Mifune, and was set in Yokohama and was a good, good movie.

C: You don't make any secret of your political preferences in any of these novels. That's supposed to be against the rules, but you've done it.

McB: I get a lot of letters from gun freaks who say, "How come you're always yelling about gun control?" That's what cops say about gun control. I only repeat what cops say. They don't like guns in the hands of the citizens. Are you talking about *Hail to the Chief*?

C: Yes. There's also a mention of Nixon in *Ghosts*.

McB: I was railing against him for a long time before he finally toppled. I had nothing to do with it, but I'd like to feel I did.

C: A good police procedural could be made out of that whole Watergate thing. I take it that you and the Mystery Writers of America are not exactly on buddy-buddy terms; in the preface to *Hail, Hail, the Gang's All Here* you lobby for ten different Edgars for this one book and it was kind of a slam.

McB: That was a little inside joke. I don't belong to the MWA. I once wrote a story called "The Last Spin," about two guys from rival gangs sitting in a basement. They had been chosen by their gangs to settle the dispute by playing Russian roulette. It's a short, short story — not a short short but a regular short, five thousand words or so. During the course of the half-hour or so they spend in the basement twirling the cylinder and clicking the gun, they discover that they have more in common with each other than they have in common with any of their respective gang members. The sad part of the story is that at the end one of them says, "Go on; this is the last spin, fuck 'em, we'll get out of here." The other guy puts the gun to his own head and blows his brains out. The story was bought for television in the year that it was published. It was published in *Manhunt*, and it was also up for an Edgar that year. I was riding in a taxicab in New York City with one of the judges — there were three judges on the committee — and he said, "You know, far and away the best short story we've read is 'The Last Spin.' " And I said, "Great." "But," he said, "we're not giving you the Edgar." And I said, "Why not?" He said, "Because you've already sold the television rights to it and we think if we give the Edgar to X, it might help him sell his stories." I said, "Oh. Is that the way prizes are given?" And I quit the Mystery Writers of America the next day.

JAMES McCLURE

James Howe McClure was born in Johannesburg, South
Africa, on October 9, 1939. His father was an officer in the
Seaforth Highlanders and served in G–2 (Intelligence), the
General Staff of the South African Army during World War
II; he is the model for the irascible but charming old retired
military man in McClure's thriller *Rogue Eagle*. The senior
McClure no doubt witnessed the pro-Nazi revolt in Johannesburg, which is described in that novel. James McClure
lives in Headington, the site of a famous public school, and
now an extension of Oxford. He was deputy editor of the
Oxford Times Group until 1975, when, after publishing his
first four novels, he quit to write novels and take an active
part in raising his two sons and his daughter, born to him
and Lorelee Ellis, whom he married in 1962. U.S. fans of
McClure will note with approval that she was born in Ohio.

McClure was educated at Scottsville School (1947–1951),
at Cowan House (1952–1954), and at Maritzburg College
(1955–1958), all in Pietermaritzburg, Natal Province, which
served as the model for Trekkersburg. He has been a newspaperman in South Africa, Scotland, and England and the reporter in *The Steam Pig* is probably a portrait of McClure
himself.

McClure's work has a scope well beyond that of other police procedurals. He has created a universe revolving around Trekkersburg, Natal, South Africa, and its two best cops, one a Zulu and the other an Afrikaner, that has had 'em beggin' for more since his shattering first novel, *The Steam Pig*, appeared in 1971. He deals with modern, fragmented, potentially explosive South Africa, a beautiful country caught up in its own ugly contradictions.

The Afrikaner soul is revealed as a banal, horrifyingly dull thing, by and large. The villain of *The Sunday Hangman* was tortured by a guilt that he could expiate only by hanging those who, he believed, deserved to die for crimes they had committed, including one policeman. The villain's guilt results from a moment of illicit sexual passion and one of the consequences of the man's guilt has been the sexual derangement of another human being, his daughter. Sex is the theme of *The Steam Pig* — sex as revenge for the victim's having been reclassified as Colored after a lifetime of living as white; her death is a direct result of the effect of frustration, not of sex but of love, upon her family and her relatives. *The Steam Pig* is a horrifying look at how apartheid has ruined the lives of one and all. The images that linger after a first reading of the McClure novels are the beggars who can come into white towns from the homelands while able-bodied men cannot; the gangsters; people slid under the beds in hospitals because there is no room in the Colored wards. The white ticket agent wallowing in drunken anguish in his cell because they have arrested him for loving a Zulu woman is a metaphor for South Africa that reverberates in the mind. Yet, even in the face of all this, McClure does not raise his voice, nor does he preach.

The protagonists are Lieutenant Tromp Kramer of the Murder and Robbery Squad and his "boy," Bantu Detective Mickey Zondi, who dresses and walks like Frank Sinatra and acts as Kramer's Dr. Watson. Through Kramer and Zondi, McClure is able to take us anywhere he wants to in South Africa.

McClure's novels reveal a bond of brotherhood between a Zulu and an Afrikaner on the Trekkersburg police force; but Tromp Kramer must keep his true feelings for Mickey Zondi as buried as a spy must keep his true allegiance, and thus we are spies inside the mind of a country that must be written about, as McClure says, as if it were science fiction.

His models are obvious, and admitted: Ed McBain and John D. MacDonald; but like all good writers his work is inimitable. A lot of it is screamingly funny, like the openings of *The Steam Pig* and *The Caterpillar Cop*. All of it is compressed, vivid, irresistibly plotted and paced, and searingly memorable. His greatness has already been recognized in Britain, where he was awarded the Gold Dagger in 1971 and the Silver Dagger in 1976 by the Crime Writers' Association.

McCLURE: The day I quit school I started work: I took the graduation photographs. My ambition at that time was to be a photojournalist. It was very much the heyday of photojournalism. *Life* was still going and big agencies like Black Star in Paris were selling photographs. I used to paint. Then photography came into my life and I worked very hard on that. I'd had quite a lot of success with photography and then I met a writer named Tom Sharpe. He was a teacher and very much older than I, but he was doing photojournalism as well — that was what he was interested in. So I worked for a commercial photographer for about a year. Then I was going to go to England, to a proper photographic school, but I couldn't afford it. *Then* I worked for Tom Sharpe. We did a lot of stuff on black townships. I didn't publish any, but he got something in *Life*. All that was too chaotic, so I went back to the same prep school.

CARR: You taught there for a while and then you spent '63–'64 with the *Natal Witness* and '64–'65 with the *Natal Mercury* and '65 with the *Daily News,* all in Pietermaritzburg. Was the last one the big step up?

McC: The big step up was from the *Natal Witness*, which is a paper just looking after Pietermaritzburg, to the two province-wide papers, the *Mercury* and the *Daily News*. The only national papers in South Africa are the Sunday papers. So the *Witness* was just a small town paper, essentially, but it's a place where many writers and other people have come from, including Edgar Wallace.

C: Was he South African?

McC: No. I don't think so, but he worked on the *Witness*. And Ryder Haggard's house was around the corner from the paper. On the papers I did pictures and copy, but I specialized in crime. I was fascinated with that side of it and it gave me a sort of in. I did a lot of court reporting — Supreme Court, Magistrate's Court — and I was sort of number two in the *Daily News* bureau. Durban is the port — it's a very big port — and that's where these big newspapers were, but we were the capital. Their head offices were where the papers were printed, but Pietermaritzburg had the provincial consulate, which is like a state legislature, where the Supreme Court sat and where all that kind of action took place, so we had to have a bureau there to cover all that kind of stuff.

C: There's a wonderful characterization of Durban in *The Steam Pig*: the city is a whore lying with her legs open to the sea.

McC: You've just touched on something there. That was my first published writing — poetry — and that image of Durban comes from one of the poems. The first nonfiction I had published was a magazine article about a Zulu sculptor, in Afrikaans, which is ironic: I failed to get my university matriculation because I failed the test in Afrikaans. You had to pass four subjects, English, Afrikaans, math, and science, and I failed Afrikaans. When I was working as a teacher I thought, "Well, I might as well get this thing." So I went and had a bit of private tuition. I wrote quite a lot of poetry that was quite well regarded. A few poems were nearly published in England. I've still got a letter from them on that; it wasn't published finally because the house stopped publishing poetry altogether. I incorporate quite a lot of the poetry into the fiction.

C: Everyone regards your work highly because it's so literate. Do you still at least read a lot of poetry?

McC: No, I don't. I'm a real slob. My interest has only recently been revived because Kirstie, my daughter, likes poetry and the other night I was taking her through all the stuff that I liked. When I was writing, it was the time of Gregory Corso and the Beat poets. I didn't write very much like them and I always remember what Steinbeck or someone said when he was asked what he thought of that bunch of poets; after a long pause he said he thought it was awfully good typewriting. I kind of understood what he meant. They published some of my poems in the University of Natal poetry journal and even had an evening when it was discussed. I came away marveling that I'd written such stuff. They made it a lot better than it was.

C: Tell me about the move.

McC: Well, I just worked my butt off and finally we left South Africa.

C: Why did you leave?

McC: You see, the thing is, I'm not an intellectual; I'm a gut reaction type and I find it difficult sometimes to explain what I mean. I'm always caught up in the complexity of things. I left South Africa for two reasons. One, I had a son, James, and I was convinced that anybody who grew up in that environment grew up neurotic because his feelings were legislated and divided. It was a curious world, and I couldn't justify it to a child because children don't accept the answer that it's a curious world. If the son of my parents' servant played with my children in the garden, that was one thing; but if we went to the beach, that black child couldn't come on the same beach. Now how can you explain that to a child? The kid calls the bluff. The second thing was, I believed it was a place you could live only if you took sides. So finally we left South Africa — Lorelee and I and James. We had eighty pounds, that's all. No job, nowhere to go. We went straight to Scotland and nearly all the money went the first week. I didn't have a job. I've never been so scared in my life because all my life I'd lived in my home town, been known, had an identity, and moved from job to job. I'd just been very lucky. I always landed, to use a South African phrase, "with my bun in the butter." I was doing O.K.

I got a job on the Edinburgh *Daily Mail*. This was 1965. That was very lucky — the fact that I got a job at all — and it was kind of scary. You move into a totally new country and you're a subeditor; you are deciding whether things are right or wrong and you've only been there a week. It was kind of scary, but as the tension of that dropped a little, I got seven quid and I bought a very beat-up government type-writer — surplus — and started writing short stories. I chucked that, moved here, and incurred another trauma working on the paper here. We had to move because we were having another child and nobody would have us — we were pariahs. Pregnant mums and rented property just don't go together in this country.

They didn't want to have us in Scotland, and I had the best references — relatives as referees. They panicked and I got fed up. I also heard a discussion that the paper was fold-ing. [*laughs*] I've just got me grip on the rock and, *wallop,* it was going. I just said one night to the guys I worked with, "Where's a decent place to live on this island?" They said, "Oxford." I said, "Great." What I didn't realize is that they were bloody graduates who had this totally romantic view of the city. A different crowd would have said Cambridge. London at that time was the most expensive city in Britain. Edinburgh was the second most and Oxford was the third most. Anyhow, I had a bit of the old McClurean luck. I just looked up the newspapers here and wrote to them. I just happened to hit the day they fired somebody. They flew me down, interviewed me, and gave me the job. So I went back there to hand in my notice and they said, "Oh no; you've been made permanent." They said, "Oh no; we don't want to lose you; we'll send you to London and we'll pay all this money. There'll be much more money in it." It was a big decision, but I came to Oxford because of the children. I don't like cities.

We came here and we lived in a house just like this one. It was far too expensive, so finally we moved into a very tiny flat down in the real cosmopolitan end of East Oxford, which was very jolly because the kids screamed all night, people fought, and you could type because typing was nothing, compared with everything else that was happening. But I wasn't doing any real writing. I still hadn't really got going. Then Kirstie was born and finally there we were: there were five of us living in two rooms. We had a small kitchen and a small bathroom, but it was two rooms otherwise. The stress really starts to hit you. The kids were in one room and we were in another, but you just never lost sight of each other and it was really pressure. It was incredible, and we had no cash at all. We only had what I'd get in my pay packet at the end of the week, and it was getting very depressing. And I watched the telly. I love the telly. It was a great compensation. It's very good, British television. And I did what everybody says they'll do. I said, "I can write something as good as that sort of thing." It was a time when they were doing a lot of documentaries about Vietnam and I was quite moved by all of this. And I find I write as a direct result of emotional things. Something moves me and then I write. I took a long time to realize that's how I work.

C: Did you know anything about the American army or Vietnam?

McC: No. I just watched everything I could and read everything I could and talked to some guys on the base.

C: American soldiers?

McC: Yeah. Just got together as much as I could. Then I

made the classic error: I said, "What I'm going to do, I'm going to have the cheapest movie, the cheapest TV play; it's going to have one set. Two sets, two pieces of stock film, and that's it. And I'm going to have three speaking parts; two of them are not going to speak anything at all that we can understand."

C: Pseudo-Vietnamese?

McC: Yeah. So that's it. That's all we get. So I wrote a play called *The Hole*. At that time, we had a television director who had made an enormous impact with a play called *Cathie Come Home*, which upset the whole of Britain. It's the one play that made everyone talk about him. People cried. They busted their sets. Well, in the end, my play was sold to TV for five hundred pounds. That was the payment on the house here. That was freedom. Bugger all, it was *room*. It was modest, but it was a real place; we had a place here. I'd been trying to write stuff and had a lot of trouble with *The Hole*, and the upshot of all this is that there was great excitement: they went into rehearsals with a guy who's quite a celebrated English actor, and then we had a director's strike in 1968. It went down the tube along with all the other plays in the same series and they never revived it. That was the end of it and I was really quite upset by that. At that time, I'd been promoted from news subeditor to news editor, digging up articles and leaders and stuff, and that's when I opted out of the dailies.

ATV, one of the networks, had offered me a writing course. They run courses for TV writers and I thought I'd have more time, so I switched to the weekly paper and found I had *less* time. So that went down, too. I thought I'd just bunch it together, you know. I was kind of disillusioned.

I was working for this guy called Anthony Price, who is a crime writer now. He wasn't then. He was a chief sub and I liked the guy because he was one of the few newsmen I'd met who was enthusiastic. That's why I went to work for him. One day I walked in and he was talking about Tom and

Jerry. It just blew my mind. We had a guy who was a crime reviewer and one day he said, "Look, before we have a pint, I've just got something to put in the post." So we went along. Then ten days later he said to me, "Hey, you remember that parcel that we mailed?" And he had a letter: "We've accepted your manuscript." So I said, "Marvelous."

That television thing had been sodded about for weeks and months and everyone had his fingers in the pie, but nobody makes their minds up and they all say, "Super, darling," but nothing happens. And again we were really poor. We really scraped along and I was getting real fed up with it all and I thought, "*That's* the way, boy." And some afternoons I used to write — just bits. I really hadn't done any short stories, nothing. I was really working too hard for my living to go any further. I used to work football — soccer — results on Saturday afternoon, about which I knew nothing. That was often catastrophic because I often couldn't tell from the copy whether the goal had been scored or not. We didn't have any money to go anywhere or anything like that. So I said to Lorelee, "I tell you what I'm going to do; I'm going to write a book." And all the memory of McBain and so on was there. It was like something I'd plugged into or sort of sensed or something. I also wanted to use the South African stuff — get it out of my system or capitalize on it. I wanted to talk about it, but I usually really dislike all books I've read by people who write about South Africa. I just want people to know about it; that's all I intend, usually. Let them know and they can decide for themselves.

C: How did you actually come across McBain and John D. MacDonald?

McC: This South African Security Branch guy had me in his office for some mysterious reason. They were very mysterious in the way they did things. And he threw these two books at me. They were both proof copies, an Ed McBain and a John D. MacDonald.

C: Where did this counterintelligence type get proof copies?

McC: I don't know where the hell he got them. And he said, "You'd better read these." Coming from a guy like that, it's almost an order. He went away for a while and I started on John D. MacDonald.

C: There you were in this bare room, waiting for God knows what, reading John D. MacDonald and Ed McBain?

McC: Well, you learn to be terribly cool. It's a game. But I was appalled by the viciousness of John D. MacDonald. It was really horrible. It was about a girl who used to push her hand into people's diaphragms and squeeze their hearts or something. Perhaps he'll deny he ever wrote it. I'll be interested to know what the name of that book was. I can't remember the Ed McBain. I think it was the sniper one. As I said, when I was teaching, I began to write a little. Once I'd opted out of photojournalism, I went on trips in my jeep. I bought an old American army jeep and used to go crashing through the bush and based a child's book on that. Then I kind of dropped all this book-writing stuff and I wrote some bad plays — like everybody does, I guess. But I guess my reading had a lot to do with what I did. My father read an enormous amount; he seldom read less than two books a day. He read very, very fast and he'd throw books at me. I remember the first James Bond landing on me and he said, "Not bad." That's all he'd ever say. But I also had this uncle who'd been an Old Bailey judge when I was quite young, so I'd been interested in that kind of stuff. That set me off and I read a hell of a lot of crime and biographies of our great barristers, and my dad read a lot of crime as well — all the Agathas and other things. So I had all this kind of running in me and then I got very taken up with journalism and really hadn't time to do anything else.

C: Back to the critical moment: you weren't going to try to influence anyone in writing about South Africa?

McC: No. I just wanted them to get a little more of what it's really like and then to let them decide. This is borne out by the reviews I get, because I get reviews in South Africa about a book that bear no resemblance to the reviews I get from Los Angeles. The South Africans lap them up.

C: Your work is sold in South Africa?

McC: Oh, yes. It gets on the best sellers. At any rate, one of the catalysts was *Cotton Comes to Harlem*, by Chester Himes. I read something about Chester Himes in which he said he just wrote it the way it was. And I thought, "That's it." It's not more complicated than that. Although since then I've gotten to be pretentious and say, "Well, I wanted a conservative market." Most conservative people read crime novels. But it wasn't that. I wanted an ordinary story that had a story of its own.

C: And so the impetus had nothing to do with wanting to rant to the right or to the left?

McC: No. I just wanted it to be like it was. So I just thought, "Well, that's it. And what shall I write?" I remember it well. I sat in that front room there at this old 1900 typewriter and had a pile of yellow paper from the newsroom, and I couldn't think how to begin, so I just wrote: "For an undertaker George Henry Abbott was a sad man. He let his job get on top of him. He let it keep him awake nights. He made mistakes." And it just started to lift off and it went off into a short story, which nobody's ever seen. It got published in a dreadful magazine. I'll have to keep quiet about that. But I didn't turn it into a short story then; I just took it out of the typewriter and it was all done in about ten minutes, the whole damn thing, and it was fantastic, incredible. I started with Abbott and then went back into the history of that funeral parlor, and there was a real piss-taking thing about the early pioneer undertaker. I started again with the same front line and I wrote right through those two weeks. I wrote seventeen hours a day, every day.

An American drama critic, Eric Bentley, said about *The Steam Pig* that that type of creation is very like Louis Pasteur finding a vaccine: he knew what he wanted, he knew how it should end, but he had only a vague idea of how to get that. What I find very odd is how it all makes sense, how things can come in very early and still have a proper relevance. Certainly the one time I tried to write a book by plan it was dreadful. I can't even remember what it was called; I threw the damn thing away. But I've certainly slowed down. I don't write books in two weeks anymore. No way. I think, in fact, I went into a very bad phase of getting too elliptical and obscure at times. I think I tightened it up very much in *The Blood of an Englishman*. I've got this unfortunate translator, Mr. Shin Ichimori of Azalea Gardens, Tokyo, who is a painstaking translator, and right now he's suffering through *Snake*. He's quite right. Sometimes it's really obscure. It doesn't matter, though. The obscurities have never mattered. You can ride on past them. But I never do that to something that's important in a story. I've largely gotten rid of those.

C: Let's go back to arriving in Oxford, for a moment. Did you find the English press to be more aggressive and nasty in some ways and less objective at the same time? They aren't working to the kind of formula that American journalists are trained to work to, the inverted pyramid, which is thoroughly objective.

McC: Yes, I found that strange. I worked inverted pyramid in South Africa and, by God, that's a good place to learn to be objective. You have to be objective because if you did political reports, your name and address went on the end of it. But, no, very few people here understand the inverted pyramid. I wasn't too terribly impressed with the raw material — the stories. So much of it is just bad; it's shocking. It's dreadful compared to the standards we worked to in South Africa. There was a whole different way of thinking about it there. You were terribly upset if anybody changed your copy in South Africa because you always had to try to get it right. Equally, if you made a mess of it, you got a hell of a ripping off; but I found here, whether it was a national or a provincial paper, people used to just chuck it in and were totally indifferent as to whether anybody changed it or not. But, wait until some editors have had a go at it and I think it's pretty good. Papers here do have a slant, though. People in this country buy a paper for its slant. But it's very interesting to look at the *Mirror*'s crossword; it tells you a terrible lot about the English. That's a down-market paper, but just try and do the crossword. It's a general knowledge crossword and it's jolly hard. What really struck me when I got here was how well informed people are, even manual laborers. But one of the big differences between English and American newspapers is that the libel laws in this country are absolutely terrifying. It's very easy to commit a libel and the consequences are frightful, so when you do investigative reporting, you've got to watch your p's and q's. There are a lot of limits to what you can do. You certainly could never produce the *National Lampoon* over here.

C: What does Sabensa Gakulu mean, as in the title of the company that holds your copyrights?

McC: That was an accident. When you register a company in this country, you give three names for the company in order of preference. I gave a perfectly sensible first two and because I just couldn't think of anything else, I put *sabensa gakulu* at the bottom. This idiot guy who runs the company registration office said, "That's the one it's going to be." So I was stuck with the one I didn't want. It just means "working very hard" in Zulu. The company thing has a great tax advantage. I can spread money from one year to the next, and the company tax is lower than income tax. It's also a great advantage in case of a libel suit because the company has limited liability. Except I wish I hadn't done it now because at the moment it's costing me more than it's saving. But you see, if you get a sudden bonanza, you're dead in this country.

A friend of mine and his wife were living in penury (his word) in Dublin, and every year they used to go to Poland

and spend their Polish royalties because you can't take zlotys out of Poland. So he and his wife would go there and stay in a great big hotel, eat themselves silly and drink themselves silly, buy as many warm clothes as they could, and then go back and live in a garret. Then he wrote a novel that MGM bought and suddenly there was eighty thousand quid. Money! So they came back to England and set themselves up, and then along came the Inland Revenue people and they took all but fifteen thousand quid. If he'd had a company . . . I'm not saying I'll be lucky and get as much as that. I'm just saying if you get sudden bumpo, you can spread it out and you don't lose great chunks of it.

C: American writers can't do that — can't incorporate, can't get capital gains. Ireland is going to be the object of a lot of reverse migration if things don't get better. Let's go to the cultural and political background of the novels. Is Trekkersburg a one-on-one picture of Pietermaritzburg?

McC: Trekkersburg is my view of it and also, therefore, not subject to the actual limitations of Pietermaritzburg. If I want to change it around a bit, I do.

C: Is South Africa just Mississippi with an army and a navy?

McC: Not really. To start with, out of every hundred people in the Union, seventy are blacks, nine are mixed race — Coloreds. Cape Coloreds is a subdivision, more Malaysian than white or black — Malaysian whites, really. And then there are three Asians and eighteen whites, more than half of whom are Afrikaners.

C: So the English-descended people are nine out of a hundred?

McC: No, around six out of a hundred. And South Africa is 471,445 square miles, larger than France, Germany, Italy, and Portugal put together.

C: Have things changed in South Africa recently?

McC: In the midsixties, I was a housemaster at a prep school and I was there one afternoon on my own. My father rang, to say that Verwoerd had been assassinated. He was the prime minister. I went bursting out of my room, wanting to tell somebody, you see, and there was nobody at school except me. I couldn't go out and tell the kids, so I went into the kitchen, where there were all these Zulu cooks working. I announced that Verwoerd had been shot. They didn't know what I meant. So I explained that he was the boss man of the government. "Ah, yah, yah, yah; got that." And I said, "He's been shot." And they said, "Oh, shame."

In those days, they didn't know a lot of things. Communications were very poor. But when I was there in '74, the black people I encountered were very different. I was eating with this family and a kid came in and knocked a glass off the table. There was an awkward moment, then somebody said. "Three ships." There was a big laugh and that was that. I noticed later during the evening somebody else using the same expression: the three ships. And again a big laugh. What might have been a display of anger just vanished. So I asked them what it was, and it was a reference to the three ships that had brought the Dutch settlers. They're on the coinage. It means: "Don't worry; the three ships are coming again to take these guys away. That's what we must think of."

C: But, of course, nobody's going anywhere, are they? With the exception of the Anglos and the Jews, who emigrate or are expelled — as was an Ole Miss law professor when I was there who was Jewish — the blacks are here and the Afrikaners are there, each in his own space in this weird political setup. The blacks are not represented, are they? In any of the legislatures, on any of the city councils?

McC: That gets into more complicated stuff, because you've got these Bantustans. You get a really cute guy like the late Butuleze, who was chief minister or whatever of KwaZulu, which is the Zulu version of South Africa. He wouldn't have gone independent.

C: Why?

McC: He was quite happy. He was smart. He embarrassed them because he stayed with it.

C: Do you think that society can go on with the blacks in their quasi republics and the whites in their four provinces? What do you think's going to happen?

McC: Hell, I don't know. If the situation is given enough time, I think it might resolve itself, but I don't think they've got the time. I think there is a lot of understanding there — a lot more than they've ever had before — that society has to change, and this understanding is there even in the present government, but the right wing keeps suppressing it, making sure it doesn't get out of hand.

C: Apartheid has gotten steadily more complex and bureaucratic as time has gone on, hasn't it?

McC: Yes, and been steadily eroded as time has gone on. For some strange reason, the vocation of nursing has apparently become very unpopular with white people, so although all hospitals were once staffed by white nurses and nursing was regarded as a very respectable profession, the numbers of white nurses are now so low you'll find black nurses in white hospitals. That was just unthinkable ten years ago.

C: Do black patients have white nurses, as they did in the Deep South even before integration?

McC: No. But you know, the most significant thing South Africa has done is form black regiments in the army. The South African police are constitutionally, if that's the right word, the first line of defense in South Africa, so the first troops who fought in the desert were the South African police. Now, they've always armed the South African police, although not very many white South Africans are aware of the fact that black detectives go about with guns.

C: People like Zondi.

McC: Yes; detectives, not patrolmen. Although today, in certain areas, your patrolman is armed and you'll get station commanders who are black who hold quite high ranks, like lieutenant and captain. These are very significant moves because they give the black and the white police a common cause. You see, it's very clear to me that black people — the black people I knew in South Africa, who were mainly Zulus — were capitalists. Their pride and their joy are their cattle and this is true even if you're an urban African. They like to possess things. They're very hard to persuade that Communism is a good idea. There is also great enmity between different tribes, which is demonstrated on the mines, where you get terrific battles on Sundays between the Zulus and the others. And what the government in South Africa has done is quite interesting. There are nine million whites and then this overwhelming mass of black people. But by setting up these homelands, these independent states, they've divided the blacks so that there is no black group greater than their own. The largest black group is the four million Zulu. And this is something that's quite resented by the smarter black politicians, who realize what's happening. They're being divided and now being ruled that way round. Pan-Africanism is more difficult now with the great distances and permission being needed to move about the country and all that. You can't visit a city without a pass if you're black. If you're white you can go anywhere you like except the black areas.

But getting back to unification of the blacks in South Africa, there's quite a lot of suspicion between them, you know, on a tribal basis. But I don't think any of them would welcome help from the north — the newly independent African states. If they're going to be liberated, they want to do it themselves, and it's that sort of thinking that makes these black regiments a good idea from the white point of view, because you already have a military people to put into these regiments.

I think the most important thing about South Africa, which was really brought home to me when I went there in '74, is that I found the only people I was easy with or whose company I enjoyed were Afrikaners, as right wing as you please, a lot of cops, people like that, and black people. English-speaking South Africans . . . We just didn't even talk the same language.

C: They're quite worried about their position.

McC: Now, that's *exactly* it, you see. Where you went there were a few invited to meals and all that, and they wanted to know what the tax was in England, what it was like living here, and all that sort of thing. The blacks were in their land, and so were the Afrikaners, and there was a lot more understanding between them — the black and white tribes. The others just don't really belong. The Afrikaners have a very rude word for English-speaking whites and Africans. They call them by a word that translated means "salty penis," because they stand with one foot in Europe and one on Africa and dangle themselves in the Atlantic Ocean; they don't have anything like that sense of commitment to their land. This was so clear so often. I'm somebody who works from the particular a lot. Most English-speaking whites don't know very much about their servants at all. It's a very complex thing. There is a degree of aggression now in the black people. They're more assertive. I was going to tell you about my friend the Afrikaner police captain. Now, this is typical of South African attitudes. His little boys are not allowed to call the gardener "boy." They have to call him by his name. And when I was at his house one evening, we were going back into the city and he called to the gardener and he asked him if he wanted a ride. And the gardener said yeah, he'd be grateful. He turned to me and he said, "Eh? Eh? You see this idle Kaffir?" And "Kaffir" is not used the way "nigger" is used. He said that he was doing well, that he was going to night school. I said, "Oh?" The captain said, "Yeah, it's bloody ridiculous. I was talking to him one day. I went out to tell him to do something, and I found he couldn't read the instructions properly. I said to him, 'O.K., I tell you what, Kaffir, I'll make a deal with you. I'll send you to night school, I will pay for your books, I will pay for your night school. But if you fail, I will sack you.'" So in his funny, funny way the captain cares about this guy.

C: You said earlier you thought life was possible in South Africa if you were able to choose sides.

McC: If you could think that either the radical right, the white supremacists, or the liberals, the radical left, were right, O.K., then you could wage that war. And I had a lot of friends on both sides, a lot of acquaintances, people I really knew, and I also remember one night some radical saying, "You're the kind we really don't need." We guys in the middle, you know. "We want opposition; we don't need people on our side like you." That impressed me quite a bit.

C: What about Janet Suzman and people like that?

McC: If I had ever belonged to a party, I might have wanted to belong to the Progressive Party because it had a qualified franchise, and that was something I could understand. Their idea at that time was that you had to have either a junior high level of education — I'm trying to translate it into American terms — or six hundred rands worth of immovable property to vote.

C: That sounds a little like what H. L. Hunt wanted in America. And they call them the Progressive Party?

McC: Well, it would have included so many blacks, actually, that South Africa would have become a black majority society.

C: How much did you have to do to get put on a plane, like the law professor at Ole Miss?

McC: That's very easy. You didn't have to do a lot to get put on a plane. I'll tell you what happened when I was teaching prep school; that'll give you some idea of the society. I taught at a prep school — a good prep school. Most of the people who sent their kids there were professional people, as we call them here: doctors and lawyers, people like that. And we had a parents' cricket match. Now, all these men were English-speaking South Africans from the top level of that local society and they shared clubs, country clubs and such like. There were twelve men who played for the fathers' team, including a professor of law and other eminent people; then we had a barbecue afterward, which was attended by staff, the resident staff, and these chaps and the headmaster. We sat around eating steak and drinking beer and chewing the fat. I can't remember it, nor could anybody, but sometime during that evening, some vague political discussion was introduced. Now, you're always very careful; you never talk politics or religion. This is a slogan you're always taught as a kid: never discuss politics or religion. There was something criticized. It was damned innocuous, so innocuous none of us could remember it. But the next morning, before school began, a very upset man arrived at school. He was one of the twelve. Early that morning, at 5:00 A.M., Security Branch had beaten on his door. When he answered the door, they said, "Dr. So-and-so, you said things last night that we don't like to hear. Don't you ever say them again." And they went away.

C: Somebody had snitched on him?

McC: Somebody out of those twelve.

C: In five hours, too. Someone had picked up the phone upon returning and the Security Branch had said, "O.K., we'll go right out." It's a society of informers.

McC: You get this informing thing that works right through South Africa.

C: What impresses me about right-wing societies, which South Africa is, or the kind of society that right-wing Republicans would like to clamp on America, is that a right-wing society acts in exactly the same way the Russians act, which is the kind of society *they* claim they're protecting us from.

McC: That's what my old man used to say, exactly that. He said that Verwoerd was a Communist plant. My father worked in Intelligence. He was a professional soldier, but that's what he moved into. He worked undercover in Istanbul and India and all that for the British army. He spoke seven languages, could write Arabic. And in the Second World War, he was in Intelligence in South Africa. He's the major in *Rogue Eagle*. My old man used to say Verwoerd was definitely a Communist plant, because he wasn't an Afrikaner, he wasn't a South African; he was a Dutchman who arrived when he was young.

C: An old American soldier asked me to put this question. It was his impression that certain South African units were not regarded as politically reliable by the Imperial General Staff. Is that right? Were they Nazis?

McC: During World War II, no South African soldier was required to leave the country against his will. All those who did volunteer wore a red flash on their shoulders, and this made them targets for this group set up by Berlin, by von Ribbentrop, inside South Africa. They're the people who sort of took over later. Now, you wouldn't wear one of those flashes unless you meant it and most South African soldiers were Afrikaners, so I doubt they were unreliable. My father was a fairly prejudiced man in many ways, and I know he would have told me about it if he'd thought that. It's perfectly true that those people who were set up by the Nazis were involved in all sorts of naughty stuff, and at one stage there was a two- or three-day battle in Johannesburg between the police and these Nazis.

C: And of course Verwoerd, who was one of them, was thrown in jail by the British and later became prime minister, and in *Rogue Eagle* is already hated himself by the Ox Wagon Sentinels, a Neo-Nazi group in South Africa.

Tell me about what happened to you when you went back in '74.

McC: When we went back in '74 to make a movie, the film company put us in the hotel that's opposite the police station that I write about. And who's the first guy I meet? Now, Kramer's a composite and he's all sorts of things, but Zondi's very much a detective I know called Mickey Zatoli. And there's old Mickey. It was incredible. I thought, "Oh, my God. I can't show my face." Then I discovered that the Kramer and Zondi books are cult books with the cops there. They love them — and a lot of sly things in them that nobody else notices. Somewhere in there Kramer says to a prisoner, "Either you come to my office or we go out to the kids' playground." Nobody else really knows much about that. That's where they torture their prisoners, you see. These guys just loved that. This guy got a big laugh. They used to use the playground equipment — they used to tie them upside down on the seesaw. Mainly they put them in the paddling pool and sort of drowned and revived them. I thought I'd brave the lion in his den, so I went over to the bar — they had a bar in the police station like we have in our police stations, a big social club in the police stations. Anyway, I went in there and boom, boom, everyone was glad to see me. "Welcome back. We didn't half love the paddling pool." And a guy I used to know said, "We loved old X. It was just like him." And I said, "Yeah, but I changed his bloody name." He said, "What do you mean?" I said, "I changed his name." And now he says, "Hey, X, look who's here!" And X comes in and the cop says, "Hey, X, he says he changed your name." And I hadn't.

C: Oh no. You could see libel suits coming in by the carload.

McC: Oh, X loves it.

C: That's even better. Let's crosscut. Your books are very imagistic.

McC: I see a lot of what I do. I try to make people see, too.

C: It seems that one of your themes is brotherhood — the failure of brotherhood on the national level, that is, between black and white, Afrikaner and Anglo, and so on, but the success of brotherhood on the particular and local level, between Kramer and Zondi. Is that conscious?

McC: No, unconscious.

C: Because South Africa has failed as a society where a man can love all others?

McC: I think it works as this. I used to look at things and I would probably come to these things about brotherhood, the failure in a broad and public sense. But in the particular it was often very real. I mean, you not only get it between cops, you used to get long and deep friendships between farmers and their *ndunos* (head men) on their farms. You used to get it between servants and masters and people who associate with each other for a long time. So all I really do is put it down again, and it has the same effect on people who read it as it had on me. It's not my intention to do it, but it's what made me interested in it. Do you follow?

C: Sure. With a good eye and an honest heart, the big themes come. The reclassification boards play an important part in *The Steam Pig* — reclassification from white to black by the government. Did that ever actually happen to anyone you knew who'd been passing as white?

McC: Oh yes.

C: What did they suddenly find that made the classification change necessary in the eyes of the government? Some great-grandpa who was black but who hadn't been reported?

McC: Often people would report them maliciously. It's really much weirder than it seems. I remember a tragedy in my home town, where a well-known white boxer was reclassified and hanged himself. I think the thing I always remember when we talk about this at all is when Lorelee was working at Grace Hospital, training to be a nurse. Grace is a big white hospital and it had two wards — one Indian and one Colored — attached. The whites had become pretty uncomfortable being put in with the blacks and they certainly didn't want to be, you see. Lorelee was working the Colored ward and she dealt with a fellow who'd been in a railroad crossing accident in a car and he was Colored. Then she was moved to med surgical at the end of the month and dealt with his brother in the white ward. They had the same parents.

C: What had happened?

McC: In this case, the white brother had "tried for white" and gotten himself reclassified as white, but his parents had always lived as Colored and so had his brother, who didn't want to leave his community and move.

C: How do you get yourself moved up in rank, as it were? Get a reclassification card? Slip them a fiver, or what?

McC: Oh, God, no. They're very incorruptible. They have all these weird tests; they press people on the end of the nose and feel how many pieces of cartilage there are.

C: *What?*

McC: Oh, you wouldn't believe it.

C: Tell me more.

McC: Among the simplest and quickest tests among the reclassification people is this one: they say, "Can you remember when you were twelve years old? If not, try it anew. Stand up." [Carr stands up.] "How tall were you? Show me." [Carr indicates a position on his chest, with palm up.] That's funny. You'd go down the pipe.

C: What'd I do wrong?

McC: If you go like this, you're white. [McClure indicates a position on his own chest, but with palm down.] Black people measure from the back of their hands to the ground, whites with the palm of the hand.

C: But it doesn't work if you're obviously African.

McC: No. It's for people you can't quite tell about. I mean, it's a lot of bullshit. It doesn't mean a thing. It's very complicated and there are lots of tragedies. Some of the worst tragedies involve families who try for white and they're made white and they move into a white neighborhood and the whites reject them; then they can't go back again.

C: How could you be made white if somebody, or a lot of people, thought you were Colored?

McC: You have to look fairly white. You see, the fact is, a lot of South Africans don't look very white.

C: Afrikaners?

McC: Yeah, I'm talking about them. White South Africans are not all white. One of the great moments of my life was at a very big agricultural show in my home town. My dad was the president and asked me to work the gates so they could keep the money and spend it on the show. I was a youngster of about fifteen. Now, the white tickets cost nearly three times what a black ticket cost. But when I looked at the people, I didn't know what they were. It didn't take me too long to solve it. If they looked likely to be white, I gave them a white ticket. Nobody bitched; nobody said, "Hey, man, I'm black." Because white tickets allowed them greater access to parts of the show that they wouldn't have had with the black ticket and they could spend the afternoon being white. If I was wrong, well, who was going to correct me? They had it on them and that was it. You know, it often occurs to me that my work is like science fiction, because I have to create a world that's very unlike other people's worlds and make it convincing, give them some idea of how it works and that this is about different ways of life, communicated differently. Maybe it doesn't strike the reader. I really believe that people should not be aware of the things you're doing. It should always look easy.

C: You're working now on a book about the San Diego police, aren't you?

McC: Yes. I admired what was being done there.

C: You told me before that you came away liking America because of the San Diego cops.

McC: I certainly like California. I find it very liberal. I know it's supposed to be wacky, but I liked a lot of their attitudes. I was a bit astonished at some of the do-goodism that seemed to be running amuck.

C: Like what?

McC: The system seemed a lot crazier than need be and I thought it very odd that part of a man's sentence for abusing a child very badly was to go and nurse the child in the hospital — so did the child and the hospital.

On the subject of the force, all California law enforcement agencies subscribe to something called POST — Police Officers' Standards and Training. If they don't meet the standards, they don't get various state moneys, so the forces are generally quite good. The styles still differ very much between the LAPD and the San Diego PD, and I wanted to know why the San Diego PD was innovative and how they'd changed, because it wasn't even a decade before when they were a pretty hard-nosed, militaristic operation. But now they're getting on very well with the community. The research was sort of digging around in the minds of the cops for the answers, and I found the changes they made in San Diego caused a terrific attrition. They lost hundreds of police, who just walked right out: they weren't going to do it. And the people who fascinated me were like the man who said to me: "Well, I guess I used to be a sock 'em, knock 'em, take names, kick-ass cop." And that's a description of the stereotypical American cop, at least from a European point of view.

C: That's what Europeans think about American cops?

McC: Yes, we do. Now, he's the interesting guy because he's still there. How much did he have to change? Because we all have sock 'em, knock 'em, kick-ass cops.

C: Even in England?

McC: Oh right. So how are we going to change this? How do you keep the guy sympathetic to change and how do you achieve it? I found that very interesting.

C: *Spike Island* was about the Liverpool police in the district that gives its name to the book.

McC: Did you like it?

C: Yes.

McC: Thank God somebody did. The Americans just pounded it left and right. Said it was repetitious, boring, incomprehensible. Most of them said I was incomprehensible because they didn't understand what people were saying. I think that's dumb, because I read things about the Deep South. I don't have to understand it all, but it doesn't bother me. But they've lost a fortune on that book.

C: Well, I don't know why because it told me things about English police work and English police officers, police constables, rather, that I never got from reading even English police procedurals, of which there are more than there used to be, but not with the gritty realism of your descriptions of that station in Liverpool. It was surprising in many ways. There was a detective sergeant who said the police force had made him into what he was. It made him feel secure so he could expand as a human being.

McC: He loved classical music because he used to be stationed at concerts.

C: He expanded as a human being *because* he'd been a police officer. That's not something you would realize about American or English police officers. And you wouldn't have any idea that Liverpool policemen are tough on other officers who are violent, who kicked around their prisoners.

McC: Yeah. They're less strict in San Diego, but they are pretty tough. It's a bit messy at the moment, the police thing here. On the other hand, there was a study done by an American criminologist who compared an American city with Edinburgh — I forget the city, but the study's cited in *Spike Island* — comparable sizes, comparable populations. The British crime figures were very low and the American crime figures were very high. He found that the Scottish department was very poorly equipped and not very well trained, and that the Americans were very much better trained and very well equipped. The conclusion of the study was that the police were irrelevant. It's what the individual society tolerates. In America last year about ten thousand people died because of handguns. In Great Britain it was eight, in Sweden, twenty-one.

C: I wanted to ask you about Zulu. Are there different levels of usage in Zulu? A polite Zulu and a plain style Zulu?

McC: Well, not altogether. There's a basic bottom-line Zulu, which isn't that bad, that everyone speaks; then they can speak it with greater refinement from there on. The thing that is fascinating about Zulus is that they didn't carve things, they didn't paint things; the Zulus' whole culture was their speech and the stories they would tell each other. It's a language of enormous vocabulary in their particular areas of interest. I don't know how many words we have to describe a cow, but we have "piebald" and "red" and "black" and so on. They have 305 words for all the refinements of shapes and mottling. And it's a beautiful language to listen to, very onomatopoeic.

They have a very structured society, and are immensely moral. You couldn't get married until you were a certain age and had done certain things. Adultery was a stoning job. They had a leader, Dingaan, who taught them very, very tough discipline — this was about the 1820s. In fact, there's an awful place on the south coast of Natal called Dingaan's Rock, where he ordered four thousand men to walk off the top of a cliff and they *did* it. He taught them to use the *assagai*, to close in and stab with it instead of throwing it, and to lock shields and march together like a Roman legion. He marched them over devil thorns and stuff until they were totally unflinchable. He was a real black Napoleon. He could have stormed up through Africa.

Back to the Zulu language: on the crest of the city of Pietermaritzburg there's a piece of ribbon instead of mantling and on it is a Zulu name, *Umgugundhlovu*. When you're a child, you're always taught this means "the place of the elephants." When we were in high school, we started Zulu and this Afrikaner teacher said, "This'll give you an interest in Zulu. *Umgugundhlovu* really means 'where the elephant farts.' " The city is down in a valley and the valley before settlement had all these thorn trees, and when the elephants were in there you couldn't see them from the surrounding parts, but you could hear them, their stomachs rumbling. The elephant has a really loud stomach rumble. *Umgugun* is the sound of their stomachs rumbling, and *dhlovu* the sound of their farts. It always made me laugh.

C: Have the Kramer and Zondi stories proceeded according to your expectations? Or has it proved tougher and tougher to work with them as time went on?

McC: It has gotten tougher. It worries me that I might not still be getting it right. It's seven years since I was there.

C: That's a good point. It's always said in America about writers like Faulkner and O'Hara that when they left the places they wrote about, the stuff ran thin. They weren't there to hear what was going on; they didn't keep up. And, of course, other critics say balderdash: they had it in their heads all along.

McC: I tend to say balderdash, too, and on these grounds — and I really, firmly believe this — when you're in it, it's very hard to get a perspective on it. It's a good thing to write about somewhere when you're elsewhere and it comes back into your mind. It's good not only because of the distance between you, which gives you perspective, but you're also aware of the difference because you're in another culture and you can rub against it. It's also simply because, I think, anything you write about should have kicked around awhile inside you. It needs a kind of maturation process; it's got to mature. But you come to the point where you've been away too long, and if you're pretending it's contemporary, then you could be getting it wrong. I keep trying to update the whole time.

C: Do you read South African newspapers?

McC: A friend sends me clippings all the time from my home town newspapers, and letters. He's very good at keeping me abreast of things. In a way the path of *The Sunday Hangman* and *The Blood of an Englishman* was dictated, in that it dealt with areas I was confident I was right about, and from the reviews I got, South African reviews, no one said it wasn't contemporary South Africa.

The hardest book, in a sort of contemporary sense, was *The Sunday Hangman*. I mean, I really sweated on *The Sunday Hangman* because about halfway through the Soweto riots occurred. I remember the kids calling me down to watch the telly and I was terribly upset. I was amazed. I was crying, not weeping. I had tears in my eyes. I was so upset by it because I knew people on both sides of the barricades. There's a sequence in *The Sunday Hangman* where Zondi talks about a dream. He's talking about running to the barricades and wondering which side he'll be on.

C: There's a section in *The Blood of an Englishman* in which Zondi goes home and Miriam, his wife, says, "I always trust in God. I have faith in God." Is that typical?

McC: Yes, that's typical; that's very real.

C: For her to be deeply religious?

McC: You see, it's a thing I deal with obliquely somewhere else. One of the great South African arguments against the blacks is to say: "Look what they do when they run amuck. Where is the first place they go? They go and they rape the nuns and burn the mission stations down that taught them." Now, Zondi was brought up in one of those missions where you had to memorize stuff and all that because of the scarcity of things. But in one of the books — I can't quite recall which one it is now — Zondi does do this; he turns on the nuns and destroys the mission. The reason is that the missions offer them equality, hope, and everything, and then when they get out into the world ... I spoke to a man who'd been through that and he hated them for it. They taught him to read and it didn't do him any good, taught him to think he was equal and it didn't do him any good. They just raised expectations, which would be thwarted. So he blamed them for it. But Christianity is a very, very strong thing; it's the Baptist church, particularly, and the Roman Catholic church. I became a Roman Catholic for a time, I think, primarily because of the effect of the Catholic church. I didn't know anything much about it, and when I was working as a reporter, I remember going to get an ordinary story up to this church one afternoon and I saw black and white people in there. You know, *weird.* They had mass for blacks in Zulu Sundays at three. A lot of whites went to that because it was really good to listen to. And it was the only place in the whole town where blacks could sit on the same benches. The Catholic church didn't make any concessions and it got away with it. I don't know what the behavior of Catholic whites was outside the church, but if a black joined them in a pew, they weren't going to shoot off into the next pew. I was really impressed by this — the fact that they had overcome it. The Anglican church in my home town went to great, painful lengths to figure out how it could rebuild its cathedral, and at one point they were going to build it on the dividing line between a black and white area so that the blacks could come in the east door. They were going to split the church up the middle. Crazy. And at the Presbyterian churches, the blacks would stand at the back.

To go back, I think the thing I meant to say to you is that I decided crime was a good vehicle because it has a discipline that's not typical of the straight novel. In crime writing there are satisfactory conclusions. It gives you a neat framework to work within.

C: It's like writing a sonnet, really: it has to be fourteen lines, but it can be Shakespearean, Petrarchan, a nonce form, or seven heroic couplets. Does it ever make you mad when people start saying, "Well, the detective novel isn't serious."

McC: I think I tend to agree with them most of the time because I think most crime novels are rubbish, but I have learned — and this is another thing that ties in with what I said about Chester Himes — about Harlem in a way I'd never learned about Harlem before, through Himes's novels, because I wasn't listening to a polemicist, James Baldwin, or some guy who's giving me the black line on something. I'd always got the closest look at life, in a way, out of crime — much more satisfactory than novels, which are so often books about writers writing about writing. I find crime fascinating. You see, it's through that that you judge a society — or that *I* judge a society: its attitudes toward crime, the way it controls crime, what it considers to be crime.

And I think there's a fine dividing line between the novel and the crime mystery story.

C: What would that line be?

McC: I don't know who draws it. I think that publishers do. I think anything, though, with a detective and a solution is a crime story. The word "mystery" does annoy me. I think it's a soft word. Most good stories involve crime, whatever kind of novel they are. Novels almost always deal with crime: it can be adultery, or it can be the finer shadings of what you mean by crime.

C: Any last thoughts? It's awfully late and you've been more than patient.

McC: I can see that ultimately you're going to come unstuck unless you start writing about what you know, not so much where you come from, but what you know.

JUNE THOMSON

June Thomson was born in Kent on June 24, 1930, and educated at Chelmsford High School for Girls, Essex, and at Bedford College of the University of London from 1949 to 1952; she graduated with a B.A. Honours in English. She has taught in Stoke-on-Trent, London, and in Hertfordshire.

In *Twentieth Century Crime and Mystery Writers* she commented about her writing: "I have always enjoyed reading detective fiction: a mystery or a puzzle has its fascination. So has the process of unraveling. Writing detective fiction gives the opportunity to examine character and relationships in a very special way — pushed to the limit, so to speak, and in jeopardy. I am interested in the personality of the outsider — the person who doesn't quite fit in with his environment."

All of her novels present the activities of Inspector Finch (Rudd in the American versions), who in the early novels carries out his duties in the Essex countryside, a beautiful but lonely place, spiritually as well as physically. Finch/Rudd has a pleasant, farmer's face and is often taken for a farmer. He is in harmony with that part of nature for which he is responsible, his manor, as English cops call it (a manor was a division of a parish, several of which made a hundred, in some places, or many of which made a county, in others). In later novels, Finch/Rudd is given special missions and promotion enough to handle cases outside his small town (*The Long Revenge* and *Shadow of a Doubt*). Thomson has chosen her locale well and her enthusiasm for it is a major part of the success of her series.

June Thomson's sense of place is one that American readers, rightly or wrongly, most often connect with American writers like Faulkner and Hawthorne and Ross Macdonald, who seem to draw their strength from the red clay hills of Mississippi or the deep, seductive woods of Concord or the sunblessed hills of coastal California. But of all the European countries, England has the most varied topography and many of the regions have only recently — and reluctantly — seen their linguistic uniqueness diluted.

Thomson's country is Essex, East Anglia, the flat alluvial part of England where once the Castle of Ely was as isolated as an island of the Philippine archipelago. Essex was the recruiting ground of some of the units of Cromwell's New Model Army. It is the redheaded, Congregational-Baptist part of England that favors Cambridge, the winds from Holland, and its Saxon heritage. It was also the home of Eighth Air Force units, many of whose members lie in the soil of the flat countryside and are honored in a Cambridge stained-glass window.

June Thomson lives now in St. Albans, Hertfordshire, probably the loveliest of the towns in the Home Counties. One of her favorite places there is the oldest pub in England; nearby is a cathedral, where the face of Archbishop Runcie, complete with horn-rimmed glasses, has been carved on the outside stringer. He peers out from among demons and medieval saints. On the way to Thomson's house from the cathedral is a concave field between two blocks of row houses. Residents call it The Bricky. The Romans dug clay there for their bricks some fourteen hundred years ago. Thomson has no trouble identifying with the people of Essex; her parents, too, lived in a thatched roof house, with a Model T outside but no plumbing inside.

Her extraordinary attachment to England and to that

part of it she knows best have made Thomson's works especially attractive to American fans of the crime novel in general and the police procedural in particular.

Her first book, *Not One of Us*, set the theme: the reaction of the closed community against the outsider. *The Long Revenge* gives the theme of the outsider a new twist. A retired secret agent has received handsomely printed cards. Inside each is a picture of the agent, a Special Operations Executive (spy) in France during World War II, standing between two German officers. Another photo is included: people being taken to death camps from that town. The inference is clear. The British SOE man is blamed not just for the deportation of people to the prison camps but for what went very wrong in that village during the war.

The leitmotif of digging (for this is what both detectives and murderers do, opposite and mirroring actions tied to the same event) is present from the start in *A Question of Identity*. It opens at an archaeological dig that has to be halted when an indisputably modern body is found in earth sacred to the Saxons. Thomson uncovers the burden of a family's guilt and how it converts them into outsiders in their own small part of the country.

Shadow of a Doubt focuses on another small community — the staff and inmates of a posh psychiatric hospital. The novel opens with an indelible image: the victim in a closet, crying as her murderer approaches. *Alibi in Time*, a punning title, is also about the death of an outsider — an almost perfect murder. In Thomson's novels, the murderer is seldom actually brought to book. The punishment is almost always the kind of ironical, poetic justice that can be more satisfying than that meted out by the State.

CARR: *Not One of Us* was your first book. Harper published it in '71. Then *Deadly Relations* (*The Habit of Loving* in America). And then you left Harper and Row?

THOMSON: They weren't interested in the next book, which was *Death Cap.* Doubleday took it.

C: Why did they change Inspector Finch in England to Inspector Rudd in America?

T: Doubleday was already publishing another English writer who'd got an Inspector Finch and I didn't realize this. They thought it would cause confusion if they were publishing two books with an Inspector Finch, so they asked me to change it.

C: How did they arrive at the name *Rudd*?

T: I had to choose a name that was roughly similar because I think they were hoping to — I don't know quite how the publishers work these things and I don't think in the end they could do it, but they were hoping to take the English plates and use them. *Rudd* basically fitted the shape that was left when you took *Finch* out. I wanted a country-sounding name like Finch that was rather simple and I had lots of names like Roach and Tench and things like that, you know. I came up with *Rudd* in the end. *Rudd* sounded nice, simple, straightforward, and had a slight sort of country quality about it.

C: One of the books I liked most was *A Question of Identity.* So much of what you write is about close-knit family groups and this was kind of the dark side of family life. You had them all together: the moron and the killer and the killer's wife, who's now living with the other brother. Is it typical of English small-town life that eccentrics have some scope?

T: I think they're tolerated in villages, yes.

C: Does English small-town life sometimes deform people into misanthropes and eccentrics and those who are a little on the dark side of eccentricity?

T: I think you get a certain amount of interbreeding going on, and I think you get people who are caught in a small village community and find it very frustrating and who perhaps don't have the outlet for their energies that they might have in a city and who get turned in on themselves.

C: Is it hard in England to be horizontally mobile? That is, can you move from York to London to get a job and then skip to Dublin and skip back to Manchester, leaving your community? Is it wrenching to leave your community, first of all, and, second, is it possible, even if it's not wrenching, to leave?

T: I think the point I was trying to make in that book is that while there is a lot more social mobility going on, there are still an awful lot of people who remain, generation after generation, in the same community and don't really move out. In fact, the village my mother lived in she moved to in 1939. She moved out only a few years ago and she wasn't really accepted as one of the people in the village.

C: Never really a local?

T: No, no, no.

C: In America, nobody was born where they live now.

T: Oh no, no. But you get this very much in English villages, that Grandma is there and you will go to church — One of the fascinating things about churchyards, English churchyards, is you will find the same names coming up, generation after generation.

C: Same first names, too, probably.

T: Yes. And particularly if it's a farming community, because land gets passed on, you see. I would say that what changes village communities is possibly a certain number of people moving out, as I moved out. But middle-class people tend to move in, buying a piece of land and having a house built, or buying a cottage and doing it up.

C: Gentrification?

T: Yeah, which is what happened with our pub. The old farm workers don't have the little bar they used to sit in because now it's all been prettied up for the middle-class people.

C: And the day-trippers?

T: Well, it depends on the village. The village I lived in wasn't a day-tripper place; it was a very ordinary little village, but you get the outsiders coming in and buying out the farm worker's cottage, putting in central heating, building a garage, laying a patio, and in that village, which was not a very pretty village. A lot of the property was in fact being taken up by outsiders coming in and setting their stamp on the place. Then the pub, which at one time had been a little bar, gets opened up, and they lay carpet and put wall lights in, and they start serving Bacardi and rum. And that's, I think, the change that takes place, but nevertheless, there's this nucleus of old families that has gone on and on.

C: It seems, sometimes, that these poor people in your books lead such desperate lives, out there in the lonely Essex countryside. Is that considered to be a rather bleak landscape in England, the Essex countryside?

T: It's very rural. Parts of it are very bleak. One of the books, *Case Closed*, is set on the marshes, which are very bleak. You can drive for a long way and not see anything. It's a very empty countryside.

C: Did you intend to write books that showed the relationship between environment and personality? In *Case Closed* there's a pathetic figure living on what we'd call a houseboat who has lost his daughter, and it seems he has just gone to pot out there by himself.

T: Yes, I think these do relate. There's a little place I used to go to on the Suffolk coast — in fact, the first book, *Not One of Us*, in a way was based on a chap there. He'd been an architect, I think. He was called Peter the Hermit and he moved into the village and he was literally living in a packing case. It was just long enough to take a camp bed and it had sacking curtains over it. He lived in this packing case and he earned a bit digging in people's gardens and doing a bit of fishing. The last time I saw him, he had moved into somebody's greenhouse. He was living in their greenhouse. He died fairly recently, I think, of some stomach complaint. He'd been living on vegetables for years and they wondered if this had caused cancer of the stomach. He had a very weird diet. But he was tolerated in the village, and all along that coast there were these old boats tied up, with men with long straggly beards and earrings, and there was one old chap with one earring.

C: There's a mention of *Lorna Doone* in *A Question of Identity*: Inspector Finch finds a copy of *Lorna Doone*. *Lorna Doone* seems to be one of the touchstones of popular English reading, apparently. One of Michael Gilbert's new books about murder in the West Country mentions *Lorna Doone* and you've mentioned *Lorna Doone*. I'm sure there must be other references. Was *Lorna Doone* a real favorite among English readers?

T: Yes. I think it's one of those classics you read when you're fairly young, you know, like *Kidnapped* and *Treasure Island*.

C: *Jane Eyre*?

T: Yes. It's part of that tradition.

C: *A Question of Identity* starts off in a little place called Holyfield, which had been Anglo-Saxon. They think the body at first is Anglo-Saxon. Then they realize it really isn't, and the woman, the errant brother's wife, buries McGuire in Holyfield because she doesn't think there's any redemption possible for her after sinning.

T: Yes, it's a very extreme Catholic view. I think I make it clear that she's a sort of masochist. The Church wouldn't have seen her sin as quite so great, but because she was as she was, she could see no personal redemption for herself. I wanted to make her obsessive about sin, if you like.

C: There were so many things in that book: Holyfield is a holy place —

T: Sacred to the Saxons.

C: — and the murder victim is placed there. The body is placed there by a rather extreme Roman Catholic, but there seems to be some sort of connection I can't really put my finger on — a tie between paganism and modern-day Christianity, which is affirmed by this burial of a murder victim in a pagan holy place. Was that conscious on your part?

T: There is this feeling of the Old Religion still going on in this country very much.

C: Have there actually been survivals of the old Druidic religion?

T: Oh yes. It's gone underground, but now it's no longer punishable by law.

C: It was at one time, then?

T: It's only recently that the laws have been changed, I think, on this. I don't think it's surfaced, but there are now people who have been interviewed on television who claim to be white witches, and people go to them for love potions and this and that.

C: Is that in the countryside mostly, in the less disturbed parts?

T: They do have them in towns, but I think mainly in the country, and certainly Essex is meant to be one of the areas in which the Old Religion hung on the longest. There are supposed to be covens in Hertfordshire, too.

C: One of the things I notice about detective fiction, the more I read it, is that it seems to be one of the last strongholds of regionalism. Do you see that? Did you want to keep Finch in Essex for the rest of his career, for instance?

T: Yes, I think so, because it's a landscape I know and I know the people. I think I still see England as a series of regions, strongly regional areas, which have a very strong flavor of their own, and although to a certain extent dialects are dying out, you've still got them. Even the landscape is different. If you go to Essex and then to Suffolk, although there are only a few miles between them, they are entirely different landscapes.

C: Readers are often impressed by the way you've created a small world. The people who wander into it, like Vaughan, the murder victim in *Alibi in Time*, seem to more or less come to grief.

T: Yes. I'm very interested in this question of the Outsider, the man who doesn't belong in society for various reasons, personality or background, social conditions, because I think they find it very difficult when they enter a community to pick up the mores of that district.

C: Are you writing about the burden of the European past in a way when you write about these microcosms into which people come and collide with the mores and the customs and even the dialect? Is it the burden of the past?

T: No. I don't think I see it in those terms. I think I am interested in the closed community and what members of that closed community can do to each other if you step outside or come into it from outside. Not belonging. I think I'm also interested in the relationships that build up, particularly between people. You see, in detective fiction, you've got to have a small world. In the past it's been the country house, with the butler and people coming down for a country house weekend. Well, this is all past now. It still goes on, but not to that extent; that's old-fashioned. But you've got to have a certain number of characters, a limited number of characters, and you've got to have, I feel, very strong relationships, because murder is mainly domestic.

C: Is it in this country?

T: Oh yes, mainly domestic. What interests me about relationships in a detective book is that those relationships have been pushed to the extreme. And then you've got a sort of mystery, you know. You've got to set this up to a certain extent, but you must limit your characters, and you limit them most naturally, I think, by using a very limited environment.

C: You have to play fair, too, don't you? You have to introduce the murderer fairly early?

T: Oh yes.

C: You can't have him jump out of a bush in chapter 10.

T: No. And you've got to be absolutely fair to your reader and you've got to put down clues, if you like, so that although they've got to be surprised and say, "Good heavens. I didn't realize it was him or her," when they look back they've got to say, "Oh yeah. Well, of course, if I'd read *that* more carefully, I could have seen that *that* was the case."

C: One of the things readers like about your work is that your clues aren't always linguistic. The archetypical example of the linguistic clue is Agatha Christie's confusing the reader as to whether Evelyn was a man or a woman. The clue in that case is linguistic. And it doesn't seem quite fair. Your clues are factual or material or physical. Dr. Cotty jiggles his clock, which leads you to a pun in the title *Alibi in Time*. That's a physical fact, a material action.

T: Yeah, and the gun in *A Question of Identity* was propped up in the corner of the room, which Finch himself realizes too late. But it's a symbol of violence. He saw it; it was there, right at the beginning.

C: And he saw a lot of other things. He saw them burning those photos and didn't quite know what the hell was going on, and the crucifix that they dig up finally becomes important. All of those are material clues. I think for too long English detective stories were written by people who wanted to play word games. They would stick in the word that was the clue, but because you were dumb, you weren't supposed to get it.

T: I don't like one other type. I don't like the clues that are too mathematical — the ones where you have to work out a timetable of trains. They're fun and they're intellectual, but I haven't got that kind of mathematical mind. I think you can look at a room, just an ordinary room, and get an awful lot about the people in it by the sort of books that are around or this and that, and you extend this into detective fiction.

C: You can make red herrings rhetorical in the sense that you put both red herrings and clues out there, but you don't concentrate on the clues; you concentrate on something else. But you've played fair.

T: Oh yes, you play fair; the clue's been there.

C: You just use rhetoric to direct their attention away from it.

T: You've put it into part of a general description, and then later on the significance of it strikes Finch. I think one's got to treat one's readers as intelligent people. You mustn't fool them. You must be honest with them. You say, "Well, here's a room; this is what Finch sees." I suppose it is a kind of trick, in that they're seeing the room through Finch's eyes. And they don't see the significance of the gun even though it is mentioned. I think that is fair. I think that is fair, yes.

C: I think of all the forms of fiction, detective fiction seems to me the most objective. Or at least more objective than a novel by a young man just out of college.

T: I don't think personally I could write about love because to me a relationship just beginning isn't all that interesting. A relationship that's gone on and has come to a point, a breaking point — and you know it's a ten-, fifteen-, twenty-year-old relationship — that's what interests me.

C: Most of the relationships in your novels are not between older people necessarily, but they're old relationships: a father-daughter relationship is an old relationship; a brother and sister-in-law relationship is an old one. Even though the daughter in that relationship is young, it's an old relationship because she's eighteen or twenty.

T: The one I'm working on now is about a marriage. The man, Max, the artist, is over seventy-five, in a marriage that has gone on for a long time with a much younger woman. Established relationships interest me more than ones that are just starting off.

C: Well, your books are for grown people. A lot of American novels are for kids; they're for twenty-five-year-olds who want to read about other people writing about their emotions. I think that's one of the most difficult things to write about, because one's emotions are one's own and we don't perceive things like "true love" the same way.

T: Oh, I agree. Quite frankly, I think a lot of life is not emotions anyway. It's scrubbing the bloody kitchen floor and digging in the garden.

C: There's a wonderful quotation from Samuel Johnson. Somebody asked Dr. Johnson why he didn't write about love and he said, "Sir, it is only one of the many emotions under the sun."

T: You know, it can't occupy your whole life. And it's awfully inverted. It's searching your psyche and your ego and an awful lot of it, I think, is an excuse for a sort of "me" emotion — "I," "I," "I," self-centered and egocentric. But I'm very interested, also, in survival, the survival of the individual. No matter how many times they're knocked down, they've got to get up again and go and dig in their garden, which is what life is about, I think.

C: That's a key theme in the twentieth century.

T: I've no longer got it, but for years I did keep a clipping out of a magazine. One whines on, saying, "Oh, my God," but this photograph shows a woman in the Warsaw Ghetto, a Jewish woman, wearing men's boots with no laces in them, standing in a gutter, holding a baby wrapped up in a bit of old blanket. And she's got her head thrown back and she is *howling.* There is this extraordinary expression on her face of utter despair. I cut it out and kept it for a long time. I thought, "I shall never be reduced to trudging in the gutter, wearing men's boots, clutching a baby." So one whines on and complains and moans, but the Jewish woman, *that's* what survival is about. I don't know if she ever did survive, but . . .

C: Endure and prevail, as Faulkner said. Not only endure, but *prevail.* But first you have to endure or you won't be around to prevail.

T: And, in fact, I think we're a lot more resilient than we're often given credit for. People survive; it's incredible what they do survive. At the end of *A Question of Identity*, the farmer goes out to milk the cows. I mean, that's life. Two brothers have just died, but his cows have still got to be milked, and the girl may come back because there's nobody else to come to. That's love as well. You've got your farm, you've got your land; you go on farming it. You pick up the pieces, you know, and you just live for another day.

C: How did you get into writing detective fiction?

T: Well, I'd read a lot, and I sort of always wanted to write and I'd written parts of books. I'd sort of tried my hand at D. H. Lawrence, Jane Austen, and so on, and Katherine Mansfield type short stories. I wrote and wrote and suddenly I discovered I'd got a book — *Not One of Us.* In fact, I lost part of it.

C: Was that the first book you ever attempted?

T: First book I ever finished. It took me about three years because I didn't take it seriously. I just wrote when I wanted to. Eventually, I was writing it in school exercise books and I suddenly realized I'd finished it. And then I lost one of the exercise books. I found it eventually. I got it typed out and sent it off.

C: Can a struggling writer in England just pick out Stodder or Constable and write a letter and say, "Here's a manuscript."

T: No. I went to an agent, actually, and in fact it was sold first in the States. Harper's took it.

C: Under Joan Kahn?

T: That's right, Joan Kahn. And, in fact, I went up to London to London Management. They liked it and said they didn't think they'd have any trouble placing it. And oh, the weeks went by and weeks went by and my agent rang me up and said it's a shame, but nobody seems to be interested.

C: In England?

T: Well, I don't know, but he obviously couldn't find a publisher, so I would have to collect it and bring it home. He said, "It's a shame to waste it; try and turn it into a television play." "Good idea," I thought, so I came home a bit despondent, with the manuscript. And then — I don't know, you know how time tends to telescope — fairly shortly afterward, he rang me to say Harper's had taken it, and then after Harper's took it, Constable took it.

C: Harper's had at that point a very big stable of detective fiction writers. Joan Kahn, I think, was probably responsible for getting them.

T: Yes. I met Joan Kahn in London. She's very nice, but she thought the next one, *Death Cap*, was too English.

C: Because of the poisoning, I guess. And he walks away at the end of *Death Cap* and leaves them to stew in their own moral juices, which is not satisfactory in America. We like a final reckoning.

T: But it often happens: you can't always prove a case.

C: A number of your books are like that. In *Alibi in Time*, nobody's ever really prosecuted or brought into prison or made to stand in the dock. Dr. Cotty crashes his car. He punishes himself. The State doesn't step in and start that awesome machinery of indictment, preliminary hearings, and so on. A lot of your books have a kind of poetic justice, or the justice of the damned soul stewing in his own juices.

T: I make a distinction between justice and the law. In fact, in the first book, Finch himself makes that distinction between the law and justice; they aren't the same. I think of this case recently of the Exit people. I don't know if you've read the case.

C: That poor man who was sentenced for helping someone commit suicide?

T: One of them got sentenced to two years and the other one got sentenced to two years' suspended sentence. Legally, he's as guilty as the other one, but the judge felt that justice would be better served by his not going to jail. At the moment they're saying we send too many people to prison. Prisons are overfull in a lot of cases in England. They should not sentence people to jail, I think. I had this argument actually with a friend of mine, who's a probation officer, over the Great Train Robbers, who were sentenced to incredibly long prison sentences. I do think that in some cases English justice tends to come down on the side of property, not life. You can get fifteen years for murder, but the robbers got sent to prison for much longer than that and in fact no one got killed.

C: Because they were armed? Somebody was hit over the head, as I remember.

T: He died later.

C: But you think if these guys had just whacked out somebody on the marshes with no property involved, they might have gotten lesser sentences?

T: That's a criticism I would make — that our law tends to be protective of property, rather than of life.

C: There's a whole wonderful subgenre of Victorian detective fiction in which no murder ever occurs, but things like diamond necklaces are avidly sought for. People are *tripping* over themselves trying to find property and that never happened in American detective fiction or American crime fiction. It was always murder and/or a search for justice. I've just now begun to realize that much of English detective fiction today is still about property. There's a Peter Dickinson novel about a woman who's trying to fix up a house in London, and it's through her acquaintance with the property laws and the eviction laws and the tenancy laws that a whole chain of things is set off. Ruth Rendell has written a couple of novels at least in which property looms very large in the plot. Are English people still concerned with property, the rights of property? Having your material world taken away from you?

T: Yes. That can be very interesting, I think. Fraud, for instance, is fascinating, but it's never appealed to me. Life rather than property would always interest me because in that way you are looking at relationships, which is what basically interests me. I couldn't get worked up about a Ford in the same way as I could about people. Most of all, people. I can see the fascination, the intricacies of a case of fraud. That kind of plot would be fascinating.

C: Inheritance laws, which Ruth Rendell did a novel about.

T: But I wouldn't be interested in the research for that, because I don't think I've got that kind of mind.

C: When I started comparing birth dates and publication dates, I found that most detective writers, surprisingly enough, land on their feet in their middle thirties or late thirties, not having written anything before that. Is it a kind of mind that matures later? Or is it the kind of personality that doesn't like certain kinds of novels?

T: I don't really know. In my own case, I was bringing up kids and working; there simply wasn't time, you know. It was only really when the family began to get a little bit older . . . I was teaching full time and running a house and bringing up kids. There simply wasn't time for me and what I wanted to do. And I suppose it was only really when the children started to grow up that I could grab the odd evening to do things. It could be that people reach a point where they can look at life perhaps more objectively, instead of being so involved with it on a personal basis. They can stand back and begin to look at it. I think to a certain extent this is why I'm very interested in the outsider theme. I think that in order to be a writer, you've got to a certain extent be an outsider yourself. You can't participate. You've got to stand back and watch.

C: Very much as Finch/Rudd is an outsider.

T: Yes.

C: Like all cops are outsiders.

T: Yes. They've got to be the observers.

C: Boyce tries to be an insider and always lands in hot water with the inspector for trying to side kind of indirectly with the local people. He doesn't keep his eyes open like a real outsider ought to.

T: Well, I suppose I've got him as a foil for Finch in a way because he's sort of terribly literal minded and he's not very sensitive and not very intuitive. I suppose he's the opposite — he's the big shouldered cop who's got his rule book out. Finch is much more sensitive and has got another ear listening as well.

C: You always describe Finch as having a prosperous farmer's face, which is ironic because he's very far removed from that, and of course a farmer is an insider. He's the basis of the food chain.

T: Yes, but Finch has come from this community. He's a

country lad, who has in a sense moved out and away from his roots. He feels sometimes he misses his roots; he broke with his past.

C: He's become a sort of artist, hasn't he? He's *from* the people but not really *with* them anymore. He's doing a very skilled and intuitive sort of job.

T: Yes, because he understands these people and in a sense the farmer's face is a kind of disguise behind which he hides.

C: A mask, really.

T: And he listens and watches. In the first book, *Not One of Us*, he does mourn his loss of his roots, the fact that he was brought up in a little cottage similar to the one he has to go visit during the investigation. He does assume this listening, silent, avuncular quality that fools people into chatting on. He uses it deliberately.

C: Did you have a real model for Finch? How much do you know about police science?

T: Not a lot, I must admit [laughs], although I've always found the police are very kind if I get stuck. Where my mother used to live, the local village policeman was always terribly kind, and though my mother lived in the village, I used to have to go down with a list of questions for the local bobby and say, "What about so-and-so," and he'd answer them. Procedure's interesting, but obviously you can't put too much into a book because it becomes a police procedural thing.

C: You don't view yourself as really a police procedural writer?

T: No. When it does come in, I do like to get it right, if I can. Obviously they're going to go through certain procedures when they first arrive on the scene of a murder. "I must get this right," I think, "without overburdening the book with it."

C: Did you actually ride with the cops or go look at what they did or consult police-science books?

T: I read quite a bit around it. One picks up an awful lot from newspapers and so on about what goes on. But basically, if I am stuck over something, I ring up this chap or go and see him and say, "Hey, what would you do now?" And he'll tell me.

C: It's good you've got an expert of some sort. But you wouldn't be interested in writing something — although they're grand in their way — like the 87th Precinct books, where endless reports and forensic results and confessions are introduced and quoted verbatim . . .

T: No, but I think that's fascinating. I'm working at the moment on some old cases and I've been up to the Colindale Newspaper Library, going back into the cases as they appeared in the *Times*. I was looking for background stuff, but the old newspapers are fascinating, and I love the little details. For instance, in the case I was looking up the other day, before she died, the woman had a supper of ham and potatoes and bottled stout. And with that kind of little detail, suddenly the whole thing comes to life.

C: Have you ever thought about writing another crime detection or detective story without Inspector Finch/Rudd?

T: Yes, I'd like to sometime, perhaps looking at it from the point of view of the murderer. I've got one or two ideas that I'd like to do without the police side of it at all — just simply somebody in a marriage wanting to get out of it and looking at it completely from his eyes.

C: That'd be interesting. That's one of the things, I guess, Americans are noted for — the kind of novel James M. Cain did so well: *Double Indemnity* and *The Postman Always Rings Twice*. The criminal-viewpoint novel has not been popular really in England, has it, traditionally? It's mostly been the police inspector kind of novel, hasn't it?

T: I think, generally speaking, yes. I work on lots of background in British murder cases. You know, there are some incredible cases.

C: I know. I've got Roughead's book on classic trials.

T: And they do tend to be domestic.

C: Is that always true in this country? You always kill somebody you know?

T: Generally speaking, there's some bond. That's why the Yorkshire Ripper case made such a furor, because this was so unusual: a mass murderer, a random killer. These are very unusual. I think part of it is, of course, that you can't get guns very easily in this country. So, in a sense, the murderer has to use a certain amount of cleverness in order to commit the murder.

C: I never thought about that. That makes murder slightly more intellectual if you can't pick up a .38 and bang away with it.

T: Yes.

C: Is that why there's so much poisoning in English detective fiction?

T: They've always had to turn to some other means to kill somebody. Oh, you can pick up a poker . . .

C: But then what are you going to do with the poker?

T: [*laughs*] Yes. But I think shooting somebody with a gun is a very dull way of killing them. And apart from that, you get into all sorts of questions and I am sure I would have to make a hell of a lot of research into ballistics and trajectories and this sort of thing which I don't find very interesting. Guns *have* been used, but guns are just not available, you see.

C: I never thought about it that way. Because you have such strict gun control in England, you really have to be ingenious to polish off your fellow man.

T: Yes, yes.

C: Is murder restricted to the, ah, smarter class in England, would you say?

T: [*laughs*] I don't know, but what I'm researching at the moment is the Wallace case, the chess player. Fascinating, absolutely fascinating. His wife was killed. There was a marvelous name in the case too — Mr. Queltrough — who phoned him up at the chess club in Liverpool and he went off. There's still a lot of controversy about the case. They think that Wallace established a very elaborate alibi for himself and in fact *he* was Queltrough phoning up the chess club, saying, "May I speak to Mr. Wallace." And he went off on the tram, two trams, in fact, and searched around for Mr. Queltrough, who lived in Minlove Gardens West. And there wasn't a Minlove Gardens West. There was a Minlove Gardens East, North, and South. He asked all kinds of people and got all these witnesses — including a policeman — who said, "Yes, he was here asking about it." And he came home and he couldn't get in. The neighbors were just leaving. He said, "I can't get in." They said, "That's funny. Let's have a look." So he eventually got in and there was his wife, battered to death on the sitting room floor.

C: Oh, Lordy.

T: They used to play duets together. She used to play the piano and he used to play the violin. You know, it's fascinating because of the relationship between the husband and the wife. Then there's this whole business of this mysterious Mr. Queltrough.

C: Was he indicted and later convicted?

T: He was taken to trial and was found guilty. It was the first case in which a union put up money for the defense. He was a Prudential Insurance agent.

C: What sort of union?

T: The members of the Prudential Insurance Company. They had more or less a trial. They said, "Well, if you really think he's not guilty, let's have a look at the evidence." So his defense lawyer went along and presented the evidence for the defense to the insurance people. And they said, "Yeah, O.K., it sounds good to us. We'll support him." And he was found guilty and the case went to appeal and he was acquitted on appeal. It's a fascinating case.

C: Is he alive now?

T: No. He died shortly afterward. He was hounded, really. This is one of those things. Was he guilty? If he wasn't guilty, he was an innocent man hounded by the law to his death, because the trial sort of finished him.

C: You know, the English system of justice is very good, but it impresses me that no matter what country you're born in, once the machinery gets cranked up —

T: Oh yeah, it grinds on —

C: You're on a fast train to conviction.

T: And you can't get off. It's a very ponderous machinery. Yet trials are extraordinarily conversational. I went to a case in the Crown court at St. Albans, to sit in on a murder case recently. It was conducted in a most conversational way: very low-key, no drama. You couldn't really believe that a man — not on trial for his life in this case; they don't hang anymore — was in the dock accused of murder. It was chatty, conversational, the judge saying, "Oh, just a minute, just a minute; would you put that another way?" Capital punishment was banned because there were so many cases in England where people had been hung, such as the Christie case, where Evans was hanged and then they found that Christie was guilty.

C: That soured people, didn't it?

T: The anticapital punishment people had a very very strong lobby. That case strengthened the lobby for abolishing hanging.

C: Have you got any plans? What are you working on now and what are you working on after that?

T: I'm working on another Finch at the moment, which I had put aside for a while. I'd like to get into radio plays.

C: That's big in England, isn't it? We've wiped them out in America.

T: I haven't heard yet, but I sent up to BBC a radio adaptation of *Deadly Relations* (*Habit of Loving* in America). I haven't heard from BBC, but what I'd like to do is do some radio work.

C: Is that fairly straightforward? Do you just get a script and send it to the BBC?

T: There's only the BBC on radio, apart from radio on the local stations. I sent in a script they didn't, wouldn't, accept, but they said if I'd like to adapt it and send in the first part, then if they liked it, they'd commission it. So I'm sort of waiting on that, and I'd like to do another Finch.

C: This'll be your eighth Finch. By now you must have an idea of who reads them. Who do you think is reading Finch?

T: I don't know. I never thought about it. I suppose people like myself. I really hadn't picked a specific reader. I think probably people slightly older.

C: I think that's true of detective fiction in general. Readers are older and a little more intelligent — that's what booksellers in America say. People who read detective fiction appear to them to be the upper division of American readers.

T: Really? I don't think they're great literature. I think they're a very interesting bit of culture, but I don't think it's great literature. People buy them to read on trains and on holidays. I think they're a way of spending a pleasant evening.

C: But just as much time and energy is poured into one of those as would be into a "serious" novel, don't you think?

T: Possibly, yes. But I think, though, that what they are saying is not terribly profound, necessarily.

C: I think it differs from writer to writer, too. Some people are really shooting for the moon and others are obviously trying to expand a novella into a novel so somebody will put it in a separate cover.

T: Possibly. I think the whole genre is very interesting because it's open to so many interpretations. I think Simenon, for instance, turned the detective novel into something more than just a puzzle. He also did work on the nondetective book, and I think it's very interesting, for instance, that Dickens toward the end of his life turned to the detective novel.

C: Are there things you can't say in "serious" novels that you think you can say in detective novels more easily or, more to the point, more efficiently?

T: No. I personally find the structure of it comforting

[*laughs*]. I don't think I'd know what to do if I just wrote a novel.

C: You like the discipline?

T: And I like the limitation. I like the discipline of it, the limitations of it. I feel more comfortable with it. But, as I say, if I just wanted to write a novel, I think, "Christ, how do I start? Who do I put in it and what do I get them to say?" I can't really think what a man or woman would say if they were sitting together, whereas if you've got a murder, your characters have got a fascinating subject to talk about. Your conversation's there. They chat about the murder. Of course they do. But at the same time you can say something about relationships, I think, which is what interests me.

C: I think that's what interests a lot of people about the detective story — that a wider range of human emotion is displayed.

T: Yes. But to me, now, I'm interested in this question of survival, of relations being something more than sex and romance and so on, which are important parts, but they just aren't what relationships are about and what life is about. You get relationships, for instance, where nothing really is said anymore, but it's still a relationship. The relationship was worn down and yet . . . I've been reading two books recently on Hardy — Thomas Hardy's two wives, Emma and Florence — and they're fascinating. He pursued these two women and all the romance, and yet when he actually married them, for some reason he was no longer interested. He was only interested in Emma again when she died. Fascinating. These are much more interesting, I think, than the dashing into bed with somebody. I'm not saying that you can't have that kind of relationship, but I think only that kind of relationship is very limiting. There's a lot more to relationships than that.

C: One hopes.

T: Yes.

JANE LANGTON

Jane Langton's first book was *The Minuteman Murder* (originally *The Transcendental Murder*). This book sets the pattern now familiar to her many fans: a tightly plotted detective story that is also intellectual, witty, and full of shrewd observations about the way men and women of more than minimum intelligence — including the villains — behave toward each other. This book also introduces Jane Langton as a modern mediator of the transcendentalist myth, particularly the myth of Thoreau. Her protagonists, Homer Kelly, sometime of the Middlesex County D.A.'s office, and Mary Morgan, Concord librarian, are co-authors, by the second novel in the series, of a book on Thoreau; as detectives as well as civilians they are much indebted to Henry David as well as to Ralph Waldo Emerson and Emily Dickinson.

The first novel gets rolling at a meeting of the Alcott Association in Concord, Massachusetts, during a festive bicentennial week that will commemorate the April 19, 1775, battle between the townsmen and the British. As history students will remember, it was during the general melee, or rather before it, that someone, no one knows who, fired the "shot heard round the world." Ernest Goss, a tweedy Exeter and Harvard type, reads letters from selected transcendentalists revealing new and shocking information about "relations between the sexes" (as he primly but salaciously describes them) in the Concord of the 1840s.

Homer Kelly, who has just published a book on Emerson, is the chairman of the meeting. Mary Morgan is in the audience. (The two have only just met.) Goss reads a letter purportedly from Margaret Fuller to Emerson:

> My dear Waldo,
> ... Thou the castle's King, I the Queen! Long have I waited in the dust to behold thy golden litter! ... O what rapture in Mrs. O'Flannigan's back sitting room! O divine divan! ...

There are other sexy epistles just as outrageously funny, including one from Thoreau to Emily Dickinson. These revelations cause the meeting to break up in assault and battery. The next day, the body of Ernest Goss, killed by a musketball, is discovered. And then a librarian is killed. How and why these people were done in comprise the rest of Langton's highly successful debut on the mystery scene. *The Minuteman Murder* also demonstrates Langton's profound sense of connection with history and with nature. And she is not only witty, she is downright funny.

In *Dark Nantucket Noon* and *The Memorial Hall Murder* and in the latest, *Natural Enemy*, Langton's theme is the desecration of the natural or the destruction of the old and valued — the sublimely ugly Memorial Hall, for example.

Dark Nantucket Noon sees Homer and Mary married and the co-authors of a book on Thoreau. Homer's job this time is to free poet Katherine Clark, who's been accused of murdering her former lover's wife on the day a total solar eclipse darkened Nantucket. The murder is connected to the spoliation of the island by greedy newcomers whose antipathy to nature is more than matched by their inadequacy as human beings and their fondness for ugliness in general.

Natural Enemy will be of interest not only to dyed-in-the-wool Langton fans but to readers of good novels in general:

again, man is posed as the enemy of the wild. A grove of trees must be cut for profit and the man who stands in the way is murdered in a particularly ironic way. The murderer is caught in a way just as ironic. The novel takes place in Langton's own Concord neighborhood, and one of the families in the book lives in the Old Baker House, which is lived in by Langton and her husband, Bill, an astronomer. Thoreau could see the smoke from the house when he lived on Walden Pond. In many ways *Natural Enemy* is Langton's finest novel. We have yet in this country to treat the care — or the destruction — of nature as a theme in fiction. The symbolism is very sophisticated and very subtle, as are the feelings of the heroine, the murderer's next victim. For those who want their fiction to reflect the fact that some humans think deeply, period, Langton is among a precious few novelists working inside a realist-naturalist tradition that has chosen to emphasize the life of the senses divorced from the life of the mind. For those who want their fiction to be stirred with more than a healthy dash of murder, as solved by those who balance the senses and the mind, Langton stands alone among her kind.

CARR: You went to Wellesley for only two years, then went on to the University of Michigan?

LANGTON: Yes, that's right. I got a bachelor of science in astronomy and then I switched to the history of art.

C: That's a real turnabout.

L: I studied that there, got a master's degree, and Bill was studying physics. Then we both came here, or rather to Cambridge, and went on and got second masters' degrees, which didn't add to our glory, but we got a lot more information stored away.

C: You went to Radcliffe. What was the article "Impostor in the Yard" in the *Radcliffe Quarterly* about?

L: That wasn't anything about myself, really. I was a good friend of the editor of the *Radcliffe Quarterly*, Ada Press, and since I'd been attending classes there because I was writing a children's book about a school like that and had said how much I was enjoying it, she said, "Why don't you write about it as an older person coming back to classes?" And so I did.

C: Did you ever actually do any work in astronomy?

L: Yes, I did, a little bit. While I was an undergraduate, I was employed by the observatory of the university for a dollar an hour — that was the right pay in those days — to take spectographs of stars that were research projects of professors, who needed to have somebody out there night after night after night, just sitting there, guiding the telescope and making sure it stayed on the star, and taking photographs.

C: A strange, solitary type of job.

L: It was nice, yeah.

C: And then you kind of abandoned astronomy?

L: I was married to a man who'd been an American boy, and it was so obvious to me from the beginning that he knew infinitely more than I would ever know or understand about astronomy, and that things came to him that were just a terrible struggle for me, not having been brought up taking cars apart and so on. So when I took a course in the history of art and it was so delicious, and I enjoyed it so much, and I understood what the professor was saying without having to go home and study it, and the things we were looking at were so wonderful, I made up my mind to change.

C: It really makes a difference, doesn't it, when you feel like you're a natural in some field?

L: Oh yes, yes, yes. I wish that I had had sense enough to major in literature, that I hadn't had a strong feeling of having to learn how to do something that was useful and salable. I wish that hadn't been the case and I had just enjoyed myself and taken what interested me, because my background in American and English literature was — is — very thin. You *can* educate yourself, but I think that those good old foundation courses, English 201 and so on, which give you some kind of framework and background, are a tremendous help.

C: Were you not forced to take English 201?

L: It was just a writing course.

C: Good Lord, how'd they let you loose without one of those long, boring survey courses?

L: Oh I wish they hadn't, I really do. Those survey courses would have given me — no matter how badly they were taught — some sort of critical standards, but when I started reading those great fat books that everybody reads at seventeen, eighteen, and nineteen, I just wanted to find out what happened.

C: That will give the present generation the cold sweats. They think big books are cruel and unusual punishment. Which ones were you remembering?

L: *The Magic Mountain* and *War and Peace* and so on. I just read them to see what happens and I still only know what happens.

C: After you got your degree from Michigan you were married?

L: Yes.

C: During the war?

L: Yes.

C: Was it hard being married during the war?

L: The war was just somewhere over there, far away.

C: You get the impression, from seeing movies made forty years later, that everyone was hanging on to the evening radio newscasts to see if the Nazis and Japs had been trounced somewhere that day.

L: Yes, I know. Of course, it wasn't like that at all. The Vietnam War was much more like that, I think, when we were all so very conscious of what was happening daily.

C: I suppose there was censorship too, wasn't there?

L: There must have been, yes. And we were all enthusiastic about what was going on and didn't question it. I was very glad Bill didn't have to be in it; he had a bad arm. No, I don't remember thinking much about the war at all. If we'd lost, things would have been very bad indeed, but I guess we just had a naive kind of optimism that somehow everything would be all right.

C: I don't think we knew we could be whipped. To cut away to something else, although it is partly related, let me tell you that I've noticed that mystery writers seem to take up writing mysteries a lot later than most poets take up writing poetry. They're usually in their late thirties, early forties. Do you have any idea why?

L: No. I didn't know that. I started the children's books, I think, because I was still really a child. And I love children's books very much, always have and always will, and it seemed a natural thing to try to do. I felt much closer to my own childhood then. I couldn't imagine writing a book for adults, but I was also at that time — I think I must have been — reading Dorothy Sayers and enjoying those very much, and I was entranced by the notion of trying to do for Concord, Massachusetts, what she'd done for — I assume those are real places she was writing about. So I guess that's how I got into that. But I don't believe I would have started with mysteries. I wrote three, or tried to write three, children's books before I finally succeeded in writing one that worked, but what I would like to do someday is write a genuine novel.

C: I think you do write genuine novels.

L: But a novel that wasn't constricted by plot so enormously, as a mystery is. Everything, everything is something necessary. You have to establish this fellow at a certain point at a certain time and it would really be a tremendous pleasure to —

C: Isn't the detective story like working in one of the classical forms of English verse? In the sonnet, or at least in the Shakespearean sonnet, there are certain things you do in the first quatrain, certain things you do in the second, including the "turnaround" line, and if you don't do it, it's not a Shakespearean sonnet — or it doesn't work, which is the crucial test. And it has to be rhymed, which is an awful constriction in English.

L: But I think the clumsiness and the burden of the mechanical things in a mystery story are — If they could be eliminated, if one could write a certain novel that hadn't attached itself to that necessity, that hadn't been burdened by that necessity, if one could write a mystery or detective novel that flowed along as an ordinary novel does, I think that would be a tremendous success.

C: Yours are very subtle.

L: Oh no, they're not subtle. In poetry, perhaps the consciousness that this is a sonnet — that the rules of the sonnet form have been obeyed — adds to one's pleasure, but when you're conscious of the mechanics in a novel, it's obviously a flaw.

C: Some of the wonderful tension in writing detective stories — or at least some of the pleasure I get — is from watching people run an obstacle course. One of the things I like about villanelles is watching somebody dance in ball and chain.

L: Yes, yes. Well, that's what I was saying, yes.

C: But you don't want the ball and chain?

L: Yes. I think if the ball and chain show in a mystery story, that's a shame. If you think, "Aha! They're bringing in the red herring now," then it's wrong. You don't want to be conscious of that.

C: Yes. You know one "fact" is a red herring; one's bound to ... I guess we're about to give away the endings of your books, but I'm not going to worry. In *Dark Nantucket Noon*, the murderer —

L: The horrible thing about that is that the dumb book is called *Dark Nantucket Noon* in the first place. I fought against the title and fought against it and fought against it. I don't like the title. I think it's boring, and when people say or write the title, "noon" is constantly changed to "moon," which it perfectly well could be, because the moon obscures the sun.

C: *Dark Nantucket Moon* would certainly have been a title one would expect.

L: And so the title is always given incorrectly. I don't care and I don't blame people for doing that: it's a bad title.

C: Kitty is walking along the beach the day of the eclipse and she actually sees the murderer.

L: That's right.

C: And she only realizes later, toward the end of the book, that one of these seals was in fact the head of a man.

L: Did the man's head disguised as a seal, or taken for a seal, get in there? When I read this again, afterward, it seemed to me they'd left the seal out. I put that in at the last minute and it seemed to me that somehow they missed it.

C: Here it is: "You what? A seal. I'd forgotten. I thought he was a seal, I'd seen him in the water on the way."

L: Oh great! I'm so glad, and there was a seal in the beginning.

C: There were a number of seals out there in the ocean and he was swimming in the midst of them. Was there another version?

L: Oh, there are always other versions, yes. It takes me many times to go through it and then I just keep changing.

C: That's really clever, though. In a lot of mystery stories the classic way to do it is to have a bunch of human beings in a room and later, when the book is all over and you've finished it, it turns out that, yes, one of the first characters you met was indeed the murderer. But that's very clever to have one of the seals be the murderer. Or what we thought was a seal. And he's hiding under the cover of nature, betraying it, in his way: one of the themes of your books.

L: Joan Kahn said how could that kind of cheerful sort of fellow have been the dastardly man he turned out to be? She said that I had to make him more plausible, and so it was then that I figured out having him connected with the *Andrea*

Doria. I remembered that the *Andrea Doria* had sunk off the coast of Nantucket; so that could be kind of a local touch to the island.

C: And the *Andrea Doria* is in the background of this whole novel.

L: Yes, that's right.

C: Helen Boatwright's parents went down with the *Andrea Doria* and Alden Dove —

L: That was all stuck in afterward, you see.

C: The stuff about the *Andrea Doria*?

L: I went to the public library and looked up everything I could find about her.

C: That's amazing. That thing stands offshore as a kind of dark presence all through the story.

L: Good!

C: Some villains also have the names of wonderful birds — Howard Swan and Alden Dove. How did this come about?

L: Alden Dove had to be A.D. That was the reason. I had to have A.D. for the *Andrea Doria*, and I like to use certain kinds of names. Finding a good name is hard, as I'm sure you know. You can't just call somebody Peterson or Cooper or Smith; the name has to have a certain solidity to it, and not sound like the name of a paper-thin character. I've got millions of paper-thin characters, but I try and try and try and keep trying this name and that name until I find one that works. But it doesn't have anything to do with their being birds. I'm sorry.

C: No deep, dark symbolism in there?

L: [*laughs*] No. No symbolism nowhere, no how.

C: As you were saying, everything counts in a detective novel. You know from the way a detective novel has to be written that when you run across the thing about Jupiter the swan losing his mate and being wounded himself that's going to figure in there somewhere and, sure enough, this nice woman who is supposedly the head of the conservation league has been out there just being — That was an awfully brutal recollection, even filtered through Alice Dove's memory, of what had been done to those wonderful birds.

L: Male swans can be very dangerous, actually.

C: They're certainly large enough to be.

L: I think one of the reasons they don't survive on our streams, even though they breed in the wild, is that in protecting their nests and their wives, they will attack very violently.

C: Human beings?

L: If you bother them, they can give you a very nasty cut.

C: They're certainly not afraid. Jupiter is almost the king of creation on that island. Let me cut back just a moment. After you began writing children's books, some of which I have read — and liked — what did the editors start telling you about doing children's books? What do they tell you that you can do in a children's book that you can't do in an adult book?

L: Oh, nobody tells you anything.

C: You're supposed to know all that?

L: There's a nice guy in town named Jay Daley. He's the director of our library, a young man who has just published his first novel, and they published it for children, but it has a great deal of explicit sex in it, more than I've seen in other books for children. I think many of the taboos that were there years ago are gone now, and there's more of a range that children have available to them than they used to have, which I think is good. I think a lot of children's writing is silly and foolish and I'm bored to death with problem novels, which seem to be very popular — the divorced father, the dead grandmother. People will say, "Well, now, we ought to have a novel about this because it will be something that people will ask for." Or "I'm getting divorced; I need books that will teach my children about that."

C: But fiction? They need fiction to teach their children? I don't know sometimes if we can escape the didactic purposes of all fiction, and certainly the history of the novel is on the side of the contractor and purchaser in that situation, because when the novel first arose in England, the nonconformist ideal was still running strong and even Defoe, like many another early novelist, purported to be giving moral instruction.

L: Or immoral instruction.

C: Yes, well, they got fascinated with what, say, Roxanne was really up to. But can we ever escape moral instruction in the novel?

L: Oh, I don't mind. I don't mind what they publish as long as there is still a market for it, a need for it, but I think the need for children's literature springs from something more than just a desire to be fashionable or to reach a certain market.

C: Then you went from children's books to detective stories or mystery stories.

L: Yes, except the third one was a detective story and then there was a wide gap between the first detective story and the second one, from 1964 to 1975, eleven years, because I wrote one that took me four years and nobody liked it and I think it was really a dud. I'm sure it was a terrible dud.

C: Was that the one entitled *Trouble in Utopia*?

L: That was one title for it, when I finally finished it. Good heavens, where have you read all this?

C: In *Contemporary Authors*; they give working titles.

L: Later I called it *When Shall These Bones Rise?* It had a ghost in it, one I was very fond of — the ghost of a real person, Ezra Ripley, but Joan Kahn didn't like it, didn't like the idea of a ghost. She thought that was absolutely forbidden in the kinds of stories that she liked to publish, and nobody else liked it either.

C: So *Trouble in Utopia* — *When Shall These Bones Rise?* — never actually went?

L: No. It's up in my attic. It was heartbreaking. I had a very small child at the time. I blame it on Andy. Also, I think that after I published one mystery, I sort of felt I could throw in anything that I enjoyed into a book, and if I enjoyed it, other people would enjoy it. And I put in too many things. I think this is my problem anyway. I write a kind of mishmash without some simple kind of unity. I'm trying to reform. But at that time I didn't know it was necessary.

C: I think your books do have unity, of theme, certainly, and other things. The first — *The Transcendental Murders* — I love, possibly as much as *Dark Nantucket Noon,* and I certainly liked *The Memorial Hall Murder.* Incidentally, I went over to Harvard and saw Memorial Hall yesterday.

L: Oh yes, isn't it great?

C: Awful!

L: No! [*laughs*] It does have a kind of awful majesty, glory, and hideousness. I'm very fond of it, and I think if it had all its gold pinnacles and its painted brick and was in good condition, you wouldn't quite say it was awful with the same tone in your voice. You might say, "Oh, it was awful," but there might be more awe and reverence in that.

C: The tower has been missing since 1956.

L: Yes, that's right. It burned.

C: Where did they get the idea for the red and green striped slates?

L: I think it probably comes from St. Stephen's in Vienna. Some German or Austrian churches had zebra striping of that kind. St. Stephen's is a big Gothic church in Vienna and I'm sure it's one of the very eclectic sources for that building.

C: I noticed the eclecticism. I wandered around the entire thing, trying to identify the individual parts, and there are various styles jammed together in that building.

L: I did a lot of looking into its background for a talk I gave to the Victorian Society in Boston. They're of course interested in old buildings and I spent an awful lot of time at the library.

C: Who was the architect?

L: Van Brunt and Ware. They were disciples, I think, of the kind of things Ruskin was doing. He was encouraging the Gothic Revival in England, including the university museum at Oxford, which was a brand new building at that time and the funniest building, but they were enraptured with the Gothic Revival.

C: And yet Memorial Hall has Romanesque Revival things in it.

L: Oh yes, yes right. Henry Hobson Richardson was coming along then as well, as I remember; I've forgotten a lot of the history.

C: The Hall was erected as a memorial to the Union Harvard men.

L: That's right, not to the Confederate soldiers.

C: Although there were some Harvard Confederates. Rooney Lee, Robert E.'s son, was one of them.

L: There were a great many; there are a great many — over a hundred. And it does seem a pity.

C: Perhaps a modest Greek Revival saloon can be built somewhere on the sacred precincts for them . . .

Your first book was called *The Transcendental Murder* when it came out in 1964. Why was the title changed to *The Minuteman Murder*?

L: That was because Dell brought it out later on, and by that time transcendental meditation had become an interesting phenomenon and they were afraid it would sound as though that was what it was about, which it certainly wasn't. I certainly wouldn't have liked it if people bought it under a mistaken apprehension that it was about something it was not. They wanted to put things like "bloodcurdling" and "violent" on the cover. They were using all sorts of adjectives that didn't fit it at all, and I begged them, "Please don't; you'll get the wrong readers and the readers will detest it because it won't be what they thought." So they did change it to something more refined and genteel.

C: You know now, after having written detective stories, that there has to be a plot behind the plot that actually takes in the happenings of the detective novel.

L: Yes. That's right, yes. The way I wrote that one and the way, I guess, I wrote the second one, I had the classic notion that you have a great many parallel plots, only one of which is actually true. And you have to veil that one and expose the others. In the more recent ones, I have not been so interested in trying to conceal who's responsible for what's going on. In fact, I really didn't try at all in *The Memorial Hall Murder*, but I didn't do it quite as wholeheartedly as I should have because I think people might be disappointed in reading it to discover that the person they suspected in the beginning was actually the murderer. I didn't mind if they did. If that was the case. I wasn't trying to invent a lot of other people who might have done it, but in the one that I'm trying to do now, the murderer is revealed — this is the book I just finished — from the beginning.

C: You must have taken a lot of time in researching Emily Dickinson's life and Thoreau's life and figuring out a way they could have met and had a child. Was it really true about that little boy who'd been elected to be the transcendental love child, if you will, being, apparently, four months old when he was christened?

L: I've forgotten completely that whole complicated part. That's an example of how *not* to write a book, I think, because it has a whole full, long chapter of explanations, and I think if one could avoid that, one should.

C: Oh, but I love that and there are other people who love that; there are people who judge you on how well the peroration goes.

L: If you could just have a thrilling exposé of one fact at the end, now *that* would be a production.

C: That was kind of the way *Dark Nantucket Noon* went. At the end you find out about Alden Dove.

L: Yes. I guess there was a letter from his wife, Alice Dove, which has a good many explanations. But with the new one, since you know from the beginning, you don't have to have an explanation at the end. My sterling example of a brilliant, brilliant finish is *The Nine Tailors*, by Dorothy Sayers.

It's such a shock. It's the morbid pleasure in a single jolt of revelation. Of course, she does have a tremendous amount of explanation, and I think if she could have avoided that, she would have.

C: You're rather bent on avoiding it now — the Big Explanation. So your attitude toward the material or how to present the material has been changed a little bit.

L: Yes, yes. I wish I were more conscious of what I'm doing. I think I'd be a better writer if I weren't fumbling around in the dark the way I am. It takes years and years for it to dawn on you that you don't have to write that way, that there could be a better way to do it.

C: I think writers ought to be a little unconscious.

L: That's right. When you begin to teach, then you have to start being analytical, and the same in reviewing. I've done reviewing recently and I've been glad of that because I really feel I've been awfully dumb and intuitive as a writer. That intuition is fine, but I think a certain amount of understanding of what the process is doesn't do any harm. I can imagine there being too much of it and losing that "careless sense of rapture" that made one begin, but I guess I'll never lose the carelessness, anyhow. And the rapture. I've got the rapture. "Rapture" is my middle name.

C: Well, that certainly gets us back to transcendentalism. You must have been very influenced by Emerson and Thoreau and their circle.

L: I certainly feel very strongly attached to Henry David Thoreau.

C: Was something here when he was just over the ridge?

L: This was the nearest house to his house.

C: He must have thought longingly about the nice fires in this place.

L: No. I'm sure he didn't. It belonged to a man named Jacob Baker and Thoreau talks about his cows, but I don't think he knew him very well. At any rate, he does mention that the nearest house is a mile away, and ours is just a mile away, so it must have been this one. I don't know what else it could have been. I do feel very sentimental about that. He must have seen our chimneys, you know, as he walked across Flint's Pond, which is over that way.

C: Is it intentional that in your books the people who are really the villains are the ones who don't appreciate nature?

L: Oh, I'm bad about that.

C: They've cut themselves off from nature. You almost know that Cheever, the president of Harvard in *The Memorial Hall Murder*, is going to be an idiot after only a few lines into that scene describing him when alone.

L: He's just so flat. As a pancake.

C: I think some people really are flat as pancakes. The banality of evil and so forth.

L: Wow. I never thought of that. But I have a suspicion that nobody's really as flat as a pancake — except my characters. The villain in my last novel I tried to make move. I just tried to give him some kind of dimension, but what does an ex–Sunday School teacher know about abnormal psychology?

C: She might know a great deal.

L: Yes, that's true. I think of those sixth-grade boys . . . But I tried to make him just a little more plausible.

C: You know something is wrong with the president of Harvard when his big thrill of the day is to watch the rays of the sun, which is the ultimate symbol of nature, hit the Great Salt, and that's all he lives for, to see those large golden rays become small, miserly silver ones.

L: He's an aesthete.

C: I don't suppose you based that on an actual president of Harvard?

L: [*smiles*] We won't say.

C: Let's talk about your latest book.

L: It's called *Natural Enemy* and one of the heroes — or heroines, I should say — of the book is a barn spider, which is in the book from the beginning and is just an ordinary spider, not like Charlotte in *Charlotte's Web*.

C: Just an ordinary spider?

L: Just an ordinary spider, and it behaves like an ordinary spider and in the end it builds a web in a doorway through which this fellow says he has just passed. "I didn't do this thing because I've been through that door; I just came in that doorway." And there's this huge round web in the doorway, which proves that nobody's been through.

C: The spider gives him away.

L: Of course, throughout the book, you're supposed to think of the spider as the natural enemy, and actually it's this man who is the natural enemy and you're aware of his being an unfriendly person, of having actually caused the death of the man who was killed in the beginning. But I use wasps to take vengeance on him at the end of the book: he's killed by wasps. You learn in the end that he wants to put a tremendous road through this wilderness or this pleasant little scene, and so of course it's just obvious that he's doomed.

C: Nature takes her revenge.

L: That's right, yes. While they're trying to stop him — they don't know he's the murderer yet, but they know he's done bad things and is going to do bad things; they don't like him and they think the only thing that's going to stop him is something huge — Homer says, "I can't stop him legally; I can't stop him in any way that I know. The only thing that will stop him is some gigantic natural event, like a volcano or earthquake or a tornado or something." And then it's this tiny spider that does it.

C: In all your novels, there's some sort of natural disaster that coincides with the moment of solution.

L: [*laughs*] Well, it's because I have such paucity of imagination. I kept wanting to put in a hurricane, and then I thought, no, I've done that. The other one was an eclipse and I wanted to do that again — but no, no, I've done that. What was left? Eventually, I'll run out of things to use. But the next book is really going to be a joy.

C: After *Natural Enemy*?

L: Yes. The next one is going to use the research I did on Emily Dickinson for *Acts of Light*. Did you know about that book?

C: No.

L: I'll show you. It's a very gorgeous book. I just wrote an introduction, but it's a magnificently lovely book. It's Emily Dickinson's poetry: eighty poems by Emily Dickinson, illustrated by my friend Nancy Berger — there are paintings that go with them, not illustrations really. I wrote something called "An Appreciation of Emily Dickinson." I had to work very hard to bone up on Emily Dickinson and found out that all this stuff about Emily in that first book is really trash, just sheer trash.

C: You mean it was made up for the benefit of the reader? Fake research is used all the time in books, you know.

L: Of course, I did make up things, but the picture I had of her then . . . It kind of sickens me when I look at it now. I have a good deal more reverence for her, and admiration and perhaps a little bit more understanding through having looked over her poems so carefully and having read about her. This new novel is going to be called *The Emily Dickinson Affair* and it's going to be set in Amherst, in her house, where I have stayed.

And there's going to be a conference going on. I went to a conference on the poet: it was her 150th anniversary — she was born December 10, 1830 — so this thing in October was her 150th anniversary. It was in Amherst and people came from all over the place. Some of it was wonderful and some of it was funny, and I thought I could use some of these types and that all kinds of funny things could be done, ending up with having Emily Dickinson sort of draw away, still an enigma and still not understood and still mysterious and still an awe-inspiring figure. I don't want to mess around with her; I don't want to be irreverent.

C: Why was Emily Dickinson so reluctant to go out into society? Were unmarried women expected to behave that way then?

L: Well, I think she was much more a woman of her time than people give her credit for. I think that, now, people who are strong supporters of the women's movement would like to see her as an advocate of women's rights, but she was not, really.

C: Let's go back to the murders. One of the things I enjoyed about *The Transcendental Murder* that wasn't present so much in *Dark Nantucket Noon* or in *The Memorial Hall Murder* was the bumbling, city-bred district attorney, who was actually terrified of trees and had been traumatically confronted with a cow when he was younger, which scared the poor man to death. Did you do that as a way of carrying on the English tradition of the bumbling policeman?

L: No. I was thinking about a man who happened to be a district attorney here, in New England, at the time. In fact, he may still be. Since I feel a lack of rationality in my own brain, I don't think I can write about people who are of keen intelligence, and therefore it comes naturally to me to write about people who are clumsy. My detective chap has bursts of tremendous revelations when I figure out that he has to make some wonderful discovery, but most of the time he is certainly not following a sensible course. I wouldn't know what a sensible course was. And the other characters, the policemen and so on — I can't very well have them doing something intelligent, because I don't know what it would be. All of my books are really just kind of fumbling around in the dark and pretending. They're a terrible pretense. Police procedurals are something I could never possibly do. For one thing, it doesn't interest me particularly. Second, I'd get it all wrong. So I'm trying to eliminate all those policemen, at least in the ones I do now. One of the reasons for doing them the way I do them is because I don't want to have to follow a sensible procedure. In the first one, I really tried that sort of thing. I was going and talking to people about fingerprints and the right lengths of guns and so on, but I decided I wasn't any good at that and that it was something that didn't particularly interest me, anyway. I heard Simon

Brett give a talk in which he discussed that. He has the police come on the scene and he says, "The police arrived and did their duty with skill," or something like that and out they go.

C: It's almost become like a stock Homeric epithet, no pun intended: "and then the boys from the lab showed up."

L: I call it the invisible policemen. They're off there in the background and you assume they're doing their job. But they hardly ever show up.

C: Homer, coming across one of the clues in *The Transcendental Murder*, has his foot bitten by a snapping turtle. I can't imagine that! Snapping turtles are big.

L: I know. The poor guy. I hate to think —

C: In real life, he would have been in severe pain.

L: That's right, yes. And she shouldn't have gone off and left him; she should have tied a tourniquet on him, but I didn't know what else to do.

C: In *Dark Nantucket Noon*, he does get some help from a Coast Guardsman and that's one of the great comic little scenes you've written. At first the Coast Guardsman thinks this guy's a nut, that he's trying to murder somebody, and then when Homer announces that he's working on a case, the Coast Guardsman can suddenly think of all kinds of atrocious ways to do people in. The attitude toward his subject really changes. Some of your stuff is wonderfully comic.

L: I think if you can be funny, you ought to be. There's just not enough laughing in life. I'm not sure I always bring it off, but if I see an opportunity, I jump at it.

C: These Gosses and Hands are wonderful creations. I suppose they're your neighbors, or people like them, and it's more observation than staying up all night devising them, but it really is funny.

L: People do continue to be absurd, don't they? In wonderful, wonderful ways.

C: One of the things that strikes me about your books is that they are really forms of Christian exegesis; they're exegeticals in the form of the novel. You must know that you are doing that.

L: Don't say anything splendid that I won't understand.

C: You use an epigraph in which God says, "The earth is mine; you're just the stewards; don't mess it up, boys and girls." And it turns out that most of the people in your novels who turn out to be villainous are the kinds of people who run around trying to put hotels and motels on Nantucket Island.

L: Well, it's an easy target. The Nantucket Island Bill never got brought up before the Congress and I understand now that Senator Kennedy has dropped it. But I wrote that novel about Nantucket in 1975, and I put something in the back saying that the bill is expected to pass in 1975, or something like that. That was very foolish, and when they brought out the second edition, I had to change it to "may some day diminish the danger." Now I understand it's been thrown out, and they're going to continue happily building on Nantucket.

C: The latest question vexing the theological schools, the seminaries — they get a new one every ten years — is the theology of conservation; they've even established a journal, but you were an exegete of the problem years ago.

L: I think lots of people were, although sometimes saving it is worse than keeping it. I think what they've done on Nantucket is awful in a way. They've made it very charming. The place where the boat comes in used to have falling-down fishing shacks, but now it's a magnificently brick-and-granite landscaped, boutiqueish place.

C: To return to the novels: I still think you're an exegete.

L: Some of the things that Jesus said are kind of important in the character of Uncle Freddy. He was in some of my books; he lives in Concord and is supposed to be running a transcendentalist school. I think of him as being a sort of Christlike figure, but to say that out loud is embarrassing because I would prefer all that to be submerged so that nobody would think of it. But he is close to me. I don't mean that I don't want people to find any Christian messages. I don't mean that, exactly, but I mean that I've got so damn many messages in the book already, and have been criticized for them. That's supposed to be bad. I can't subscribe to that at all. I can't help it, I can't help being that way.

C: The history of the novel is on your side.

L: Is it? Good. But right now there are people who talk about not sending messages; but "message" is my middle name. At the end of each chapter I say, "Do something like this" or "This is the way to behave, children" or something like that.

C: There's a wonderful scene in *Dark Nantucket Noon* in which Jupiter the swan comes back after Alice Dove has been missing and Alice is dressed in men's clothes. I just couldn't help but think that was a kind of blazon.

L: Oh yes. Leda and the swan, yes.

C: Well not only that, but that kind of foreshadowing technique: Adam comes up with the solution to the mystery and there is the reuniting of male and female — Kitty and Joe, Mary and Adam. And then you might even take it a step further and see Mary as the new law and Adam as the old.

L: I won't say that was absolutely out of my mind. I did call the swan Jupiter because Jupiter the god did turn into a swan, and I did think of Alice as being a funny kind of Leda. I don't know if anything is adumbrated there. I kept meaning to say something about the use of Christian symbols — or not — and also about the confusion of certain kinds of handsome landscape with mere wealth: people who write about long drives and Tudor brick and sweeping lawns and so on.

Something I do want to get into my books, or try to get into them, or wistfully hope to get into them, is what I guess is a transcendental view of nature, which is really a mystical response to it. The whole trouble with mystical talk is that "mystical" and "talk" are antithetical. You simply can't dis-

cuss mystical responses without sounding foolish. That's why
I hate people who sit in lotus positions, and dislike all talk of
gurus and gazing into space and consulting one's soul, and
feel so mistrustful of transcendental meditation. But Emerson and Thoreau were specialists in this art and actually got
down on paper their excitement about what they were looking at. Emerson, I think, was at bottom an idealist. That is,
he took the philosophical transcendental position that what
came through the senses was merely an illusion, and was
only meant to fire off the imagination like a match. But I
don't think Thoreau cared a fig for that, although somebody
could probably find a passage somewhere that proves me
wrong, in that bottomless well of his journals, where so many
marvelous paragraphs swarm unhooked and are lost to the
index. I'll show you, if I may, a quotation from Thoreau to
show you what I mean — the transformation of sense experience into exaltation:

> I had a vision of these birds as I stood in the swamps. I saw this
> familiar — too familiar — fact at a different angle, and I was
> charmed and haunted by it. But only as by the sound of a
> strain of music dying away. I had seen into paradisaic regions,
> with their air and sky, and I was no longer merely a denizen of
> this vulgar earth. Yet had I hardly a foothold there. I was only
> sure that I was charmed, and no mistake. It is only necessary to
> behold thus the least fact or phenomenon, however familiar,
> from a point to a hair's breadth aside from our habitual path
> or routine, to be overcome by its beauty and significance. It is a
> wonderful fact that I should be affected, and thus deeply and
> powerfully, more than by aught else in all my experience —
> that this fruit should be borne in me, sprung from a seed finer
> than the spores of fungi, floated from other atmospheres, finer
> than the dust caught in the sails of vessels a thousand miles
> from land! Here the invisible seeds settle, and spring, and bear
> flowers of immortal beauty.

That's Thoreau on birds seen in winter. A "hair's breadth
aside" has become a byword for me in writing fantasies for
children. My real children have unreal experiences merely

by standing a hair's breadth aside and seeing the "beauty and significance" of ordinary reality. To me, this response is lost to contemporary life, since nobody knows how to say it anymore without being embarrassed. But it is out there all the time, staring us in the face, like giant traffic lights two inches from our faces, and somehow we keep looking to the side and saying, "What traffic light? I don't see any traffic light."

And here's something else. We discussed *Acts of Light* earlier, and forgive me for quoting from myself, but here is a sentence or two from the thing I wrote about Emily Dickinson for that book. "But her poetry also affects us with a special force because it expresses something that is *missing* from our own, a transfigured vision of the natural world. 'The Breaking of the Day/Addeth to my Degree'; 'You'll know it — as you know 'tis Noon — /By Glory.' Lines like these stimulate in us some shriveled organ of awareness, feeding an unconscious starvation. Her ecstatic sense of 'sum' in witnessing the bird's song or the red blaze of the morning has a rare excitement for readers accustomed to a bleaker poetry of melancholy subtractions. We begin to suspect that we too have been receiving bulletins from immortality, undecipherable without her magical translation."

This is pure pomposity when attached to my little mystery stories and children's books. All I mean to say is that it is this view of nature rather than the sweeping-drive-Tudor-brick view of nature that I hope to stick in sometimes. I said that beauty of setting was wrong, sheerly for its beauty — who cares about beauty? Because so often it can only be equated with wealth. Homer Kelly says in *Natural Enemy*: "Here they were, the same crowd. Grouchily Homer imagined their comfortable domestic establishments. They all lived in picture book farmhouses, only every blade of grass was like a dollar bill, and the weathered fence rails were so much beaten silver." But when Thoreau says — and I'm giving a free rendition — "I looked at a walnut the other day, and saw that it was made for joy," that has nothing to do with real estate values and comfortable suburbs. And there is the sky over every city street — the traffic light going on and off in our faces. That's what I meant.

There's the whole other half of nature, which is its horror. You don't get the one without the other, although the transcendentalists didn't have much to say about that. Thoreau says in *Walden* that he willingly puts up with it — I think it's a passage about a mouse in the jaws of a cat — although elsewhere he says the universe is fundamentally wrong. My spider is an example of both aspects, her miraculous web on the one hand and its grisly purpose on the other. There is an enigma: the two parts of the natural world. We are all wretchedly aware of the second part. I keep wanting to take people by the shoulders and shake them and make them see the first part. [*laughs*] Perhaps I shouldn't shake them so hard that their eyes cross and their teeth fall out.

C: Let's stick with "hair's breadth aside."

GREGORY MCDONALD

Gregory Mcdonald's first novel, *Running Scared*, was not a detective novel, although there have certainly been worse titles for a detective novel. *Running Scared* was about a rational suicide and its aftermath, and was one of the opening shots in the war for a new consciousness in America, a struggle that has not yet been completely abandoned. And then Mcdonald wrote nothing for a long time. He was a newspaperman on the *Boston Globe*, from 1966 to 1973, covering the upheaval he had seen coming as it abrogated or expanded the old limits of social and literary and sexual expression.

In 1973 he decided to quit the newspaper life and to write. The order of those infinitives is crucial. It's one thing to try to write amid the chaotic pleasures and muted disasters of newspaper life, or of any life, even if it be quieter and better ordered, as almost any life outside newspapers must be. It's another to burn your bridges. Greg Mcdonald made it, and to that leap into the emotional — and financial — unknown we owe one of the most interesting protagonists and one of the most interesting styles to come into American fiction in a long, long time.

Mcdonald describes himself as a postcinematic, postpsychiatric writer, and his style takes for granted a storehouse of images in the minds of all readers who have experienced movies and television at any point in the past thirty years. Naturally, he concentrates on dialogue. But for those who thought *Fletch*, his bombshell of a first detective novel, for which he won an Edgar, was antidescriptive, let them try it again.

Mcdonald's prose style, or rather his highly developed method of employing dialogue, is not oblique and reflects his own moral vision. His books *appear* to be attempts to shirk the duty of fiction, which is to build a formal construct that realizes the possibilities of the medium to the fullest of the writer's ability and, within the needs of the situation, creates the affect desired. But, of course, the essence of the workmanship is that the scaffolding is placed behind, rather than in front of, the edifice. Mcdonald novels would not play if one converted them to scripts by patiently eliminating all exposition and retaining only the dialogue, which is precisely how John Huston got a screenplay from Hammett's *The Maltese Falcon*. They wouldn't play; they are novels. They behave as novels and do the work as novels and, most importantly, they are structured as novels: the plot presents the story, rather than the other way around. And when Mcdonald moves the plot forward, establishing character and creating dramatic effect solely with dialogue, he is not only revealing his mastery of the craft but also making tangible and visible his high opinion of the American reader.

Fletch is a sixties rebel marooned in the "me," "me," "me" generation, but determined not to inhabit any Alamos. He floats. He drifts. In the first novel he is offered $20,000 to kill a man who claims he is dying. This will, incidentally, more than cover the $12,000 in back alimony Fletch owes two ex-wives. He's intrigued by the man and takes on the hit — thus setting himself up for one.

Mcdonald disavows any intent to point a moral in *Confess, Fletch; Fletch's Fortune;* and *Fletch and the Widow Bradley* and in the Inspector Flynn books, *Flynn* and *The Buck Passes Flynn.* But he is a moralist — as opposed to a propagandist for morality. To write about, to spend time transforming into fiction, to merely *mention* murder, despair, dishonor, and fraud is to make a moral comment.

Confess, Fletch is probably the most interesting and convincingly peopled book after *Fletch*. Fletch, who doesn't like it in Rio, returns to Boston and rents a place, where he finds a corpse, insisting in its stolid way on joint occupancy.

This book introduces "Inspector" Flynn of the Boston PD. The third book one should pick up immediately is *The Buck Passes Flynn*, the action of which is already in high gear by the time Flynn discovers that a small town in Texas, a fishing village on the Massachusetts coast, and a section of the Pentagon have been wiped out by the simple device of letting each person in those places — man, woman, and child — wake up to find that each has been left a suitcase containing $100,000, in cash.

And now, in keeping with Mcdonald's postcinematic stance, his credits: born in Shrewsbury, Massachusetts, on February 15, 1937. Chauncy Hall and Harvard University, A.B. 1958. Married Susi Aiken in 1963. Arts and humanities editor and critic-at-large, *Boston Globe*, 1966–1973. Writing since then. He lives in Lincoln, Massachusetts, not very far from his fellow writer Jane Langton.

CARR: I read somewhere that you used to captain sailing vessels.

MCDONALD: That's how I paid my way through college. I skippered sailing vessels about thirty thousand miles. Just at that time in history — I was in college — a lot of people were making money in the oil fields of Oklahoma and Texas, and they thought it would be prestigious to have a yacht. But they didn't know much about them and they would get them into trouble here and there around the world, and what I did was build a little ship trouble-shooting business. I would pack my suitcases and fly to wherever it was and take over power of agency of the yacht and get it out of trouble. They would get it stuck for legal reasons, or I would take care of mechanical problems, and I even once sailed out under gunfire. It was a very profitable business.

C: How did you like Harvard?

Mcd: That's a large question. I got accepted there when I was sixteen and I wish that I'd had another year or two under my belt of being alive. But I had read very comprehensively through my youth. When I was growing up, my daddy had a library of about twenty thousand books in the house, and by the time I was sixteen and the house had broken up, I had my own little library of about two thousand books, so I was well read by the time I went to Harvard. What I did was concentrate on English, the dead language, simply as an excuse to go about it irresponsibly. Courses in psychology and philosophy and theology and a lot of other -ologies were more my interest. In fact, about the only things at Harvard that I absolutely had to read in a course were the works of Chaucer, which I put off until my senior year. I hadn't read him before because I hadn't liked him before, and I still don't like him. He's a very external viewer of human beings.

C: Harvard was smaller then, I imagine.

Mcd: Each class was a thousand or less. Harvard College was about four thousand. At that time in history, Harvard professors were getting paid very well for traveling back and forth to Washington as consultants here and there, and, therefore, personal relations with Harvard faculty were rare. There were three men that I admired enormously, whom I feel I took something from and had some personal knowledge of. One was Howard Mumford Jones, another was Paul Tillich, and another was George Buttrick. In fact — a funny story — when *Running Scared* came out, my wife and I were living deeper in the country, further west of here, and we had to come all the way into Cambridge to get a *New York Times* in order to read the review of my book. We went to the kiosk there, in Harvard Square, and by golly the review was in. So we bought copies and I took them over to the steps of Widener Library and I was all geared up — I had even brought a pair of scissors from home to clip the reviews out. I was sitting there on the steps of Widener Library, clipping, when down the stairs walks Howard Mumford Jones. My God, I was embarrassed. He subsequently wrote me a letter, which was just great, on the book. Something on the futility of filling up libraries.

C: How old were you when *Running Scared* was published?

Mcd: I was twenty-three when I wrote it. Let's see, *Running Scared* is now old enough to vote. It came out the same month that my elder son did, June 1964. My wife agreed to marry me in Puerto Rico, not knowing either that I had gone to Harvard or that I had written, and in fact I had gotten pretty disgusted at the writing business. I think the main thing that had broken my head was that a very important publisher, whose name I won't mention, had read *Running Scared* and wanted it very much, but the offer they made was that they would publish it under an imprint they would make up for that book alone. They wanted the profits from it. They wanted the historical prestige of having published it, but they didn't want it under their imprint because it was a very controversial book. I said no to that, and I think I really didn't read or write for about three years after it. After we were married, and we were living in the country, in western Massachusetts, we collected our common luggage — mine was in the basement of my brother's house in Connecticut. While I was out one day, she was going through my luggage, straightening things out, and came across the typescript of *Running Scared* and sat down and read it. When I came in that night, she just said, "I didn't know about this. This is shocking, and you'd better do something to get it published." I told her I just would not deal with a large American publishing house ever again. Some months subsequent to that, an old friend dropped by and told us about a small publishing house that he had visited, and after he left my wife insisted that she would send that manuscript to that small publishing house, Ivan Obolensky, and she did. We had just moved into that community. We couldn't afford a telephone and by the end of the week the poor people in the post office thought that these nice young people were from large families that were dying like flies. We were getting five or six telegrams a day at the post office box and we didn't know it. Finally, we picked up the mail on Saturday and realized Obolensky wanted to publish that book. It literally took him only three or four days to make up his mind to do it. The critics have since referred to *Running Scared* as sort of the first blow of the revolution of the sixties. It appears to be about rational suicide, and what it really does do, or what I intended to do and I think did do, is indict all of the institutions that were then in their full power — the churches, the universities, psychiatric institutions, and families — as being just incredibly cold. They had turned that generation, my generation, into punchcards, and it was a very heavy indictment. It was extremely controversial, and the mail and the response we had to it when it first came out was thoroughly shattering. But when Avon published it for the fourth time — I guess that was in 1977 — incredibly enough, there wasn't one complaint.

C: By then the ground had been broken and all sorts of truths had been revealed.

Mcd: It does prove to you that the world does change and that that revolution did accomplish something.

C: I think it did. You graduated at the very tail end of those materialistic years. It was horrible at certain southern universities and it couldn't have been much better anywhere else.

Mcd: Well, it was very strange. About half my class were very much 1950s people. They were aiming for the corporation and corporate life. A good friend no longer with us joined the CIA. I think less than half were able to get into the new technology, the new morality, some of the new understandings, the new music, and so forth. It was a very strange class. When I was a journalist, old Eli Goldstein once came up to me at a party and said, "You know what you're doing, don't you? You're really interpreting each age to the other." I took that as a very high compliment. I hadn't realized that was what I had been trying to do, and I think that's what I was doing. You know, I was the first guy to wear blue jeans at Harvard. That was a terrible scandal in those days. I was wearing blue jeans because I was coming in off the sea, stinking and soaking wet, and wanted my breakfast on Monday mornings and had not had time to change. But that was a pretty radical thing then.

C: Who were the American writers in the late forties and fifties whom people looked up to when you were beginning to write and were thinking about writing?

Mcd: Why do you say American writers?

C: Well, that's another part of the question. Were they American or were they European?

Mcd: I think the writers who made me say "wow" were people like Thomas Mann and Dostoyevsky and Turgenev and Sartre.

C: Camus maybe?

Mcd: Kant, Kierkegaard, and very much Camus. I'm reluctant to say Camus because by odd coincidence I had read everything of Camus except *The Stranger* when I wrote *Running Scared*. Some critic referred to *The Stranger* in reference to *Running Scared* and I was shocked. I had never read it. I went out and read it and was even more shocked because the title that I had had for *Running Scared* was *The Estranged*. Therefore, I'm deeply indebted to Camus, so much so that I'm slow to use his name. I have these oblique things. I had never read *Miss Lonelyhearts* when I wrote *Love among the Mashed Potatoes*; then after I wrote it I was scared to death and did read it the following December. I had the remarkable reaction to it of saying, "My God, the poor guy sure missed a hell of an opportunity." I read so much at Harvard that Howard

Mumford Jones suggested that I might get literary indigestion. I really specialized in the short novel, the novella. I was a great fan of people like Eudora Welty and Steinbeck.

C: I'm going to ask you a leading question. I'm good at that.

Mcd: Good. I need leadership.

C: Is it not true that a lot of criticism of crime writing or detective writing or suspense fiction is sometimes hunting in the wrong field when it considers them as traditional novels, because so much of crime and detective fiction is in the *conte* or novella form?

Mcd: Yes.

C: They're marketed as novels because you can't market a novella. A lot of detective writing is superb as examples of the novella form or the *conte*, but runs into real trouble living up to the standards set for Victorian triple deckers.

Mcd: Well, there are things you cannot suspend forever. There are two forms of literature, both of which I work in, that you cannot do at great length. The first one, of course, is humor. Humor has got to be short. The second is the detective form. After three or four hundred thousand words, you begin to say, "Who cares who killed Cock Robin?" Because you've got too many things going on. The detective novel is a thin frame. It is better as a novella, which is one reason why again they make such good films so frequently.

C: But there is, however, room enough for character development, I think.

Mcd: I think that's the first job.

C: Fletch is a fully developed character even by the standards of criticism usually reserved for the Victorian triple deckers. He's as fully developed as any of Dickens's or Trollope's people.

Mcd: To me, the character comes first, and from the characters come movement, the electricity. And of course from the characters comes the humor. I know that all writers do not feel this way.

C: There were, of course, the English writers in the twenties who were writing detective novels who wanted the plot first, and a lot of plot, because they were writing punning or funning detective novels.

Mcd: Quite right, and they were looking for the gimmick; they were looking for the twist and so forth. I'm always amazed when people speak well of my plots because to me plots are not terribly important.

C: But your novels are very well plotted; there's no deficiency there on your part.

Mcd: Thank you. Once in a while I come across a situation in which it would be better for me if such and such happened in the plot, but the character tells me, "Hey, man, I wouldn't do that." And I do go with the character at that point, always. Always.

C: There's a real talent to writing funny detective stuff and yours is funny. How do you build the humor in your detective novels? Is it character, dialogue, situation, or some wild combination of all three?

Mcd: No. Again, it is character. I believe it's character. It's not situation, not that I look down on people who create what are basically humorous situations, but to me writing about the ordinary person is not terribly much fun and it's not terribly interesting to ordinary people reading it. There has to be some slight edge to the character in a detective novel, some eccentricity, a peculiar view of the world that other people agree with, but maybe haven't crystallized. And it's this slightly offbeat view of the world that I think makes Flynn the character he is, and the same with Fletch and some of the characters around them.

C: Isn't that the essence of humor? The people whom we perceive as humorous, in a creation like a play or a novel, have extreme attitudes that they look at devoutly and seriously. We think it's funny because we're not able to go that far.

Mcd: They see that the world is absurd, which it is. They have this slightly detached perspective. They have a view of themselves and then of the world.

C: Right, but first of themselves.

Mcd: Yes, and they don't feel that the two have to agree. I really think that most people — at least, most Americans — feel that they're out of step with the world and they're wrong. My characters, probably because of my own Scottish thickheadedness, say, "I've got a world view and it doesn't jibe with what the world's view is, but isn't the tension between the two fun?" And that's where books come from.

C: That's a good word — "tension." That's really what makes writing work sometimes, and I think in a shorter form, like humor or the detective novel, it has to be there because otherwise you do lapse into social criticism, the emotional burden of the bourgeoisie and all that. One of the reasons, I guess, detective fiction is looked down upon by so-called serious critics is that there aren't many ordinary people in it. I would suppose that's one of the reasons.

Mcd: Well, there are some very strong selling points to mystery fiction. The first is that it really is the greatest opportunity that a typewriter gives you for social criticism, instead of — as you sometimes see in academic novels — people sitting back discussing what's wrong with the world in great long vast passages of purple prose, which has become incredibly popular in the last ten or fifteen years. The mystery novel happens in the streets and in homes and in families, and instead of great long explanations as to why the telephones don't work or why a certain government bureaucracy doesn't work or why the buses don't work, you *see* that the telephones and the government bureaucracy and the hospital system are not working. The second thing that is, I think, very appealing to the readers of this genre is that our lives are chaotic and we have to have the belief that we can make sense out of them, that we can order them, and more simply than other literary forms the mystery novel does order chaos. For the most part, things come out O.K. in the end and all the lines are tied. It is marvelously reassuring to people, which is why, of course, the famous hand in *Flynn* has caused such a stir and controversy; people get really quite angry at me and scream at me sometimes when I'm out in public about the hand in *Flynn*, because there is no resolution to the problem of the hand. And that's exactly what I was doing — exactly what I wanted to do. I wanted to break this thing down, but that was just one small, little experiment and the reaction to it has been considerable, because the people in that book lose their reassurance that you can perfectly order life — you can't. Of course, both Fletch and Flynn couldn't have existed ten or fifteen years ago. They're both extremely — totally — new characters. They are postrevolutionary. And I'm speaking of the revolution that happened worldwide in the late sixties and early seventies.

C: Of feeling and culture and politics all at once.

Mcd: Fletch and Flynn are also postcinematic and they are postexistential and they are postpsychiatric and they are postideologic, which is why they have this incredible popularity worldwide.

C: What do you mean by "postpsychiatric"?

Mcd: In saying "postpsychiatric," I mean that both Fletch and Flynn are beyond the point of scab picking, of discussing relationships, of worrying about them, of trying to attain that which much of Western civilization came to believe in from, let's say, 1920 to 1960, and that is something called normality. They don't believe in it and they don't try to attain it and they don't give a damn about it.

C: And normality is more or less what a psychiatrist or a psychoanalyst tries to have you turn to from your disordered state.

Mcd: Quite. My characters enjoy the disordered state and they accept it and consider that that's what life is. Each of them reacts to a situation in, I think, a very postrevolutionary, postpsychiatric way. That is, when they see a problem or they have a problem, instead of internalizing it and picking at it like a scab, they accept it as it is and enjoy the tension of it, enjoy the difference of it, and it gives them energy, rather than taking it away.

C: Flynn's an eccentric guy anyway. Anyone who was the son of an Irish consular official in Munich — how many Irish radicals in Boston remember that Ireland was neutral and maintained relations with Hitler? — and who was out running through the woods with the Hitler Youth and then came home from standing watch to find that the Nazis had disposed of his parents and then went to British Intelligence ... The implication, anyway, is that he went to work for British Intelligence. He says his life's a blank after that, but the implication is that he was mixed up in some intelligence work when he was an adult. Correct?

Mcd: It is correct. Flynn's statement is that by the time he was twenty, he'd had enough truth. He accepts everybody's truth, but he doesn't see it as necessity. The latest book, *The Buck Passes Flynn*, has a line in there that both the editors and the copy editor have called me about. I received three calls asking me to take the damned line out because they weren't understanding it, and I stuck to my guns and said, "No. I want that line in; you can take out the rest of the book if you like." The line is essentially that Fletch always believed his ears, but seldom believed what he heard.

C: Well, I understand. That's a Zen saying, in a way.

Mcd: Thank you. You can be my editor any day.

C: You did lay off a long time between *Running Scared* and the Fletch novels.

Mcd: *Fletch* came out exactly ten years after *Running Scared*. And then it was *Confess, Fletch* and then it was *Flynn. Fletch's Fortune* and *Love among the Mashed Potatoes* both came out in July 1978.

C: Why did you turn to detective fiction? You've probably given the answer before.

Mcd: I'm not sure I've ever been asked for it before, to tell you the truth. Why'd I turn my hand to it? I don't really know. I think for about three years before I left journalism, the character Fletch was growing in my mind and I saw the opening scene and I saw the resolution and I saw a lot of things in the middle; it became clearer and clearer to me the three years before I left journalism, and Fletch just appeared as he did in the book *Fletch*. It was really Fletch who had to come out and he came out in the mystery form. That sounds like a silly T. S. Eliot's midwife kind of answer, but it's the truth.

C: Chandler said at one time there were things he could say when he wrote detective fiction he didn't think he could say doing something else and he knew he had to say them, so detective novels were what they flowed into.

Mcd: The night that we were driving into New York City for the Mystery Writers of America award dinner, my wife asked me if I wanted to win the Edgar.

C: You didn't know before you showed up?

Mcd: I knew I'd been nominated. I answered her quite honestly that I wasn't sure I wanted to win the Edgar because it might brand me as a mystery writer. And to a certain extent it has, but on the other hand there seem to be people who are not mystery readers who read my books. I'm very proud to be a mystery writer. I'm very proud to be a mystery writer, indeed. The only thing that scares me is that the mystery books are so hugely popular and sell in such huge figures. Then along comes *Love among the Mashed Potatoes*, which has some remarkable things in it, in both its form and its structure. In fact, there are more characters per page in that book, I think, that come off than there are in any book of its size in history.

C: That's part of the problem probably.

Mcd: Yeah. Maybe. I wish people would see it without coming at it from the Fletch and Flynn world.

C: Let me ask you something else. Borges says that the history of literature can be viewed as the rise and fall of genres. Is that what's happening with the sudden burst of popularity for detective novels and the beginning of critical acceptance of some of its writers? Do you think we're seeing here a shift within the culture to a form at least like the detective novel, something both objectified and ritualistic?

Mcd: I think art follows philosophy very closely, and it does reflect very closely what is going on in the world if it is successful. I think what we're seeing now are heavy preoccupations with the kind of themes that are best treated by the mystery novel.

C: So you think the odds are that there will be a shift to a kind of externalized fiction, like detective fiction, rather than the old inward-dwelling, near-sentimental novels that exist almost without relation to society and the world?

Mcd: I think what really has happened is that since World War II, an awful lot of at least American fiction has been going higher and higher up into the ivory tower. It has become increasingly academic. An awful lot of authors, in order to survive financially, have gone to the university. It is a natural thing for them to want to appeal to the people with whom they are having their nightly sherry — the other academics around them — rather than to the people who are the readers in this world, the people who are out doing hard work. And I think they have become really far removed from where the people are and what the people are thinking about and want to know about, and I think there is a terrible reaction against that.

C: Can everybody identify with a detective hero? Can they identify with Lord Peter Wimsey?

Mcd: I think so. In writing the Wimsey novels, Sayers very carefully built in his propensity to use slang, and he was, after all, a democrat; that was his charm. And Bunter, his man, was really his only friend and certainly his equal, although his servant. Yes, I think that we can identify with him. And the thing about the mystery story in general is that every day we confront something that is not immediately understandable. You sit down with a mystery novel in which something happens in the first chapter that you don't understand and you'll see that man, that person, that mystery writer, resolve the problem for you by the last page. And that will at least fill you with the spirit in which you can come to understand the mysteries in your life.

C: What was the reception among publishers and agents — or however you worked — to *Fletch*? Was it difficult to place?

Mcd: I'll tell you how that came about. I finished that novel on August 3. It had been the tradition of my family to go up to Vermont on August 1 of every year for a month, and my family very faithfully packed up on the last day of July, but Daddy was still upstairs in his study at his typewriter. The first of August went by and the second of August went by and the third of August, and they actually went out and sat in the car, including the dog. And this was right under the study window. I was hearing them and I couldn't avoid seeing them. They were even honking the horn and it was that day that I wrote the last chapter of *Fletch*.

C: So the end of *Fletch* is sort of like the end of writing it.

Mcd: Absolutely. I was going somewhere. I wasn't sure where, at that point.

C: Didn't have a bag of money with you, though.

Mcd: I certainly did not have a bag of money. I left the manuscript on my desk and made a phone call to my old copy boy at the *Globe*, Chuck Martime, who was a great friend. I have since been his best man and we're still the greatest of friends. He had a key to the house, anyway, and I said, "Chuck, if you happen to come by, would you notice that on my desk is a manuscript, and if you've got a spare hour, would you Xerox it and send it to somebody? I'm gone for a month."

C: Just anybody? Those were his instructions?

Mcd: Yeah. And Chuck being Chuck said, "Wow, sure." He came by while we were in Vermont and Xeroxed three copies, and he, not knowing what he was doing, sent the three copies out to three different publishers. One publisher sent it back with the envelope open, so the pages spilled out all over post offices from New York to Lincoln. We got ten pages back of that copy. Another publisher sent it back unread with a little Xerox note in it saying, "We do not read unsolicited manuscripts." The third publisher, Bobbs-Merrill, by the time I got back had called up and made a very modest offer for it. So that's how that came to be.

C: That could have been a horror story.

Mcd: So *Fletch* was sold without an agent. William Morris came to me as *Fletch* was being published, and that's how I came to be with William Morris.

C: That was fast on their part.

Mcd: Well, yes.

C: You said you were here doing the last chapter that last day. How do you work? Do you try to end each chapter perfectly and put it on the line, then do another one and put it on the line? Or do you take the whole book at the end and squeeze it and hammer on it?

Mcd: No. I work in a way that I've never heard of anybody working in. I had an old teacher in prep school who told us that instead of trying to develop a good memory, you should try to develop a good "forgettory," and I certainly took his advice to heart. It was his statement that anything, any knowledge, can be looked up in a book, including your own name, and if you walk around all your life tying the mind down and being proud of all the facts and figures you remember, you're not freeing your mind to create and drink in new images and facts and figures. This is so true that I'm just incapable of remembering a telephone number or a title or a name. I've become rather famous for it. When an idea begins popping up in my mind, instead of making a note of it or whatever, I try to suppress it. I figure if it's any good, it'll come up again. And if it isn't any good, it's gone and it should have. I also find that over a period of a year or two years or three years that every time the idea pops up, it pops up fuller, you know, as if it were trying to be even more appealing to you, to get you to pay attention to it. I go through this process for two or three years and, in fact, what I do is literally write the whole book in my mind, memorize it pretty much word for word. That's one reason I write short books.

C: Your memory just isn't that long?

Mcd: Yeah, and any sections of it that I forget in the process deserve to be forgotten. Then it gets to the point where it becomes irresponsible, and I will sit down with it and I'll try two or three pages of it. What I'm looking for there is the tone and the pacing. Then I will put those pages aside for two or three months until I begin to be able to see them with detachment.

C: A lot of inner maturing of the idea.

Mcd: Then I may get them out again and see if the tone is right at all. Finally, after doing that a few times — the idea is irrepressible and it has its own energy and its own force — I will sit down and start working with pen and paper. Then, by the time I get to the typewriter it's really an editing process, so that the manuscript itself turns out fairly perfect or, according to the editors, there's not a lot of work to be done at that point.

C: I couldn't drive any wedges in it if I were an editor?

Mcd: The editor of *Love among the Mashed Potatoes* was really quite marvelous, and it was fun to work with him, but he used to go screaming at me because when he was in the process of editing the book — and he is a very bright editor and a very bright man — he was perfectly sure that he'd be right about one word on page 18 and he'd move that word or remove it and then he'd discover on page 119 that that word had been essential and he had to put it back. I'm not speaking well of myself; what I'm saying is that I have the high art of laziness. I do things the laziest possible way. There's a very thin line between laziness and efficiency. So all this process, which sounds terribly intellectual, is really just a matter of getting the work down to doing as little as possible.

C: So that finally, at the end, it's crystallized, and all you have to do really is feed it out of that internal computer onto a piece of paper and make sure the grammar's right and it looks good on the page and it's typed.

Mcd: It's pretty nearly that process. It's almost a matter of dictating it to myself at that point. You still find an awful lot wrong with it. Getting sentences to work right and getting things down even further from that point is a big object, but it's pretty much that process.

C: Do you find that your stuff is written for the page or written for the ear?

Mcd: My goal is to cause people to hear with their eyes.

C: Totally different from reciting aloud.

Mcd: No, I don't want to recite it aloud. I want people to read silently and hear it.

C: Your books, obviously, depend heavily on dialogue and the rhythms of American speech.

Mcd: *Fletch,* I think, sets a precedent, a mathematical one, if nothing else, in the lack of what I call prose in it. It is almost 98 percent dialogue, which I was aiming to do.

C: There are places where you could have rolled on forever describing things.

Mcd: Let me just speak to that for a minute. I refer to my writing as being postcinematic, and I'm saying something here that I've been thinking for the last thirty years, which crystallized when I was a bachelor living in New York. A woman lived below me with her family and used to come to see me sometimes. She came up once with her baby, who was then eighteen months old, and the baby toddled over to the television set I had in the room and turned it on, and with a twist of her wrist scanned all the channels at once. I realized that by eighteen months she was able to, by twirling the dial quickly, establish which was a news program, which was a variety program, which was a drama. Now, the average American, by the time he is eighteen years old, has seen twenty-one thousand hours of film. This is something one must take into consideration. Sir Walter Scott was writing for an audience of people who were born in valleys and in their lifetimes might not go fifty miles from their hearths. Therefore, when he was describing a street in Paris or a street in Edinburgh, he had to tell the people everything that was on that street: what it looked like, what it smelled like, what it sounded like, what the street did, how it functioned. Now today, whether people consciously know it or not, from thousands of hours of film they have in fact trillions of images. This was driven home to me when I was in Los Angeles. If you stand anywhere in Los Angeles — except Watts, which should have been filmed — including almost any private home out there (at least every single private home I've been to), you look at something and you've seen it before. It has been filmed. The contemporary writer has got to take this into consideration. There has been this technological revolution — again, you've got to refer to McLuhan — and that all is now in the mind. People are not perhaps as linear as they once were. They are seeing things at twenty-four frames a second. Therefore, when the author is describing a street in Edinburgh or in Paris, he not only doesn't have to say everything that is on that street, he is a damn fool for trying, because everything he says is taking away from the image that the person already has of that street. He's taking away from the reality of it.

C: But what if they are the wrong images? So much of what appears about New Orleans on TV and in the movies is stuff that we who live there find ridiculous. Maybe the natives of Paris and Edinburgh feel that way, too.

Mcd: Then absolutely what you must do is correct that image. But you do so much more effectively by dealing with what is known than by dealing with a fresh —

C: Hinging it onto something that's known?

Mcd: There is no such thing at this point as a fresh and innocent mind — a mind without images. What I frequently find myself doing is sitting down and reading people — you know, the sort of American writer who gets the front page of the *New York Times Book Review* — and at some point early on in the book I'll say, "Oh God, you aren't going to tell me that, are you?" And out come seven pages of something that I already know pretty well and I've seen pretty well. It takes away from the reality of whatever it is he's trying to get across to me rather than increasing it.

C: A bad imitation.

Mcd: Bad imitation: that's right. To me, the author's trick is to point the finger and then get the hell out of the scene. Let the characters take over. If there is a footstool between them, let them refer to the footstool so that the footstool has some reality to *them,* and thus to the reader, rather than having the author say, "Hey, there's a footstool between them." And it's terribly key that it comes from that more detached point of view. Now, having said that, I'm going to correct myself and say that when I am writing about New York in the 1940s, at that point I will let the descriptive paragraphs roll.

C: That's precinematic?

Mcd: Sure. Or if I write about Paris in 1960, I will button down the descriptions so that you will be seeing what I want you to in some detail. But if I'm trying to tell you what happens quickly between people on a street in New York, I will get that description down to five words if I can.

C: Can you say a little more about technique? Where, for instance, did you learn yours?

Mcd: I think every writer — American or otherwise — has taught himself. You cannot, you cannot, you *cannot* become a great anything without starting from scratch. Having used the word "great," I feel ridiculous talking about myself. But when I was a boy, to use my son's favorite phrase, I threw out all the rules and regulations of grammar. I didn't see any point in commas or periods or quotation marks or whatever else.

C: Been reading a lot of that section in Faulkner's "The Bear" that goes on unbroken majestically, enduring and prevailing, for a dozen pages before the sentence ends, had you?

Mcd: Yes, I'd been reading a lot of Faulkner. And I threw all that stuff away and then I wrote millions and millions of words, literally, beginning at the age of eight.

C: Experimenting?

Mcd: Yes sir. What I'm interested in with grammar, besides clarity and so forth, is of course the rhythm, the sound of it, and those things are tools — hammers and nails and screws — and are absolutely essential. But I don't think any writer or composer or painter who doesn't reinvent the art himself can succeed.

C: If we could bring back one of those pages, would it look like *Fletch*?

Mcd: No.

C: Not a bit?

Mcd: No, not a bit. Not a bit. In fact, when Avon was bringing out their edition of *Running Scared* in '77 or '78, I asked permission to copy-edit the New American Library Signet Classic edition, because there are typographical errors in there, including on the first page, which had always bothered me. Avon was always proud of its physical book so they gave me permission to take a red pen to it. I went down to the Cape and spent a week and realized how terrified I was to read the book critically. I took a little bit of it each morning, in small doses, and I realized two things immediately: one is that I wouldn't write *Running Scared* that way at all now, and second is that the version that's printed is just the way *Running Scared* should have been written. It really couldn't have been written in any other way.

C: In other words, without the style and tone, there wouldn't have been that book?

Mcd: Right. The conscious decisions I made about that book in writing it — that is, the long paragraphs being essential to the theme — I would now probably try to refine down into simplicity. The theme was so shocking that it couldn't have been done that way at the time. It was right for me to do that book at that time in the way I did it, and it would be impossible for me to do that book in that way now.

C: That's frightening in a way, isn't it?

Mcd: Well, it's a lesson to writers that when the time comes to write something, write it. Because the time not only comes, it goes.

C: I've tried to tell writing students that. They want to see how much smarter they'll be next year. And they will be, but the passion or the obsession is gone by then.

Mcd: I met a man at a dinner party in England six weeks ago who was pleasantly making a joke of the fact that he had been working on one book for five years and now he's at the point where he has to go back and look at the beginning. The terrible thing is, he's afraid he won't recognize it. He was seeing himself in an endless cycle with this book.

C: Between *Running Scared* and *Fletch* you spent time in the newspaper business.

Mcd: Yes sir.

C: Did those years on the *Boston Globe* hammer your style into shape?

Mcd: Absolutely. There's no question about it, and again, like everybody else, I didn't really realize it until later. A couple of things were happening. One thing was what was happening at the newspaper itself: they kept increasing the size of the body type. If you were to try to read a 1940 newspaper now, you'd have to get out a magnifying glass. We're very spoiled by larger print now. We don't even notice. It happened so gradually. This meant in practice that the column kept getting shorter, and that certainly tightens you up. The second thing that was happening was I learned — or rather I used my proclivity — to get out into the street and to get what people were saying. I would start the column with a very simple deduction as to who they were and where they were and then let them rip, let them speak, use their dialogue and monologue, let them speak for themselves. Sometimes it was the journalistic trick of giving them enough rope to hang themselves. Sometimes it was simply a means of getting something said that would create some understanding by its being said. I would not change the grammar or the syntax or anything, and this is certainly a technique that I've carried over in the Fletch and Flynn books, that is, to let the writer set the stage and then get the hell out, get away. I don't think the writer is more interesting because he's a writer. I know I disagree in that respect with a great many American writers who are still in the psychiatric mold. There's an easy analogy between that way of thinking of the writer as the most interesting person and the *auteur* theory of film making, in which the director went to stage center and became the star of the film, rather than the writer or the actors or the set designer or the costume designer. The writer really ought to get out of the way, if he has anything to say about people.

C: You're collaborating with the public consciousness and the public tongue, in other words.

Mcd: I think the first job of the writer is to define human need and to try as well as he can to answer that need, to bring some understanding to it, and I'm talking about all kinds of human anxieties, whether they are sexual, political, whatever. *The Buck Passes Flynn* is a book that very simply addresses the real anxieties that are created by runaway inflation. That's why I wrote it. I have the conceit that in doing that book I am being somewhat responsive to the anxieties that people are having right now. Another reason why I think the Fletch books have done so well is that we have a great anxiety about what the media are doing in this country.

C: With good reason.

Mcd: A particular school of journalism has grown up in the last fifteen years, and there are two major magazines that subscribe to the theory most enthusiastically, and are therefore most culpable: it is the school that constantly puts in such things as "a Washington housewife says" or as a so-and-so said. You know that it's all made up. It's the reporter trying to get something across.

C: When did you leave the *Globe*?

Mcd: I quit April 20, 1973, the seventh year there to the minute, so I must have begun April 20, 1966.

C: You would have been twenty-eight. Had you done journalism before that?

Mcd: No. My daddy was a journalist. That's another place where Fletch came from. I had been hearing these stories of journalists since I was knee-high to a grasshopper — to use a Southern expression — and the whole idea of embodying the spirit of journalists became very large in my mind. And, of course, then as we were sitting around the city room at three o'clock in the morning telling each other tales, along came Fletch as this fictitious character, this person who would tell the photographers where the body was and ask them to wait till the widow got home. You know, of course, a "fletcher" is an arrow maker.

C: Right. In Scotland the trade was the basis for a family name; *flecha,* in Latin.

Mcd: So that also is where Fletch comes from.

C: Fletch really reminds me of old style journalists, maybe not that old, but of the early fifties, when my brother started working for the *Memphis Press-Scimitar.* They would send people around to the homes of people who had just had a relative drown or die or blow up, and the reporter would go to the front door and ask brilliant questions like "How does it feel to be a widow?" while the photographer went in the back door and into the bedroom and stole a photo from the dresser of the late departed.

Mcd: You think that's what Fletch would do, but he

doesn't. Fletch is a journalist to the point where he presumes that everyone is lying to him and that this gives him the right to lie back. But when it comes time to write the story, he sits down and writes the truth, and then gets out of town as fast as he can. My father, to get back to that, had been a news analyst and commentator for CBS Radio from the depression to the end of the Korean War. He was Irving T. Mcdonald — he was named after Washington Irving. He had started in the print media when he was in college, and then he was a stringer for this and that. His family was half-military and half-show business, or half-vaudeville, as in fact my mother's family was sort of, too. My granduncle on my mother's side was Buffalo Bill Cody and my grandfather on my father's side was Colonel Henry Mcdonald, who raised his own troops out of the Springfield Valley and charged the Spanish at Santiago in Cuba. I have since worked out that Cody and my grandfather must have known each other when the Union Pacific railroad was being built, because Cody was a scout for them and my grandfather was in charge of the troops in that area. My father, working his way through college, had the job of being Will Rogers's plant in the audience. He was the shill, the local yokel who would stand up and agree to be lassoed and so forth, wherever they were, and he was a friend of Rogers until he died. So my father wrote a few juveniles when he was in his twenties and worked very early in the film business with a couple of brothers named Fox.

C: Wow.

Mcd: Yeah. He thought he was a wealthy man when he was twenty-five and got married and was on his honeymoon in Bermuda when he got a cable from Aaron Fox saying, "We're out. The money men have taken over." And thus Twentieth Century–Fox came into being and my father was out of the film business. He went to college at a place in Worcester called Holy Cross. It was a place where he could get his way paid, so he was a journalist during the time that I knew him. But not one of your ordinary newspaper — press — journalists. He was the man who came and went in the Packard car, and you could tell it was Sunday because he'd be wearing a softer shirt with his three-piece suit and tie. It was a very formal and very, very busy life for him.

I went to the *Boston Globe* when I was twenty-eight. I had already written *Running Scared* and therefore they took me in at a rather high rank.

C: You'd never actually done newspaper writing before, had you?

Mcd: No.

C: Did they quickly cure you of what they at least regarded as faults?

Mcd: No, no. They ran it as I wrote it. There was no editing of any sort of anything I wrote. There was only one story of mine that they pulled and that was on Genet's *The Balcony.* They pulled that out because they thought I was making an unfortunate analogy between something that was going on in *The Balcony* and the Roman Catholic mass, and they thought it might be offensive to the Roman Catholics. They pulled it. It cost them three thousand bucks, and they apologized to me within six months of having done so because they realized that they were wrong. I had a hell of a fight once about using the word "pregnant," if you can believe it. Up to that point, at least in the *Boston Globe* (I don't know about other newspapers), a man's bare legs had never been shown in the newspaper. They had run boxing pictures from above the belly button up, and they had to come around quickly. I was the first one in the major media to write openly against the war in Vietnam, and I got beat up in the *Boston Globe* parking lot for it. It was done by the unions — the men downstairs, the printers and mailers and drivers. For a period of more than six months I had to mail in my copy and I had to meet with the editor at various sneaky places around town. I had to be kept out of the offices of the

Boston Globe. And finally the day came when the *Boston Globe* was the first newspaper to editorially go out against the war in Vietnam. I knew it was happening, of course, and I was just about eighteen inches off the ground. I felt very good about that, and during those years I spent time with everybody from Richard Nixon and George Wallace to John Wayne to Abbie Hoffman to Gloria Swanson to whomever you care to mention.

C: That sounds glorious.

Mcd: It was glorious. It was enormous fun. It was hugely seductive fun. You know, I worked hard and I worked continuously, but I felt I was doing well and doing something good and getting some things said and getting things understood. At some point I was made the arts and humanities editor, which meant the chief critic, and the critic-at-large columnist for the daily and Sunday editions. I did that for about three years. Then I left without a word of my next novel on paper.

C: Care to explore why?

Mcd: Because it was seven years. I was getting very restless. It was sort of catching up with me. I found that I was really beginning to repeat myself and I was becoming almost a historian of myself. It was one of those situations where I would think and think and think and think as to what would be a new story or a new angle, and after I'd worked it out, I'd realize I'd already done it. Those were the best days to be a journalist in this era. But the era came to an end. The second thing was that it was during Nixon's administration and the government was all over us.

C: That's right. You all were on the hit list, weren't you?

Mcd: Yes sir. We couldn't go out to lunch without a government man being in the office in the afternoon asking for our expense account for lunch that day.

C: Literally?

Mcd: Literally.

C: Were they really shadowing you people? What did they

think you'd done besides publish the Pentagon Papers and trifling little stuff like that?

Mcd: Well, they wanted to know with whom we'd had lunch.

C: I hope you didn't tell them.

Mcd: No. You'd say you were having lunch with a guitarist and you would have had lunch with a painter; you'd just be doing it to be contrary. And then there came the great economic freeze, which was enforced upon the newspaper. One night, on top of all this other, I asked my boss why I couldn't have a raise. I told him I had two kids and that I deserved it and needed it. He said, and his answer was exactly this, "Well, what the hell did you think you were doing when you were making the government angry at you?" Those were the days that are incredible even now. I had a friend who was a lobster man off an island in Maine who was perfectly ready to take me over to Nova Scotia at any time.

I don't mean to be dramatic about it, but those were scary days. And they came to an end. I was extremely restless, and I guess the fact is that I had written a novel that had meant something and I had been successful before I went to the *Boston Globe*, so clearly it was better to try it again when I was thirty-six, rather than forty-six or fifty-six or sixty-six. So I quit, cold turkey, on my seventh anniversary, to the second — and went into debt, borrowed money. I didn't have a dime. Well, I did, in fact. I had a little *Running Scared* money left over, but that had always been a $10,000 cushion for the family in case something happened to one of the boys or something. But I borrowed money with the idea that I'd spend a year trying to write something and only that. And I knew the statistics against that succeeding.

The original publisher had gone out of business. As critic for the *Boston Globe* I certainly could have used some contacts in the theater and in the publishing business, but I didn't. So it was at that point, after having quit, that I started *Fletch*, it all being very much in my mind. Within eighteen months, believe it or not, I was able to pay back the money at 9 percent per annum interest. It was real luck. I mean, for that year I did not take a deep breath and I didn't sleep; I was just tight as a tick because I knew the statistics of my succeeding were negligible.

C: Did you also think you'd served your hitch in journalism and it was going to be no different from then on out, I mean, stylistically?

Mcd: I figured I had said what I had to say in that medium and that it had treated me well and I had treated it pretty well and at that point there was no indebtedness between us. That was very definitely so. And after all, I was as well paid as you could be in the newspaper business at that point and I still wasn't living as well as my father had, nor were my kids living as well as I had, and there was really no way to get ahead. I really felt there were bigger canvases that I wanted to draw on.

C: Would you advise a young woman or a young man who thinks maybe she or he has a novel somewhere hidden in the soul to go into newspapers for two or three years?

Mcd: No. I wouldn't because I know some terrifically talented, bright, able people in the newspaper business who are obliged by the business to fall into the trap of writing formula stories. It actually becomes a mind set you can't escape. No matter what you try to write, you can't get out of it. I avoided that because I came in at a higher level, having been a novelist, because I was writing for the magazine — I even committed poetry in the magazine. From that point I was able to write whatever I wanted to, just as I wanted to write it. I still can write a news story according to the formula, but it wasn't what I was obliged to do every day, and if you're going into journalism, you'd better expect that that's what they're going to oblige you to do. And it is a trap. Although when you realize what some of these journalists are able to create, sometimes literature, on deadline, it can really be pretty inspiring.

C: There are things in your novels, themes, metaphors, structure, and — that horrible word — symbols, that lead to climaxes increasing in intensity — all that good stuff used in retailing fiction — that you couldn't have gotten from newspapers.

Mcd: I think that life is a process of testing the walls of our own existences and of really becoming freer and freer and freer, from the time you're a little kid and you want the freedom of being a big person. And I still think of myself as a journalist. I miss the business very much indeed; I would like to do journalism again some day in my life, but I think that it was time for me to free myself of the restraints of journalism. You know, I feel the same way about mystery novels, which is why I do a book like *Love among the Mashed Potatoes*: I want to be free of that confinement of being only a mystery novelist.

C: Is there growth beyond fiction? For you?

Mcd: Oh, yes. The basic love with which I was born was a love for form and for function, and I really began exploring this love first with music. If I live long enough, I will be very surprised if I am not playing with forms in music and painting before I turn up my toes. Someday people are going to report that I've had a heart attack and died, and it just isn't going to be true. I will just have died of the heightened excitement with which I was born.

C: Let's talk about Flynn. One of the things I like about him is that he's not a real cop. As someone says, there is no rank of inspector in the Boston Police Department and he has this dummy, Grover, who follows him around and connects him to the p.d. He's a figure of literary convention much as, I think, the so-called grittily realistic cops of certain police procedurals are.

Mcd: Flynn came into existence before the *Confess, Fletch* book.

C: Right.

Mcd: And he came so alive that I thought that I wasn't

going to let him go. When I notified my agent and publisher that I was going to try a Flynn book, they yelled and said, "No, no, no. Not at all. Please don't. He's Irish and he's forty and he's married. Where's the romantic interest?" But he likes his kids, and therefore I did it. The agent didn't think much of it, but he handed it on to the publisher, who, I think, was probably not too much in favor of it. The sales manager of that publishing firm stole it and took it home with him and came in in the morning and threw it on the publisher's desk and said, "Finally, the son of a bitch has written a book for me." And they offered me more money for that than they had for the Fletch books. I guess one of the contrary things that got me working on Flynn was that you always hear about the Irish cop in detective literature. Frankly, I've never met one in detective fiction. It's like that old thing of the butler doing it. Try to find a book in which the butler actually did it.

While I was playing with the idea of Flynn as a man of wide background and whether I would get away with this or not, during that year I happened to meet four or five men of backgrounds comparable to the one I was building for Flynn.

C: Were they cops?

Mcd: No. They had worked in various forms of police work, including intelligence work, international intelligence work, and they were in and out of all those scenes, including local police issues.

C: That's dreadful to hear.

Mcd: These people do exist. In fact, to a large extent. They're scary. They do exist. An awful lot of them came out of the World War II era and a lot of them came out of there very young. So that did justify my going ahead with the character and giving him that wide background. Because it's not my purpose to create a completely incredible character who could never have existed.

C: What about the hard-boiled detective?

Mcd: First of all, I think the hard-boiled detective is something that happened at a certain time in history. In the later thirties there was the depression. Earning a living was a pretty hard job and the world could smell a massive war coming on, and I do believe that toughness in a man was greatly admired — the ability to recover quickly from being belted. I think it was something that people admired, respected, wanted to read about, wanted to know about. They wanted to be assured of that kind of masculinity. That era to my mind is gone, although there are writers who are still writing as if we were in the thirties.

C: And at the same time there were Peter Wimsey and Nick Charles, and S. S. Van Dine's character Philo Vance.

Mcd: The people of wealth and sophistication, the martini drinkers, showing people there was intelligence in the upper classes and that you could trust the upper class to solve things.

C: That was really one of the functions?

Mcd: Yes sir. You can trust the upper classes. They will still be able to raise up an officer corps.

C: How about now?

Mcd: There is always a class structure. You cannot have a society without a class structure, of this I'm thoroughly convinced. It just depends what the class structure decides to base itself on, whether it's lineage or money. I believe that the American class structure is the most incredibly complicated and sophisticated one that has ever existed on the face of the earth. Extremely subtle. There is still a class of extraordinarily wealthy people, but they have learned not to give big balls. The class structure that I think exists now is one in which the people who are most admired are people of intelligence. Education is not always the important criterion.

C: It sure is different here from the South or from England. Are you saying that Fletch and Flynn justify the existence of a class or a group of people who are both intelligent and able to take action?

Mcd: Right.

C: They're exemplars of that class?

Mcd: Right. They consider themselves separate from any authoritarian sort of structure. They consider themselves to be individuals, which is very much an American characteristic.

C: Have you gotten to the point of explaining individualism to the masses in detective novels? If those novels were once explaining that the upper class can be trusted and they were once explaining that male prowess was good, are those novels now in the position of explaining individualism and intelligence to the masses?

Mcd: Something that is intriguing to me, and that I find myself wanting to express over and over and over again, is the extraordinary intelligence and the extraordinary fund of experience in unlikely places. I don't know about you, but I keep running into it and I guess it's a new thing or partly new: the garage mechanic who can quote Yeats, and does; the taxi driver who has a book by Schopenhauer on the seat beside him; the farmer who has the fastest, wittiest mind that you could possibly come across, much better than anything you would hear in Las Vegas or on television, but who actually spends his life driving his tractor. The people in any community recognize these people, and they do exist, and the people do separate them from the community and give them an extra prestige and honor and so forth by a variety of subtle means. Their lives become more difficult, frequently, especially in an egalitarian society, because they are special. But the world has been through such flux in the last forty years that you can speak to the most unlikely person on the bus or anywhere and find in this person a wealth of experience, a wealth of developed wisdom and knowledge and the development of certain expertise, physical and mental, that would have made any one of them an emperor six hundred years ago. That's what I think Fletch and Flynn are.

C: Fletch and Flynn are unique in the annals, as it were, of the American detective novel. The ending of *Fletch* is probably going to be imitated again and again in the coming decades.

Mcd: It already has been. I've seen four or five this year.

C: I didn't know that.

Mcd: I wish I didn't.

C: Here is a guy who's going to leave with a bag full of money belonging to a man who asked Fletch to kill him, and Fletch in a way did kill him; he certainly killed him metaphorically. And now he has the money and is taking the guy's place on a private plane going to South America. He looks over and sees this nice-looking woman and her child, who are waiting for the man who's lying back there dead where Fletch left him. Fletch doesn't say, "Here, madam. Have a nice life with the money." He doesn't mail a check for back alimony; he doesn't call the authorities; he just leaves. The hero as having become existential man.

Mcd: Leaving the woman there has bothered many people — his not being generous to her — but you have to realize that in Fletch's mind she has a priori accomplished a murder.

C: He says that, in fact.

Mcd: Yes. The only regret I have about *Fletch* is that I wish the last line were still in it. In the editing process I agreed to have the last line taken out, and I've regretted it ever since. It was, as I remember it: "And he had written three good stories that week." That was what was so important to him — not flying away with the money.

C: Were you interested in the painter Tharp at one time?

Mcd: There is no such man.

C: Thank God. I thought there was some obscure American painter I hadn't heard of. I was depressed.

Mcd: I was playing a game.

C: I'm not opposed to games. Did anyone complain that suddenly our barefoot boy had developed an interest in art in *Confess, Fletch*?

Mcd: That came about in various ways. First of all, when I wrote *Fletch* I had no idea of carrying it on as a series; if I had, I wouldn't have left the son of a bitch in Rio with three million bucks. That created an enormous problem for me. I had to think about it for months. I finally had to resolve it by realizing that if Fletch didn't care about money when he didn't have any, he shouldn't care about money when he has some. The whole thing of the series came absolutely from fan letters and the mail saying, "Let's have some more Fletch." When I decided to do a second Fletch, it was very much in my heart that I wasn't going to do a Fletch book again. I was only going to do a second Fletch if it could be as good as the first, which is why the second one unprecedentedly won the Edgar award as well. That meant as much or more to me than the first one, because it was a little symbol that I had written a second book as good as the first. You must realize that Fletch is a chameleon. He blends.

C: Like a lot of good reporters.

Mcd: Like a lot of good reporters. So when you see Fletch in *Confess, Fletch* he has money. Someone pointed out to me that in *Fletch* he was a very intelligent person and that obviously he'd had some intellectual experience. You remember in the Fletch book he goes back to his own apartment after you think that he's living in the room at the beach and you see some good photographs on his walls and so forth.

C: That's a shock because you'd thought he was a real bum.

Mcd: Yes. But it really was all there in the first place.

C: The foreshadowing is in the character, I guess, because he's got to be smarter than a beach bum to solve all this.

Mcd: Yes. Here's a man who doesn't have to do heavy lifting every day and he's got the intelligence, so why shouldn't he be interested in the visual arts?

C: You said before that you had complaints about *Flynn*, that people complained because it didn't have a neat resolvable ending. Was that a book that you intended to be more of a novel of character, which would mean the plot was not as important, or had you tried to write a puzzle mystery?

Mcd: No. The whole mystery in *Flynn* does resolve itself. Maybe in that book all the pieces fall together too quickly in the end, but it's all there. The hand I built in quite on purpose, as a sort of postexistential declamation that not everything does exist in the moment and that there are things that are not solved immediately. I don't know if you can call it a kind of rebellion. You can call it a kind of statement, you can call it a kind of resistance, but with the hand business I knew perfectly well from the first minute what I was doing and why I was doing it.

C: Did the Flynn book sell as well as the Fletch books?

Mcd: Somebody sat me down in New York at some point a couple of years ago. You know how they love demographics. They showed me, to my surprise and their surprise, almost as if I'd planned it, that Fletch is extremely popular on both coasts of the United States and popular in the middle and Flynn is extremely popular in the middle and popular on both coasts. Flynn is also very popular in the world where people are still growing children and dogs and cats and cows and watching things grow, where family is important. So Flynn in many cases is more popular than Fletch.

C: Did you like the third Fletch book as well as the previous two?

Mcd: Hell, I can't answer that.

C: No favorites?

Mcd: I think that some of the things I was trying to do in that book I did do.

C: There's a hilarious send-up of the press establishment in there.

Mcd: Like Robert Frost said, it's a brave thing to write anything and it takes even more bravery to write the next thing and more than that for the next thing and so on.

C: Do you feel that pressure especially when you have created a series character?

Mcd: Seven or eight weeks ago I was at a meeting in Stockholm and I was called upon to make a speech — this was at the International Crime Writers' Conference. I think I was maybe the youngest person there. Therefore, what I said in my speech was extremely insolent and I sort of mumbled it, hoping that nobody would hear me. The point I was trying to make was that a novel ought to be a novel. I know, as you do, that a great many people make fortunes from writing the same book over and over and over again, and this is the trap of the series. I am at this point of good conscience, in that each book, I think, is a novel. And that really isn't a matter of pride; it's a matter of my own interest. If I did what some series writers have done, which is to write the same book over and over and over again, I'd go out of my fucking mind with boredom. I'd be a hell of a lot richer, but I'd be bored. If there's a Fletch book out this year (there hasn't been one since 1978), I think I'll be breaking new ground with it. In fact, I think I'm dealing with something that has never been dealt with in fictional literature before [the book is *Fletch and the Widow Bradley*]. If you write the same book over and over and over again, then people can say that one book is as good as another; but if you are experimenting and trying, you know you can't bat a thousand all the time. I find so far that people coming along saying that they like this better than that says more about them than it does about the books.

C: Simenon was asked once when he was going to do a big book and he replied that all his books together were one big book.

Mcd: That reminds me of the man who came to me about a year ago. He was very eager at the thought of being my agent and he said, "Boy, *Who Took Toby Rinaldi?* is the first evidence we've had that you can write paragraphs." That's what he said and that was the end of his forward motion, as far as I was concerned.

C: So you've taken at least a little criticism for your style.

Mcd: I looked at him with my eyes crossed, realizing that he had no idea of what you go through in taking information that could easily be given in paragraph form and turning it into dialogue. God, it shocked me. No, I wouldn't imitate Simenon in that response. There are some things outside the mystery genre that I have done. There are more that I'm going to do and want to do. It is rather difficult because Americans believe in the star method, and the publishers and critics are very quick to typecast. I firmly believe that if I wrote Genesis right now, they'd say, "Where's the body?"

C: I hope the triumph of the visual image doesn't drive novelists back to things that are absolutely untranslatable, like Proust's long work and Faulkner's *Absalom, Absalom!* Those are absolutely untranslatable, and I think there's room in fiction for realistic novels with images that excite the visual capacities of the imagination.

Mcd: I think I have a different prognosis for the world of film from anybody else's, certainly anybody I'm reading. We now have cable coming upon us with the possibility of fifty-two channels at least, just in this house. When you've got that much of anything, people stop seeing you. Television has already become very similar to wallpaper. We have hundreds of thousands of gorgeous stone walls in New England. Nobody ever sees them. When you have so much of anything, the product necessarily becomes cheapened just by the quantity. I do believe that the filmed image — and I'm a great lover of film — is already so omnipresent that minute by minute it is losing its impact. I think this is also partly because it is — as McLuhan said — a passive medium. I don't know if it is still true, but at least it was true for the first twenty years of TV in this country that every year per capita book buying increased.

C: It still hasn't slackened off.

Mcd: I think it's going up and the actual television audience is decreasing. There's just too much of it.

C: Any last thoughts about literature and morality?

Mcd: I think the simplest statement about morality that there can be is that we're all in the same car, together.

C: And it's going to crash.

Mcd: And it's going to crash. And how am I going to help you through the crash. I don't think there's anything that should be coming down from the author.

ROBERT B. PARKER

Robert Brown Parker was born in Springfield, Massachusetts, on September 17, 1932, the son of a telephone company executive. He was educated at Colby College in Waterville, Maine, and after service in Korea with the army, from 1954 to 1956, he was graduated from Boston University with an M.A. in English in 1957. He began his business career with Curtis-Wright as a management trainee, ending it as the co-owner of a small advertising agency, Parker Farmer, in 1962. At that point, he went back to Boston University to begin work on his doctorate in English, which he received in 1971. He taught from 1962 through 1979 at Boston University, Massachusetts State–Lowell, Suffolk University, Massachusetts State–Bridgewater, Northeastern University. He was able in 1980 to retire on the strength of the popular and critical success of the Spenser private eye novels. He won the Edgar Allan Poe Award from the Mystery Writers of America in 1976. His wife, Joan Hall, whom he married in 1956, is a staff development specialist for the Massachusetts Department of Education. She has an M.Ed. in early childhood education and guidance and has taught at Endicott College.

Parker's dissertation, interesting reading in itself, is entitled *The Violent Hero, Wilderness Heritage, and Urban Reality: A*

Study of the Private Eye in the Novels of Dashiell Hammett, Raymond Chandler, and Ross Macdonald.

Parker created his own detective protagonist because Chandler was dead. Or so he wrote to Chandler's biographer. But Parker is not copying Chandler. Nor would he find it very easy to do so. Chandler was the pre–World War I product of an eighteenth-century education received in a seventeenth-century school, taught by men who had lived most of their lives in Victorian England. Chandler had the viewpoint of the Augustans; Parker is the product of his independent admiration for the romantic writers, including James Fenimore Cooper, and modern American writers like Robert Frost.

Parker wrote in his dissertation: "The crime is the occasion of the story, but the subject of the story is not the detection, but the detective." And so it is in Parker. The books taken as a whole give us a fascinating and more often than not moving story of a man who, as Parker said of himself in *Three Weeks in Spring* (when he and Joan learned she had breast cancer and would have to undergo surgery immediately), realizes, first, the world is essentially haphazard and must be dealt with as it comes and, second, we have to deal with what we have and not with what we fear.

Spenser burst into the detective fiction world with *The Godwulf Manuscript*. A fourteenth-century illuminated manuscript has been stolen from a Boston university whose president is a masterpiece of venomous characterization and represents one of the real duds in the minefields of academe. As with all good detective novels written in America, the weaving of the novel is broad in warp and thick in woof and there are some wonderful portraits of spiritually defunct academics and tough, embattled cops who have virtually lost control of a big, tough, embattled American city. The city — Parker will stick with it: it is his version of Boston — is the same one where, in the spring of 1982, a young black kid was acquitted of murder on one day and testified the next day that he had in fact done the murder; therefore, his accomplice was innocent too. Both got away with this legal maneuver and a Commonwealth's attorney said flatly that the boy "got away with murder."

It is the kind of city that needs a tough, compassionate private eye whose report of his life and times resembles the faerie prose of Fitzgerald as much as that of Chandler.

Parker's style also calmly and with great assurance declares its independence from the tight, white-lipped, teeth-clenched English that has been the style of address for tough guys since Hemingway and all the others who drove ambulances and came back to tell us war was hell. Marquand, John Crowe Ransom, Chandler, and others who actually saw bayonets jammed into bellies didn't bother; they'd been there.

There are a number of new and good things in this debut: like other detective novels, it carries on the tradition of regional writing that had fallen on hard times before the detective novel revived it, but the region — Boston — is new. And Spenser doesn't hesitate to sleep with his client (not to mention the client's mother). This may not be highly ethical or even very good for business, but it is at least different and a refreshing change. Again, Spenser seems to genuinely regret having to use violence, an attitude that is held in real life by more than a few men who have discovered after plying it the ultimate emptiness and uselessness of violence as a steady diet. And if disenchantment with the larval stage of the American white middle class that shows through is more reminiscent of a tired professor than of a tough old private eye, then the fault is minor.

Not least for being last is Spenser's consciousness of the weakening of his knightly flesh: "Sometimes I wondered if I was getting too old for this work. And sometimes I thought I had gotten too old last year."

In *Mortal Stakes,* which Geherin rightly describes as brilliant with "vivid characterization, serious exploration of theme, graceful and witty writing," Marty Rabb, who is a Sandy Koufax–class pitcher, is being blackmailed by a sportscaster who works for a gangster. The resolution of the dilemma violates the detective story formula and there are diametrically opposed opinions about its fitness. The reader will decide, of course, but, as always, Parker is pushing at the boundaries of the formula, expanding its limits.

A Savage Place finds Spenser in Hollywood, as sassy as ever, just as vulnerable, and even more apt to take the law into his hands. But it works magnificently. In his latest, *Ceremony*, Parker again manages to ring some changes on the genre while presenting a fast-paced, well-written, tough-detective yarn. With every new Spenser novel, Parker's following has grown, and future dissertations will have to reckon with him as a legitimate successor to Hammett and Chandler.

CARR: Why are people reading detective fiction?

PARKER: I suppose it has something to do with form, which allows the detective novel to present, if not a contained universe, at least a containable universe, and it is one of the last refuges of the heroic figure, the man who triumphs or who at least doesn't get defeated. He doesn't often triumph, but he is not finally overwhelmed. It's the refuge of integrity and commitment and courage and the romantic hero figure. Spenser as well as Marlowe is a figure of romance.

C: I think the early nineteenth century made that distinction between romance and maybe a serious sort of philosophical novel, although I think some people in the romance camp were doing things modern critics like Lukacs respect, namely Sir Walter Scott, who is still read and admired.

P: I would distinguish romance from the others the way Northrop Frye did. Rather than opposing the romance to the serious novel, I would say that a romance is as serious as a nonromance, but romance is a form; it's not a value in and of itself, it's a descriptive term. A romance is a novel in which the hero is perhaps superior to other men, but not to nature.

C: But people, especially academics, resent romances.

P: Well, academics resent almost everything because they can't do anything.

C: I'm glad it was you who said that.

P: There are exceptions, obviously, but by and large academics are the worst people I've met. Perhaps I feel that way because my expectations were different; I didn't become one until I was past thirty. I went in thinking that this was so much better than advertising and other things I'd been doing for a living. Finally, I was getting into dignified work with a goal that one could admire, with people who were committed to something other than selling aspirins. I found out that they don't like to teach and they don't like to write and they don't like to read. They just like to talk about tenure and promotion.

C: Let's go back and pick up some of your biography, some of the good bits that won't be in the résumé. You graduated from Colby in 1954 and spent two years in the army.

P: I was the radio operator for Headquarters Company B, 3rd Battalion, 19th Infantry Regiment, 24th Division, serial number US 51306950.

C: How did you like Korea?

P: I didn't like it at all. I was there for sixteen months and we had intrusions from the other side and did security for the Neutral Nations Inspection Team. We were up on the DMZ and the Truce Zone there for a while and there was a certain amount of danger, I guess. My major problem was that I wanted to be home with Joan Hall, the former Joan Hall, of Swampscott, and now Joan Parker. It was arduous and occasionally dangerous and often uncomfortable, but men in groups I've always enjoyed.

C: The male-bonding experience.

P: All that. And that was pleasing. I don't know many

people whose military experience is not one of the central ones of their lives. The people who were in the military who are my age spent what is now 4 percent of their lives in the service, but it probably occupies 30 percent of the conversation. I mean, there's still army talk now, after thirty years, and you see it in the VFWs and the American Legion. It is a centralizing experience. There's lots to say about it, but I don't know that this is the time or place to say it.

C: Did you play football?

P: No. I wasn't very big in college. I got to be much larger in recent years, mostly from weight lifting and stuff. I always weighed about 160 pounds in college. When I came back from Korea and got married to Joan, I weighed 151. I would've gotten married before I went, but she wouldn't marry me before I went.

C: Well, she had some taste, anyway.

P: Yeah, I always admired her for that. And then after the master's degree, I worked for Curtis-Wright Aircraft in Woodbridge, New Jersey, briefly. I was in a training program and they were developing a solid fuel missile called the Navajo. Two weeks after I started the training program, they fired the Navajo and it fell over. The next day, we were all out of work. In December 1957, I went to work for Raytheon, right here in Massachusetts, in the missile systems division as a technical writer, and then moved on to Prudential as a copy writer and industrial editor.

C: Were you writing for what someone once described as an "internal organ"?

P: Yes, yes. Precisely. I edited a couple of house organs that were sent to insurance salesmen. They were management tools, as I was. They were to promote sales. The idea was to show how Joe Smith had sold this amount of insurance. "These are Joe's tips on how to do it."

C: Did you ever feel like committing suicide after a hard day at the internal organ?

P: Well, I'm not suicidal, but if I were, I would have been, yes. As it was, I felt like beating up the entire office, or coming home and kicking the dog. I hated it. Then I tried founding my own advertising agency with a friend of mine named Mel Farmer. We both were all right writing copy, but neither of us wanted to go out and sell the business. Neither one of us could stand it, so we quit, and he went off on his own and I went back to school in 1962 to get a Ph.D.

C: When I was doing the bibliography on you, I found a book on advertising by a Robert B. Parker who was born in 1932. I rushed over to the Tulane University Business Library to get it, but, alas, it was not you.

P: You're the second person to come up with that. The other person didn't check it any further and assumed that was me and made a fair to-do about it, and didn't want to be told it wasn't me. It was worked into a thesis, I think.

C: But back to the Ph.D.

P: Joan told me to do that. I was not happy with my work and I'd always wanted to write, but I had Joan and David to support at that time and she was pregnant with Daniel. She said, "Why don't you become a professor so you can write?" And I said, "You have to have a Ph.D." She said, "So get a Ph.D." And I said, "But I have a few people to feed and two cars and a house in the suburbs and nobody's working if I quit." She said, "Well, we can work it out." So we did. I got my GI Bill reinstated.

C: It was possible to do that?

P: My congressman helped. He had been John Kennedy's roommate at Harvard and Kennedy was president at the time, so . . . But they were happy to give it back; I had just let it lapse. I hadn't used it within the required length of time. I had used one year of it for the master's degree, so I had three years left.

C: That was a good, solid break.

P: It was. I got a teaching assistantship at B.U. and my father gave me some money, and then I worked twenty hours a week for my old partner, Mel Farmer, who was then the audio-visual director at Arthur D. Little company in Cambridge, the consulting firm. I wrote a script for the film on the gravity feed oil burner nozzle. We did movies. Then I'd narrate them. I didn't know what I'd written and I didn't know what I was reading when I narrated it.

C: So the voice of Robert Parker is now locked in some corporate vault narrating the near-Eisensteinian epic on this nozzle?

P: *The Maintenance and Operation of the Gravity Feed Oil Burner Nozzle.* We also did one on some kind of supply system technique for the navy, which I remember. We did that with animation, with little ships on a board. Click one frame, move the ship. And I narrated that, too.

C: How was it at B.U.? Did they have a good doctoral program in English?

P: B.U. was terrific, I thought. Silber, the president, contends that if B.U. were located someplace other than in the shadow of Harvard, it would be recognized as one of the country's major educational institutions. And I think he's right. I think it's very good. I didn't enjoy getting my Ph.D. That would be like enjoying a root canal. Academic hazing is bizarre, but I liked the faculty at B.U. and I liked what I learned there and I thought there were some excellent teachers. All told, it was a very good program and I benefited greatly from it.

C: How long were you in academe?

P: I started my Ph.D. work in September 1962, when I was a teaching fellow at B.U., and I resigned effective January 1, 1979, from Northeastern. I was a full professor when I left, tenured. It's like the old Groucho Marx joke: "I wouldn't teach at a university that would give me tenure."

C: What did you teach?

P: A course called "The Novel of Violence," which I did not title, but was my dissertation essentially. What it really should have been called was "The American Hero."

C: What did you think about the way literature is being spooned out to the young?

P: I think it's not being done well. I'm not sure I know how to do it well because the average kid doesn't want to read it. That's the starting problem. But what I do think is that the average instructor chooses literature that needs to be explained to the kid. Otherwise, what has he got to do? And I would, too. I mean, you don't want to go in there and look at them and read aloud with them. You've got to have a problem for you to solve in order to justify your existence in there. So the kids are given things to read, and one of the standards for selecting the reading list — I don't think I've ever heard anyone say this, but I'm sure it's true — is that the kids won't be able to understand those books without expert guidance. So you're hitting them with stuff they won't be able to read without you, and I really don't know the solution to that. The other problem, of course, is that they get the same thing over and over again. A kid who goes to a decent high school and then on to a decent college may have read *The Great Gatsby* five times by the time he gets through and have been bored all five times.

C: Weren't you able to write very much as a teacher, because you were probably conscientious?

P: No, I wasn't conscientious. I had my priorities very clear. I was teaching in order to get the chance to write and I tried not to cheat the kids, but I was a writer who taught, not a teacher who wrote.

C: A friend of mine says one cheats everyone when one writes.

P: No. I don't. I'll cheat the writing before I cheat Joan and the boys, but I'll cheat the students before I'll cheat the writing. It's a nice, orderly system. I know what's important. And I wrote the first six books while I was a professor. The first book came out at Houghton Mifflin in 1974 and I didn't leave teaching until 1979. I quit teaching when I moved from Houghton to Delacorte. I also changed agents at the time. Again, my previous agent, good fellow and all, had among his clients James Clavell, and you know when Clavell called and I called whose call got through. He was simply too busy to work on my case the way I wanted it worked on, so I changed agents and publishers.

C: Does it help your career eventually if you break from your old publisher, regardless of who it was?

P: Probably, because it's the kind of business where you get a new client or writer and they whoop it up: "We got Parker away from" whomever. And they'll give you more money to change. [*David Parker enters the kitchen.*] There's my handsome son, right there, looking bright and lively. Hi, Dave.

DAVE: Hi.

P [in his mock-pompous tone]: I'm doing an interview here, son. You must be used to this by now, being a celebrity child. [*back to normal*] So I think it would behoove any writer, if he feels that it's not going as well as he'd like it, to change publishers.

C: Did academe seem to you a world in which things were not being done right?

P: Oh yeah. I thought most of it was done wrong. I'm sort of Aristotelian in my view of life. Aristotle defined things by their function, and it seems to me that the function of a college is to educate the young, but that was maybe eighteenth on the list of priorities. If you're going to be a professor, shouldn't you be trying to educate the young? Yet discussions about whether to keep freshmen English, for instance, revolved entirely around what we'd do with the freshman English teachers if we didn't teach it. That kind of thing used to drive me wacko. Somebody once said that one of the reasons academic infighting is so vicious is that the stakes are so small. There's so little at stake and they are so nasty about it. More than any other group I've ever seen, academics don't seem to know how to act, and there *is* a way to act.

C: With some sort of honor and compassion and just plain decency.

P: I mean, the people in the 24th Infantry Division knew much more about how to act than my colleagues. There are exceptions, but if I were in real trouble and I needed real help real bad, it would be to the academic world that I would go last.

C: Did you have anybody in mind when you created that horrible guy who was president of something like B.U. in *The Godwulf Manuscript*?

P: No, I didn't. I made him up entirely out of whole cloth. He doesn't resemble anyone at all that I knew. Since that time, at least five college presidents have been identified. But I had somebody in mind when I created the nasty little villain, an academic professor. I can't remember his name now and I wouldn't say, anyway. There is a cop in one of the books that has a certain facial gesture that I've observed in an acquaintance of mine. His lips seem to be a little out of sync with what he says. Now, that little part that I saw in this acquaintance of mine I put on this cop. The friend of mine is otherwise totally unlike the cop. Or someone in a novel will look like John Cassavetes; I think it's useful to be able to see them. I try to make them up, but the reader should be able to see them, too.

C: Let's go back a minute. Had you wanted to write fiction since you were a mere lad?

P: Yes.

C: In the wilds of western Massachusetts?

P: Yes. My standard line is that as soon as I found out I couldn't hit a curve ball, I became a writer.

C: Did you ever try to publish fiction when you were an undergraduate?

P: No. *The Godwulf Manuscript* was the first piece of serious adult fiction I attempted.

C: Any poems? Any critical dicta?

P: Nope, nothing. I didn't have time to do it. I had always wanted, in this order, to be a husband, a father, and a writer.

C: You're a good man. Most people would have reversed the order.

P: No, I still would put it in that order. It would be an easy choice. If I couldn't have all of it, I'd give up the writing first. And I had the good fortune to realize my priorities rather early on. Joan and I got married when I was twenty-three, and we had David when I was twenty-six and Dan when I was thirty. By thirty I had all I'd ever really set out for, and I was satisfied with that. And then all I needed was to find a job that didn't make me vomit. This doesn't make me sick, sitting home and pounding the typewriter. But when I had my wife and boys to support, I used to try to write — late at night or on weekends; all that crap that people try to do — and I found, at least in my case, that I couldn't do that, that I need long stretches of uninterrupted time in order to write. I needed four hours of time to get done two hours of writing.

C: There was an English writer at Hollins when I was there who seemed to be able to steal fifteen minutes and scribble down a few more sentences of his epic.

P: I think there are people who can. Joan doesn't write, but she can work in little stretches like that. If she's got ten minutes, she can sit down and work on something and then stop and pick it up again. It's a matter of concentration. On the other hand, she doesn't notice much on the periphery, whereas I notice everything. It's just two different head molds. When I do a writer's conference and they ask me for advice, that's one of the things I try to say to people: you have to find a way in which you can write, and you can't walk around thinking you ought to be able to write this way or that. You've *got* to write the way you can.

C: You would tell young people to not necessarily emulate Robert Parker or William Faulkner or Raymond Chandler, but just to try to find what —

P: Try to find the physical circumstances that are most efficient for you. I can't hole myself up in an office for eight to ten days and do a book. I'm very mechanical. I write three or four pages a day. I set myself a page count.

C: Is that a good day — three or four pages?

P: No, that's every day. That's not good or bad.

C: It's every screaming day?

P: If I say three pages a day, then I do three pages a day. If I say five, I do five. My page quota depends on my deadline and schedule.

C: Do you ever feel better one day than another about writing?

P: No, not really. Occasionally, there may be things going on so that I am either too busy or too angry or too unhappy or too sick or something to write. Like everybody else in the world. But no, normally when I sit down at the typewriter each day, it's not better or worse. It's something I do for — it's my living. It's what I do. I type out my pages.

C: Do you ever have really inspired days when every ball you hit goes over the fence?

P: [*laughs*] No. You can tell that by reading my stuff.

C: No, that's not true.

P: There's very little inspiration to it. I am very organized, as my wife and children will tell you, with some humor. My closet is always neat. I know where my tools are and all of that. My desk, my office are very orderly. I don't work well under other circumstances and so my approach to writing is very orderly. I outline first, I do a scenario, and then work up a chapter outline.

C: I'm going to bring up something I asked some other writers. I asked them why detective writers — I'm not trying to influence your answer, I just want you to react to this — start so late, or relatively late. They said detective writers started late because they may not have been solely interested in the life of the senses and feelings, so they wait until they can write about something solid, something they know about. The women who write as Emma Lathen know banking and the securities exchanges; Dick Francis knows racing; Gardner was an attorney. There are other examples. Why did you write detective fiction rather than so-called serious fiction?

P: Detective fiction is serious fiction.

C: Right, but I mean according to the lights of cataloguers in libraries.

P: I know, there's no good way of talking about it. I set out to write — I can remember sitting with Joan and the boys at a Holiday Inn pool in Ottawa, Canada, in 1970. The boys were swimming and I was talking to Joan about myself. I do that often. That's why she went to work, I think. I was telling her that I didn't know if I could write. Well, I knew I couldn't write *The Sound and the Fury.* Neither could Hemingway. I don't mean that's either bad or good, but I couldn't do that. I don't have that kind of talent. But I could write *The Big Sleep,* or approximate it. I said I know how to do that. I said I can do that and I'm going to work on that first. As I say, I'm quite orderly. I got the Ph.D. I got tenure at the university. Now it was time to write the novel. I was teaching nine hours a week, so I was able to squeeze in a few free moments.

C: You Yankees don't work very hard, do you?

P: Oh God, no. I used to drive people crazy in the academic world by saying, "I'm used to work and this ain't it." It's bizarre. They don't get paid much, but they don't work much. Anyway, it was time. I had finished this all up. I was almost forty and it was time to write the novel. I don't know that I could have written it when I was thirty.

C: Could you have written anything when you were thirty?

P: I don't know. I didn't try. My guess is no. It seems to me that I wrote it when it was time to write it, and I knew how to do this so I did it, and I like to do it. It's also an opportunity for me to talk about things I want to talk about. I did a writer's conference with John Updike this summer. It's always fun to be the other novelist on a panel with John Updike, you know. He's a very nice guy. But I noticed, for instance, that he and I have a different assessment of the way we respond to literature. He talks about serious literature as containing ideas that illuminate. I read serious literature for the same reason I look at a Picasso painting. I like the way it looks, I like the way it moves, and the idea of illumination is not very pertinent to me.

C: But Spenser's gestures and actions illuminate.

P: I'm willing to say that you can get some good information from my novels. You can get good information from Harold Robbins's novels. There's illumination in Jacqueline Susann. She can't write very well, but the point is that I don't believe illumination is the standard of judgment, good or bad. You can get wonderful illumination from something that's not very good.

C: Do you think that culture should reinforce moral values?

P: Oh hell, I have no idea.

C: Your writing does, which is why I ask.

P: Again — and I don't mean to say something derogatory — that's a critic's question, not a novelist's. Or at least not mine. I write about someone who has moral values and expresses them. No, I wouldn't even say moral values. I'd say that I've worked out a system by which I can live in this world with some dignity.

C: A private code, in other words.

P: Yeah, sure.

C: Spenser in *A Savage Place* backs away from really lecturing a woman after he sees her through the window making love to the man who will later kill her. I don't think he would've restrained himself in the earlier novels. Wasn't Spenser out front with it in earlier novels, especially in *The Godwulf Manuscript*?

P: Well, he's older than he used to be.

C: O.K. And the character changes in the imaginary world in which he lives.

P: He has to. I admired Rex Stout very much, but what I always thought was a bit lacking in Stout was that Archie and Nero never changed. Stout got to be over eighty years old and Archie was still thirty-two. I don't want Spenser to be sixty-seven years old and still jumping through windows and kicking down doors. I started writing the first novel in 1971, so I would've been thirty-nine when I began *The Godwulf Manuscript*. I began it in November 1971 and now I'm forty-nine. But things change and perceptions enlarge; I don't consciously set out to make Spenser grow and I don't consciously mention his age anymore, which is how I plan to deal with *that*. If you follow the books, obviously we've established that he was in the Korean War, for instance. He has to be at some given point a certain age, so he's got to be close to fifty now, if you've followed along, and people don't want a fifty-year-old detective. I don't either. Marlowe was forty-two in *Playback* and had been thirty-two in *The Big Sleep*.

C: You mentioned an outline and a scenario. Do you do what some scriptwriters do, which is to write a kind of walk-through scene without all the good stuff in it, then walk through another scene?

P: No. I just do a little treatment or whatever, a little three- or four-page summary of the story idea, and then I work up a chapter outline, which is maybe five or six hand-written pages to the chapter. The outline for a chapter might say, simply, "Spenser drives to Smithfield, explains to Susan," or whatever.

C: At what stage does the weird humor come in? What draft?

P: I only do one draft. When the outline's done, then I write it and compose on a typewriter. And what comes out of my typewriter is essentially what you read. The changes are minor. They are almost exclusively copy-editing changes. I've never been edited. I've never changed anything.

C: Do you feel you should've been edited, or that someone should've at least sent you a note saying what a brilliant dialogue you had there in chapter 3, or something to that effect?

P: No. I'm happy with the books.

C: Oh, I am too, I'm not saying that.

P: I think that editing wouldn't have improved me. I'm improved *greatly* by copy-editing because I don't spell well. Copy editors take care of a lot of stuff. They don't catch everything, though. Once I had Spenser drive north, take a left, and head east. But no, there are never any soars of the imagination or any great vaulting feelings, and no great declines into depression either. The excitement is in thinking it up, in starting the book, and to the extent that it's inspired, the inspiration is in thinking it up, but then thinking it up is mechanical. I don't write when I'm inspired. I write the same way that people go to work each morning. When I finish one book, I begin another. I have two children to educate.

C: Did you ever wake up one day and have this wild, swinging feeling that you'd glimpsed something, some eternal verity?

P: No. I like to write and I'm very satisfied with what I do and I have a great feeling of pleasure in having constructed these books and I'm proud of them and I think I'm the best there is at what I do. I'm not afflicted with modesty, but . . . There are many people who write better than I do, but none of them is doing the kind of stuff I do. I can't manage the language as well as John Updike; I can't do anything as well as William Faulkner, probably including drinking bourbon.

C: He didn't do that very well, apparently.

P: I guess not. All the practice he had, too.

C: Lost every game.

P: But I know what I can do, and I'm confident of that and I like the feeling of having done it. I also like to do carpentry. The house we lived in prior to this I built pretty much myself. I like to cook. I like to make things and these are some of the things I make. I'd like to keep on doing it, but there's never the ecstasy of creation or the despair of failure. It's what I do.

C: An every-day-at-the-office type of thing.

P: Yeah.

C: You wouldn't put on a pore ole Southern boy who's come all this way?

P: Sheee-it no. No, this is — I'm telling you the truth. I like the way things dovetail and I like a certain amount of celebrity. But only a certain amount. Hence my unpublished telephone number. I like to be recognized on the street. The perfect way of getting recognized is the way it happened to me recently: I was at a restaurant one night with Joan and the waiter brought us over a drink from someone who had recognized me and admired me and bought me a drink and left. If they come over and say, "I like your work," and I say, "Thank you," then what do we say? And I like to have someone say "I saw your picture in *People* magazine," or whatever. That's fun. I like to go to Hollywood. I don't so much enjoy Hollywood, but I like to come back and have people say, "What was it like in Hollywood?"

C: What were you doing in Hollywood?

P: I'm writing a screenplay of *Wilderness*, for Universal and Michael Phillips.

C: Your plots have a kind of workmanlike construction because although they are not the most complex in the world, they do fit together nicely; they're all plausible. Brewster is an awful son of a bitch and it's plausible someone should want to kill him. The people in *Wilderness* are plausible and their actions are plausible. There must be some satisfaction in doing all of that well.

P: The plot is what interests me the least. I'm interested in character, primarily in Spenser's, and I guess I'm interested in relationships. Anyone who's read most of the books knows that there are certain recurrent relationships that interest me, including, to the extent the form permits, parent-child relationships.

C: There's no mystery in the books in the same sense that there's a mystery, a puzzle, in the works of Allingham, Tey, John Dickson Carr.

P: There's no puzzle of that sort to be unraveled, in the nineteenth-century ratiocinative sense. There *are* mysteries, which are in some way unsolvable, and there are problems that have to be resolved and people to be saved, but there's never much worry about who took that missing statuette or what happened to the rare, priceless jewel box or any of that stuff.

C: As the author of *Watteau's Shepherds*, which is about British detective fiction from 1914 to 1940, points out, these writers were having us on. A book was a private joke or an intellectual exercise.

P: That's one of the things I like least about the ratiocinative detective story: it wasn't serious and most of the people who wrote them weren't serious. I'm serious in my books. When *Wilderness* was coming out, I was having a drink in the Ritz bar with a figure in the literary world. He was asking me what the next book was and I told him. He said, "Not another Spenser novel?" I said, "No, a mainstream novel, a novel-novel." He said, "Well, you're finally going straight, aren't you?" I said, "No. To the extent that I have art, the art is in the Spenser books." *Wilderness* is an attempt to find a new market, try a new thing. It's not a hack job. That is, whether it's good or bad, it was written with as much seriousness as anything else. I'm working on a non–Spenser novel as soon as I get through with the screenplay called *Love and Glory*, which is a love story with no violence, no "physicality," none of that.

C: Do you resent it when people say that detective fiction is somehow not serious, not adult?

P: Yeah, sure.

C: What's your standard reply?

P: I don't bother.

C: Is there pressure in creating a series character?

P: Well, "pressure" might not be the word I'd use. There are specific problems with a series character. Some are mundane, but nevertheless they're real problems and include the question of how much you say about the protagonist in each book. You do know each time out that some people will have read each of the preceding books, but that some people will be reading you for the first time, so they've got to be informed of Spenser's attributes. You have to establish the relationship with Hawk, the relationship with Susan, some of Spenser's physical accomplishments, all of that, without doing it over and over.

C: But unless Spenser joins the priesthood or moves to Des Moines, there really isn't much you can do once you've established him in his locus and in his age group and given him six feet of muscle.

P: You can't change him after you've established him because it would be bad art. You can't, even if it would make a wonderful novel, have him suddenly abandon Susan in the face of danger. He does go around. In *The Judas Goat,* he was kicking around in Montreal and Europe. He'll go places where I go. In *Ceremony* he's in Boston again, with a little excursion to Providence. The next one after that, *The Widening Gyre* — the title is from Yeats's poem "The Second Coming" — will take him to D.C.

C: Has regionalism returned to American fiction today via the detective novel? All of the protagonists are tied to one locality.

P: I would suppose so. I don't really know more about the current literary scene than you do, so your guess is as good as mine as to whether regionalism has returned as an acceptable literary motif. I think that partly because I am writing romance, I need to root it in very hard, gritty, real, circumstantial realism and that leads to regionalism because you want to imbed the character in such a web of credibility that his slightly larger-than-lifeness is not bothersome. Chandler did that. Hammett didn't do it all that much. Chandler was the one who rooted the genre in southern California.

C: Isn't every detective writer who has a home-town hero following Chandler, who had a home-town hero as his protagonist? Marlowe almost never got out of L.A. He went to Mexico to check on his buddy in *The Long Good-bye.*

P: Never further than Bay City or up in the mountains in *The Lady in the Lake.* He never went anyplace. That's right. And the war came and went and he took no notice of it.

C: The tone and the atmosphere of *The Lady in the Lake* owe a lot to World War II.

P: Yeah. They're tearing up the rubber sidewalk in front of the Treloar Building down there on Olive Street in L.A. There's a soldier in the mountains. I don't know and who's to say? Obviously, a lot of us got it from Hemingway, too, that kind of concrete detail or the illusion of it. He made a little go a long way.

C: Some reviewers have said you've fallen in love with Spenser.

P: Yeah, somebody said that. Again, it's critics' talk. It doesn't mean very much, really. I'm fond of him; I wouldn't really want to spend a lot of time writing about some guy I wasn't.

C: No, how could you? But have you sort of let him develop certain mannerisms, certain dependable things you can fall back on?

P: Not consciously. I try to avoid that. But Spenser is a guy who has been around now for eight or nine books and he obviously has — as we all do — things that he's interested in, mannerisms, attitudes, and so forth, and there is a conscious effort to avoid having them become mannerisms, let's say. I don't know if I succeed in that or not. If someone means that I'm unwilling to let him be human and weaker, I would deny that. He rarely is completely successful. What I do know is that you cannot, finally, for the sake of your own preservation, pay very much attention to what reviewers say if you're reviewed widely. And I'm not condemning reviewers.

C: Although I'm not sure they've all read what they're reviewing.

P: I know some of them don't because they reprint the jacket copy as a review. The jacket copy is rarely critical, you know. But if you get reviewed nationally, every suggestion that could be made will be made — improve your dialogue, improve your plotting — and finally it doesn't seem to make very much difference what anyone says.

C: Is there any one critic alone in his or her generation whom you listen to?

P: Not in that sense. There are people whose writing has enlarged my understanding of my own work. As I say, I'm not one of those who say a critic is a legless man who teaches running. Sometimes he is, but a legless man can teach running. There's a difference between being able to see whether it's being done well or not.

C: To be fair you have to say that.

P: I'm competent to make an evaluation of "The Waste Land" even though I couldn't have written it.

C: No, but you're a consumer of it, and that's one of the points in favor of reviewing: that it's an aid to the consumer.

P: I think that people have sometimes seen things in my work that I was not as aware of until they'd seen it. I have learned from that, though you don't want to pay too much attention to that or you start thinking about it. But by and large most reviewers don't do a very good job.

C: And I think they have a crush of work.

P: I think so, too, and a review is, after all, always for the furtherance of the reviewer's career; that's why he does it, or she does it.

C: Or should be, because they're certainly not going to be making any money from it.

P: That's right. I've done it. I've done reviews for the *New York Times*, the *Washington Post*, and the *Boston Globe*, and I did it to further my career. There's nothing wrong with that. I won't savage another writer, even if he or she deserves it.

C: I think Auden had the right idea about that. Until we're all dead and they've thought about us a hundred years, who's to say who's ahead?

P: So I try to find a way around it if I didn't like the book very much or — well, the worst review I ever did was of someone who's dead.

C: And you can't libel a dead person. Back to editing: you have never been strenuously edited, right?

P: I send it in; they print it.

C: Was that true of *The Godwulf Manuscript*?

P: Yes. Maybe I rewrote one page at the suggestion of Austin Olney at Houghton Mifflin. I don't remember now, but I remember cutting a paragraph or something. But for all practical purposes, I send it in, they clean up the punctuation and spelling, and print it as it comes.

C: In a way you're free to try all kinds of amazing innovations in the genre if you want to, because some of those guys are sitting around saying, "Hmm, weighs five pounds; print it."

P: Yes, that's absolutely true. I think it is common knowledge that editing in modern publishing is acquisition editing, not the Maxwell Perkins kind of editing. Publishing is a business and a lot of people who work in publishing are not paid very well, either. I suspect that's because there are so many women in the business, who are being taken advantage of from the standpoint of pay. But you need to remember that after the novel comes out of my typewriter, that's the last time a literary or aesthetic judgment is made on it. Everything after that is essentially commercial. But I'm glad about that. I don't want to revise. I do know some people who are being edited. At least two writers I know — they're not household names — have revised their last novels at the behest of editors. My situation may be an accolade to the perfection of my first draft, you know.

C: Let's not sink in it up to our knees. I wanted to refer to your more distant predecessors. Sir Walter Scott is at the back of all this detective and male adventure stuff, isn't he?

P: Sure, sure. And of course Cooper and Twain in this country. Scott and the earlier Arthurian heroes are all knightly figures. There's a doctoral dissertation by a guy named William Kenney, which traces the detective hero up from the Arthurian romance, and he's probably right.

C: In *Early Autumn* you've got that miserable kid that I would send to a camp for retardos, but Spenser is trying to make something out of the poor guy, and at one point he tells the kid that eventually he will read James Fenimore Cooper.

P: I'm fond of Cooper, although I don't admire his prose style.

C: No, who could?

P: But finally, when you're through wading through it and feeling sort of superior to him because he was such a klutz of a prose stylist, you look back and realize it worked. You remember Leather-stocking and those corridors through the brushless forests. It works, however badly he did it. Hemingway put the origins of American literature at a much too recent point. It wasn't out of *Huckleberry Finn* that American literature came; it was out of the Cooper novels.

C: Yes. *Huckleberry Finn* is a badly constructed book and suffers forever from what the movie people would call a logic problem: they want to take this slave away, they can only get him away on the river, but the river flows south, into slavery. Maybe that's why Twain took so long to write it: he saw the problem. But you're right. Cooper was the start even if, as the story goes, he was just trying to bring Scott to Upstate.

P: The fact that he was called the American Scott may be coincidental. The story I remember is that his wife was reading aloud to him some early nineteenth-century novel and he said, "I can do better than that." He probably didn't succeed. But he got the myth of America, as D. H. Lawrence remarks. He got it and he fixed it, and we have all spun out of it ever since. But when I say it works, I mean that one of the reasons it works for me is that I read them all in the order he suggested. He wrote an essay in which he suggested the reading order, so it was like reading one very large saga, painful as the prose style is.

C: Although not as bad as Dreiser.

P: Oh no. Dreiser and Eugene O'Neill are the two worst professional writers I've ever read, in terms of management of the language. You know, Kenney traces the development of the Arthurian heroes through Scott and the detective hero — and through the western hero, although I think that's arguable. He even makes the point that a lot of Marlowe's values are upper-class aristocratic.

C: But doesn't a buck private in an infantry company have the same values — honor, courage, and integrity?

P: Well, yeah, but I think Marlowe was something of an elitist.

C: But not as bad as dear old Peter Wimsey. Let the record reflect that Mr. Parker choked on that. How do you view that moment in the genre?

P: It reflects a world view that isn't available any more, that is, the detective being intellectually superior to his surroundings. It makes an assumption that the world is amenable to logical deduction. Their triumphs are ultimately triumphs of the intellect, based on the view of the world that the nineteenth century inherited from the eighteenth, that is, that the world was an intricate machine, but amenable to human control and to reason. Somewhere around 1914 that world view disappeared and it hasn't returned. Consequently, what emerged one way or another in Hemingway and in James M. Cain, and in Hammett and elsewhere, modified in this country by the frontier tradition — [*in his mock-pompous voice*] c.f. my doctoral dissertation — was a view of the world as not being amenable to human control. Logic and reason were not terribly useful. They were better than nothing, but what really mattered, finally, was the ability to endure, as intellect was replaced by toughness.

C: But Spenser uses his mind. And a lot of the bad guys are frantically using their minds, even if only to defraud someone. But I guess that's not what they live for and what they get their pleasure from.

P: Nor is it what makes Spenser at least not lose. Finally, it is that he is committed to a vision of life — [*back to his mock-pompous tone*] see, I used to be a professor — he's committed to a Vision of Life, which includes sentimentality. He's as sentimental as Holden Caulfield or as Huck Finn, but what makes him different from Holden Caulfield, say, is that he's also tough enough to maintain a sentimentality.

C: O.K. But what's the difference between what Spenser does when he beats up Red Brewster and what some homicide detectives do when they take in murder suspects and beat them over the head with thick ledgers or bash their heads into the walls so hard that a wall is dented. Apparently when some detectives catch young blacks suspected of murder, it's routine to beat them until some kind of confession is forthcoming.

P: Well, a basic difference, and I'm not persuaded that's always a bad approach.

C: But just from the viewpoint of police efficiency, it's a bad thing because you never know if you got the right man.

P: But the difference is that Spenser is not an instrument of civilization. What you want from policemen is obedience. You want them to manifest the intentions of the civilization that employs them.

C: That's a literary convention, too, though, you know.

P: But that's what you want; that's the ideal, whereas Spenser is not part of the establishment. When a cop beats up a murder suspect, the government is beating up on a citizen. When Spenser does it, it's just him and them.

C: The whole thing about illegitimate power bothers me, because he has some power by virtue of his being big and tough and having a gun and being pretty swift on his feet and being able to do ten miles a day.

P: And he uses it.

C: If the cops weren't here, we'd probably have to shoot people like Spenser.

P: Or he'd shoot them. Sure. Well, as he says about Hawk in one of the novels, Hawk probably shouldn't be walking around loose. The point is that Spenser's reaction is to an imperfect world, a fallen universe, if you like, and it's the best he can do. Neither he nor I would argue that that's right. *A Savage Place* is in many ways a tragedy. He loses.

C: He gets the villain to make a confession, however inadmissible.

P: He lost the girl, though, and it was his job to guard her. She gets her head blown off. And that's what he cares about. He doesn't care about justice. He cares about people, however sentimental that cliché is.

C: In *A Savage Place*, there's one jarring note, or maybe it just jarred me because I was in the newspaper business a long time. When the young woman goes in to talk to these guys who are determined to tell her nothing, she's been insulted and hurt and she's scared, but then she starts to cry because these guys threaten to call her boss. If one of my reporters had done that, I'd've fired her.

P: Well, I think part of my point was, and it may well be a jarring note, that she was not a tough old broad. It was the maleness of that rejection, not the threat of being fired; it was the recognition of her isolation and that her only ally, Spenser, was a man too. My wife's work takes her into that kind of situation too, but my wife does not break down and cry; she creates crying. Joan doesn't get ulcers; she gives them.

C: But what I liked about the scene was that it was a wonderful adumbration of her death. And the novel really is that girl's tragedy.

P: It's hers. And it's Spenser's because he can't prevent her death, can't save her or help her, and that is after all what he does; that's his profession. He would be a catcher in the rye if he could be, but he can't be. So his paroxysm of violence at the end, in my imagination — nothing is more boring than writers explaining their work and I won't do very much more of it — is the result of, I think, not so much the quest of justice as the release of frustration.

C: Extra innings?

P: Yes, and an attempt to somehow mollify himself a

little, to relieve some of his feelings. It didn't work and that's what Samuelson, the cop, understands. Samuelson understands that and that's why he lets him go.

C: For a man who's written as widely and as well as you have, there are very few jarring notes, which is one of the great things about your work. You can pick it up and you're comfortable with it, and it has what a friend of mine used to insist every great novel needs, and that is charm. And that's not a Southern expression with negative connotations. But in *The Judas Goat*, when Hawk and Spenser are whaling away at the Man Mountain McGoon — Zachary — spraying all that blood, snot, and slobber all over the place, I thought, "My God, what is Parker doing here?" Using your hands just doesn't spell street fighter to me.

P: Well, it mattered not only that they beat him but how they beat him.

C: You mean, on his own terms?

P: Yeah.

C: But there were two of them.

P: Yeah, but he was a good-sized fellow. They did the best they could, or the best I could.

C: I like all the little wisecracks Spenser makes. Tom Hart at Houghton Mifflin says you must've been the kind of kid who sat in the back of the class and made wisecracks in the fifth grade.

P: Joan and I used to go to PTA meetings when the boys were small — that's a dreadful evening — and we'd walk in the classroom and immediately go sit in the back and put our feet up and chew gum and snicker at each other. But sure, I guess I was that. Humor is a distancing trick, of course. And it's a controlling trick.

C: And with Spenser it's strictly verbal; the humor's not in the situation. Spenser is a man who wants to be distanced, I think, in his own life, too. I mean, here's a man who's sitting in a seedy office, or relatively seedy: the detective Spenser reading about the poet Spenser, which I thought was overdoing it a little. And the detective from Seedyville flies off to Tinsel City. There must be a kind of schizophrenia in that kind of life. Or do you think not?

P: I think not.

C: So much for leading questions.

P: I don't have anything to say beyond my saying that I don't have any sense of paranoia or schizophrenia. I don't feel it in myself and he comes out of me. His goal is autonomy. I just want people to leave me alone, not put their hands on me. Autonomy is Spenser's goal and he does what he can do. If he could write, maybe he'd write. Someone asks him why he's a detective and he says, "Because I can't sing and dance." People do have to do what they know how to do.

C: Do you think people look with more favor these days on the writers who cover several fields? It's unthinkable that Chandler could or would ever have done a book like *Three Weeks in Spring* or written a non–Marlowe novel, but your career has shotgunned all over.

P: *Three Weeks in Spring* is a special case, obviously, and what it did for me, among other things, is make me understand that I could write other things.

C: That's a beautiful book, by the way.

P: Thank you. Joan's 100 percent, by the way, a question that no one wants to ask, but everyone thinks. It's been six years and they call it cured after five. But back to the question: I will periodically do other kinds of books because they're an opportunity to try something different. I think writing a non–Spenser novel occasionally makes the Spenser novels better.

C: It was interesting to me to see in *Wilderness* what the character didn't have that Spenser had and what the big tough guy who's the paid gun didn't have that Hawk has. And what the wife doesn't have that Susan Silverman has. This is a dumb question, but I'm paid to do this: which set of characters would you rather work with?

P: That's a *dumb* question. No, I'd rather work with Spenser and Hawk and Susan. They're a little idealized, but I've been with them for a long time; I don't have to think them up.

C: Would it drive you nuts to have to come up with a new protagonist each time out?

P: I would think that would be harder, and also you lose a lot of opportunities to do interesting things. If you stay with the same stock company, you have a chance to do what Faulkner did — although the comparison is ludicrous — you can keep messing with the characters until you get them right, and I'm going to keep at it until I get it right.

C: He meets Rachel Wallace, and in another book she recommends him; Hawk appears from book to book.

P: It's a chance to modify and develop and change. In a series, if you do it right, the character can grow, as you do. After all, I'm not what I was ten years ago, and I will probably be even more different ten years down the line. In some ways I'm going to be better and in some ways I'm not.

C: Are we going to see Hawk and Susan and Spenser get all good and gray headed together and shuffle off on Sundays to the Boston Common to relive good old times, or are you finally going to come to the end of that series because Spenser can't jump through windows anymore?

P: No. I assume I'll keep at it until I die. I don't know how else to solve the problem. We'll just see as I get older. I'm still physically capable of doing most of the things Spenser does. I don't mean beating people up, but I can run as far as Spenser can, though not quite as fast. I can bench press quite a lot, though not as much as he can. Sometimes the question arises: isn't he a little too remarkable? No, he isn't. I only make him a little better than I am. And I know people who can do better than he does. I have a friend who used to be a tackle with the Boston Patriots who can do everything that Spenser can, but better.

C: Do you think you relied too much on Hawk in those

books, especially *The Judas Goat* and *Promised Land*? Do you think you relied on him too much as a foil for Spenser in that (a) Spenser might not need a foil and (b) Hawk is probably too close to Spenser to be a foil and (c) Hawk is a little sweeter than any black thug I ever saw in police court?

P: No.

C: [*groans*] My next question —

P: Hawk is interesting to me. Hawk attracts a lot of attention, interestingly enough — people ask me where I got him and why he's in there and what he does — in disproportion to the number of appearances he makes.

C: They've never seen black people before?

P: Well, I don't know, but they're interested in him. He's in many ways their favorite character. They're sometimes more interested in him than they are in Spenser. One of the reasons he's in there is that I don't have black friends anymore and I miss them. I used to, in the army and growing up. Secondly, he is, without any racial pun intended, though with a deliberate recognition of his darkness, the dark side of Spenser; he's what Spenser might have been if Spenser had grown up in a society that treated him the way society must have treated Hawk.

C: Or maybe Hawk's just ba-ad.

P: There's that. But I can work on the differences and similarities between them for as long as I want to. Susan and Hawk are both in there in some sense for the same reason Watson is with Holmes and Archie with Nero Wolfe. They serve, as does the whole novel, Spenser's purposes, and everything in there is done primarily to let us know more about him.

C: When I read *Early Autumn*, I soon realized there was no detecting; there was really not much danger. It was really a chrestomathy on the subject of raising kids.

P: [*as David Parker enters*] Well, I had a lot of experience raising feeb kids. No, really, it was a way to talk about how to live; they're all ways to talk about how to live.

C: One of the things I react negatively to in your books is the amount of instruction, though.

P: Your objection's not the only one I've heard. I don't know that that's the way it comes out. I'm not being evasive; it may be so. Periodically, some reviewer bitches about the amount of talk.

C: No, I don't mean that. I like *longeurs,* almost anybody's *longeurs;* it's one of the few things left that separates fiction from the screenplay. But the whole purpose of *Early Autumn* is to show a man giving a boy a few pointers on Life and I thought, "Well, why don't we have a book on child management and get on with the program?"

P: I'm perfectly willing to concede that I may not separate fiction and exposition well on some occasions, but one of the reasons writers say so many dumb things is that they're trying to explicate the inexplicable. And when they are asked questions about what they do, they are again forced to explicate the inexplicable. So I never have said anything about what I do that seemed to ring quite true to the inner person who does the writing. I really don't have much response to the charge that sometimes there is too much instruction. Maybe, but it's probably going to continue, and that's the way it works.

C: Well, we're not going to quit voting for you on that account. And speaking of voting, are you in the Mystery Writers of America? I understand they summon you to the meeting when you're going to get your award, but you don't know you've won until the magic moment.

P: Well, theoretically, that's so. But they want you there and so they do not exactly say that they're going to give you the award, but you know you're going to get it when you go there, and the other people probably don't. They think they might. The first I heard of it was when my editor called me up and said, "The Mystery Writers of America want to give you an award." And Houghton said they'd pay my way down. So I went down and I remember being seated at an appropriate table with other people. As this guy was showing me to my table, he said, "You'll be glad you came." And I thought, "I think some of the suspense is waning here."

C: One last point, about style. I like your descriptions of people and things because they're both funny and to the point. Do you think there's room in the detective novel for careful description, or should the novel just race along from one section of dialogue to another?

P: You need a certain amount of description to give the book dimension and reverberation and the sound of music beyond the distant hill, and that's how Chandler got it; it wasn't the dialogue. There's no other way to do place than to describe. What was it Conrad said? His job as a novelist was to make you see. Hmm. So far I've managed to compare myself to Conrad, Faulkner, Henry James. But, anyway, I think description is necessary. I don't read too much detective fiction actually, but I think one of the things that people fail to do is to take the time to describe. No writer likes to do description. It's so easy to write dialogue. De dum de dum de dum and then say, "Oh shit, here's a building I have to describe." I think you need a certain amount of discipline. I can't think of too many books in which context isn't important. But my goal is not simply to get the reader to see what it looks like but to make use of it as a thing to give dimension and reverberation. I think without that a book can be thinner than it should be.

C: Any last message for the world, Mr. Parker?

P: "Buy early and often." Or, "I do this for money."

C: Do you think there's an outside limit to a man's writing career?

P: I don't really have any idea. It doesn't feel that way to me.

C: What do you see in the future? More Spenser novels?

P: I'll do as many Spenser novels as they'll publish.

C: May he prosper and flourish.

EMMA LATHEN

Mary Jane Latsis, who holds a doctorate in agricultural economics, and Martha Henissart, who holds a law degree, met at Harvard University in the fifties, where they discovered that they were both fans of the mystery novel, particularly what is now called the Golden Age (or genteel) mystery novel. They joined forces — and the first three letters of their last names — to become not two fans but one writer: Emma Lathen. They entered a mystery-writing contest and lost, but their first novel, *Banking on Death*, was published in 1961. After going through a succession of not-very-helpful editors, their perfect grasp of their milieu, their deliciously feline Augustan prose, and their sharp eyes received a well-deserved accolade from Lord C. P. Snow, himself no mean writer of mysteries, in the *Financial Times* of London in May 1970: "She is probably the best living writer of American detective stories. . . . The detail . . . is investigated with the enthusiasm of Balzac. . . . She is very witty, in a wry and downbeat manner. The whole of her writing is in fact exactly what in our vanity we like to think of as proprietorially English."

Lathen (it will be more convenient, and certainly appropriate, to consider Latsis and Henissart as a corporate personality) has preserved the benign and therefore highly entertaining aspects of the tradition: technical knowledge; unity of character and action and time, if not always of place; and the avoidance of the quotidian banalities of life, and of graphic descriptions of sex and violence.

The protagonist of the Lathen novels is John Putnam Thatcher, vice-president of Sloan Guaranty Trust, the third largest bank in the world. The protagonist of another series of novels they have written as R. B. Dominic is Ben Safford, a congressman from a district in southern Ohio. John Putnam Thatcher is probably more familiar to mystery fans for the simple reason that he has been around longer and appears in more books. Thatcher was born and raised in Sunapee, New Hampshire, and was graduated from Harvard. In the earlier books, he is described as having fought at the Marne in World War I, but this line in his vita has been suppressed in recent years, as it would make him between eighty-three and ninety years old. No one really cares, anyway, how old a series hero is, as long as he's over twenty-five. Lathen is wise to give the general impression that Thatcher is at the upper end of middle age. We know he is a widower and a grandfather. His essential prop in the howling chaos of Wall Street is Queens-bred Miss Rose Teresa Corsa, a "virtuoso of wordless communication" and a sort of Greek chorus, despite her Italian name, to the sometimes ostensibly foolish carryings on and absentmindedness of her boss, John Putnam Thatcher. Thatcher is a sharp denizen of Wall Street. Here, the authorial voice describing Thatcher's outlook: "Wall Street is, at bottom, a collection of endearingly childlike innocents, always expecting the good, the beautiful, the true and the profitable. The shrewd eyes, manly handshakes and expensive tailoring that deluded the public (and a goodly portion of the financial press) did not fool Thatcher for one moment; he was one of the few men on the Street not constantly surprised by the turn of events — *any* turn of events." Thatcher has also "seen excellent lawyers become alcoholics, Secretaries of State, and worse."

A major strength of Lathen's books is the style. Lathen is one of the few writers who could use the word "defenestration" with confidence; moreover, her audience expects that she shall. The diction, the post-eighth-grade sentences, the amused sanguine outlook of Thatcher all contribute to the tone of each novel, and whether you consider the tone to reflect the author's attitude toward his audience or toward his material, or to simply mean "color" and "atmosphere" in the writing, Lathen is the most interesting exploiter of tone in the whole field. Notice this snippet from *Pick Up Sticks:* Sylvia Hazen, a financial *Wunderkind,* arrives on a motorcycle to have cocktails with John Putnam Thatcher: "thigh-high boots reached thigh-low pearls; green-rimmed sweep-around sunglasses echoed a brief emerald shift. On the stool beside her, she has deposited a crash helmet and a brief case.

"Ah well, thought Thatcher, another new experience."

Lathen's books are always about some facet of business America, and since those who have the gold make the rules, Thatcher can go anywhere and ask anything. Lathen is thus able to treat society (for whose life is untouched by money?) as an organic whole. Lathen is earnest. And while she is not necessarily convinced, as Balzac was, that behind every great fortune lies a crime, she is thoroughly convinced that the greedy of the earth (and her corporate types come in all shapes and sizes of bank accounts) can be depended upon to employ crime to maximize profitability and expedite the liquidation of assets.

Among the early novels — from the new-editor-for-every-book phase — *Banking on Death* and *Accounting for Murder* are particularly good, and it's interesting to see how the style has become more and more polished and hard hitting and how Thatcher has become more active. Also instructive is how Lathen now gets more from her great supporting cast, including Charlie Trinkam, the pompous and essentially shlemiel-like Ken Nicolls, and the indispensable Brad Withers. *Murder Makes the Wheels Go 'Round* is about felonious doings in the auto industry, although even what is revealed here wasn't as bad as it got in real life. In *Pick Up Sticks* fraud and eventually murder plague a real estate development company; the solution depends on an expert knowledge of land law, New England folks, and how salesmen close sales. *By Hook or by Crook* is about the Americanization of the Parajian family, dealers in fine Oriental rugs, and the murders that occur in the midst of a classic Golden Age crisis: a "missing heir" problem, the solution of which depends again on Thatcher's keen understanding of men in the marketplace. *Going for the Gold* is a fascinating look at the disruption of an Olympic village by a blizzard of forged traveler's checks and is full, as usual, of shrewd insights about the zone where greed and honor are in constant conflict.

CARR: When did you all start? Was it '61 or even earlier? Had you discussed the idea of collaborating prior to that?

HENISSART: No, technically we started in 1960 and then the book was published in 1961.

LATSIS: Yes, that was the beginning.

C: Did you enter into this with some trepidation? I guess using a pseudonym is more convenient if there are two of you, but Ms. Henissart was probably in practice as a lawyer at the time.

H: Oh yes. We were both fully occupied at the time.

L: But there wasn't any trepidation. And as for the pseudonym, it's so much easier to have just one name.

H: Oh yes, it was much easier to have the one name. No one has ever mastered the name of either one of us, anyway. And we had to have anonymity.

L: I think actually we entered into this with unbecoming confidence, to be perfectly honest. Don't you think so?

H: [*answering L*] Oh yes. Like almost everyone of our generation who was a mystery reader, we had grown up reading mysteries and having a great profusion of quite interesting ones, and then we ran out of them and we said to ourselves that no one was writing the kind of mysteries we'd grown up reading.

L: So let us do it. "We shall become classics in our own time," we said.

C: Well, you have, actually.

L: Well, there you are. Just goes to show.

C: Had you all been reading Allingham and Sayers and Tey and also Chandler and Hammett?

H & L: Oh sure, yes.

C: One thing has struck me about the people I'm interviewing, that they started writing mystery stories way past the time, usually right after being graduated from college, when most people started writing "serious" novels about sexual liberation, the Marxist line as applied to the struggle in Selma, et cetera. Why do mystery writers start relatively later than the people who write what are called serious novels?

H: Well, I can think of a nice, unflattering unreason.

C: O.K.

H: Unflattering to them, not to mystery writers. By and large, you have to have *some* acquaintance with *some* content material to write mysteries. As you know, almost all youthful writing is autobiographical for the excellent reason that the only thing they've ever noticed or known is themselves.

L: But they're inexperienced and they have no contact with the world. Now, often this changes by the time they're thirty-five.

C: I'm fascinated with your subject material, probably because my father was a banker and I'm now working for a law firm, but does that subject material turn off people who want to read about tough guys in the slums beating up drug dealers?

H: Oh I think readers have long since split mystery into the genteel and the sex and sadism categories.

L: Certainly that isn't to be regarded as a dark confidence.

H: Good heavens, all you have to do is look at a lot of media today. They've got a big claque. No, there are plenty of people who read both genres, but they regard the two as distinct.

C: And then there's the police procedural kind of thing, which may or may not be sex and sadism, and often isn't.

H: That can be anything: Elizabeth Linington, Ed McBain.

C: Did you always get nice reactions, warm feelings, whatever, from the editors about the work? To the extent that they loved it and were going to make it successful?

H: Ahhh . . . No.

L: In a word.

H: We started to write at a time when the game of musical chairs in the publishing industry was at its height.

L: "Hi there, I'm your new editor."

H: That would be the first letter.

L: Followed two weeks later by, "It's been wonderful working with you, but I'm moving down to the corner magazine and you'll shortly be hearing from — "

H: "My replacement."

L: "Robin." Hi, Robin. "Hi."

H: We didn't have an editor in any real sense for years and years and years.

L: Not for a long, long time.

C: I noticed you switched publishers.

H: Oh, worse than that. We never had an editor for more than one book. And for the most part, less. No, obviously we're exaggerating. There were at that point an awful lot of serious-paperback houses who were enlarging their editorial staffs. There was a big employment upheaval. And most of the editors were not interested in what we were writing.

C: Had either one of you worked in banking?

L: I wrote bank letters.

C: Really? Advice on investments?

L: Well, outlook, economic forecasts, and then some industry studies, things like that. I am responsible for several long-lasting errors that have been perpetuated in Massachusetts statistics. We did a study of the economic impact of the summer theaters for the vacation industry of New England, for which there was no information, so I made it all up, you see, and it's now passed into the lore. I believe computers have taken it in now.

H: Well, you're a standard footnote, aren't you? Unimpeachable authority.

L: I'm the bottom line from which this absurd structure is built.

C: How did agricultural economics get into that?

L: Well, after all, agricultural economics, you know, is a subset of general macroeconomics. They are, generally speaking, the same. There are agricultural economists who are red hot on the corn-hog relationship or the economics of a particular crop, but I wasn't that. I was an agricultural economist in the sense of incomes. And that was a big component of the gross national product. It really is as big a component as trade. So it's really a misnomer to say "agricultural economist" because that always suggests someone who's a big specialist in dairies. I know a cow when I see one, but ...

C: Yours is more like one of the black arts.

L: That's a deflating, but very just, comment.

H: I was in corporate finance before international trade, but, as you know, the big problem in international trade is getting financing, and so in both guises I was in and out of banks all the time, financing manufacturing activities and distributive networks abroad and very often joint ventures with foreign principals.

C: You met at Harvard. How did that come about?

H: Probably trading mysteries. No, I say that. How?

L: I remember. I had just come back from Rome and someone had given me an introduction to somebody who knew you. Wasn't that it?

H: Of course, what I'm inclined to say is that probably it was my using the ladies' room over in Littauer. In the early days of my being at Harvard Law School.

C: When did you first decide you wanted to write fiction? Fiction in general, rather than having John Putnam Thatcher in mind?

H: That happened at exactly the same time. We never really considered any other form of fiction.

L: No. Although that's something I've always been interested in. The world of writing people. The world of people who are interested in fiction, fascinated by writing in college. I was an undergraduate majoring in economics, Martha majored in science, and the two were different worlds and they were quite far apart.

C: But I think some of the best writers have studied anything but English as undergraduates. How do you collaborate? What are the mechanics of it?

H: We have a very strange method of collaboration, simply because when we started to write, we were employed full time and we very often were apart, or one or the other of us was on a Christmas trip. We put together a plot outline, and then we write alternate chapters simultaneously. That is, I'll be writing chapter 5 somewhere and Mary Jane will be writing chapter 6 somewhere.

C: That calls for a really great outline.

H: This was really for efficiency of production under the circumstances that prevailed.

C: Was there any clash between styles?

L: In the beginning there was. It wasn't really a clash, but there was a difference. But we've been doing it now for a good many years and I think there's been a general similarity in the original process, and of course we're very, very practiced in ironing out those differences. I can no longer tell, in some of our earlier books — if I ever look at them — who wrote what.

C: A textual analysis would yield nothing?

L: I don't think it would.

184/THE CRAFT OF CRIME

H: Certainly, I don't think it would after the first four books. I speak as one who has never reread any of these, but certainly there's no doubt that at the beginning of our collaboration, a significant portion of our time was spent ironing out stylistic differences.

C: Long sentences versus short sentences?

H: And that problem no longer exists, but I would assume there are still some traces of it.

L: Actually, I don't think the differences were so much syntactical. I think in many ways they were attitudinal.

H: Right.

L: There was sort of a different approach, but I think basically, perhaps because we both read so much of the same sort of things, the real sentence-by-sentence question was never truly a great problem. We both wrote a kind of standard English.

H: Well, that's a very valid point, but our reading from childhood up has been the classic regimen.

C: Which was?

L: Everything from Jane Austen through Sherlock Holmes.

C: Victorian literature, which is generally similar in impact and structure to this, though. It's really interesting. I like the structure of the typical John Putnam Thatcher novel and also the novels you write under the name of R. B. Dominic.

H: Oh, have you read those?

C: Oh yes. I love those. Val Oakes is one of my favorite fictional creations.

H: He's one of mine, too.

L: Someone said we shall never see his like again. Let's face it —

H: We haven't seen his like in the United States Senate! For generations.

C: I was afraid of that. I was afraid there was no real model.

L: But let some of us maintain our illusions.

C: Have you all spent a great deal of time in Washington on one pretext or another? Observing these people?

L: I worked there for a couple of years. And I've been back on special assignments.

C: The *Wall Street Journal* did an article on you and quoted you to the effect that as funny and ridiculous as some of those lines of dialogue are, you probably heard them — some of the things the constituents say to Ben Safford.

L: Oh, you can't go around making up every idiocy.

H: It is not possible, I think, to manufacture an idiocy that does not already exist in full flower.

L: In that respect, creative work is a misnomer; it's just data gathering at its best.

H: No, it's very true. I've forgotten which critic said that the older you get, the more you realize that the most outrageous characters in Dickens are walking the streets! It's true. It's true. You don't believe it at twenty-five, but as the years roll on . . .

C: One of those novels that I really liked was *Attending Physicians*. And one of the things I want to get into is that some of the real villains in those novels have been women. The woman who went after Dr. Steve Rojack was his mistress and was involved in the whole murder scheme along with Rojack. You guys came down pretty hard on her all the way through the book. I was beginning to smell villain all over her after that description after the first description of her clothes.

H: What was she wearing?

C: I've forgotten, but the tone let you know that it was horrible, and a lot of ungentle fun was being poked at her.

H: I picked up a wonderful outfit on the MTA today that I'm going to immortalize in a book. I studied it carefully.

L: I'll give you a hint. If you ever see little toes peeping out with very careful nail polish, *that* woman is a murderess.

H: We've got to be careful.

C: Do your politics get into the novels sometimes? There was a guy in *Attending Physicians* who gave a long and idealistic speech on doctors' being educated, trained, and paid by the federal government. I guess they get in there sometimes by osmosis, but your views do seem to be planted in your novels here and there.

H: Well, that speech was planted deliberately, but we make no effort to keep our politics out.

C: That's interesting, because a lot of mystery writers are rather conservative.

L: You mean politically?

C: Yes.

H: Well, after the last couple of elections, you'd have to say they were just mirroring the general population.

C: I know, but even before that American detective writers were conservative. I'm thinking of the Raymond Chandler, or Chandlerish, attitudes toward chivalry. That kind of thinking comes from a conservative political outlook.

H: Well, certainly it does. That comes from the Western, frontier tradition laid in modern times. That is your alienated loner detective, such as in the Gary Cooper and Grace Kelly movie, *High Noon*.

C: Which people now view as a morality play about the witch hunt for Communists in the fifties.

H: The cop is a descendant of that, on the same stamping ground, except with throwaway guns.

C: I liked the John Putnam Thatcher novel about the clothing plant in Puerto Rico, featuring, as usual, all sorts of terrible things happening and featuring this wonderful Puerto Rican woman, Annie, who was a charismatic figure and came down to set things straight and verbally stomped this little revolutionary Castroite Trotskyite antirevisionist who — let the record reflect the authors are grinning.

L: You're sentimental too, I see.

C: I am, kind of.

H: Well, that's one of our favorites. While we were researching that, we were kicked out of the ILGWU [International Ladies' Garment Workers' Union] offices down there. It was a pleasure.

C: To be kicked out, you mean?

L: Yeah. The door was held open and we were told never to darken it again.

C: Did they know why you were there? They knew you were gathering research for a novel and they didn't like your style, or what did happen?

H: What happened was that we finagled our way in there and then somebody higher up discovered we were there and — I don't blame them — did not like it.

L: Well, it was very simple. We walked in and a very charming young man, a Puerto Rican national, unburdened himself and told us *all* about the union, and I mean people and how many organizers there were and where they were — this, that, and the other. We were going along great guns when all of a sudden the door opened and in walked Sid from New York, who said, "What's going on here?" and he said, "I'm just explaining to the lady — " "Out!" It was a learning experience for José. I think I can tell you what Sid said to him after we left.

C: Too bad you didn't put that in. But that would make it another kind of book.

L: We don't write that kind of book, no.

C: No, right. What we've got here is a family reading experience.

H: Nothing that an eight-year-old shouldn't be exposed to.

C: You could've chosen a number of people for your protagonist. Why did you choose an investment banker? I love John Putnam Thatcher, but I'm just thinking of people you could've chosen.

H: Well, we chose one that would be better for our purposes. What we really wanted to do was to be able to explain any institution that caught our roving fancy.

C: And a man like that can go check any one of them out.

L: And to go back to Gary Cooper, there was also an attempt to take the modern American man *off* the horse and make him part of an institution rather than the lone gun. There have been so many people — the lawyer, the doctor — and in the end they're all the same.

H: In modern American writing of all sorts, and it's simplistic. That myth affects all the institutions of modern life.

C: Yes, that's true. Mary McCarthy said once in an essay on *Anna Karenina* that at least you could learn how to make strawberry jam reading that book, and yours are not so much mythological in intent. You deal with life as it's actually lived, mainly in financial institutions and in the corporations, but those are surely as important as strawberry jam, and more complex, and you know how they work.

H: Well, I remember — it doesn't derogate from his greatness — but I remember the critics saying that Hemingway was incapable of dealing with anything but individuals and as a result his characters moved through an unpopulated Paris. They were the only people there.

C: Yes. Frank O'Connor said he wrote about a world inhabited by tourists and waiters. I think you're to be congratulated on not only how well you handle the world you've created but also your choice of worlds: very few people realize that there are bankers like Brad Withers and Charlie Trinkam, but there are obviously people like that in banking and in other corporate worlds.

L: In America most people go to work. There may be societies in which this is not true, but most people go to work, and they do not go out to a field to dig up radishes: they go into a big, big institution of one sort or another, and we try to catch the flavor of that kind of life.

H: Yes. Most of us don't go into a one-man enterprise in the morning when we go to work.

C: Where he talks to his faithful secretary, Della Street.

H: Or Effie.

C: I guess one of the things you're doing is working away from literary conventions, one of which is the single man, or rather lone man or lone woman, going into a little law firm or a little detective firm. Those are certainly old, old conventions.

H: Well, you know, there isn't a Victorian novel that won't teach you a great deal about Victorian England after you've read it.

L: Yes. I like to believe, when I'm having delusions of grandeur, that we are Trollopean more than anything else just in trying to give a picture of a complex society.

C: Oh, I think that's true. There are wonderful disquisitions in Trollope — I'm thinking now of *The Eustace Diamonds* — on how to write a will, what can and what can't be inherited, inheritance *in rem* and *in personam*. Trollope asked a barrister to check it out and report to him, and he relayed this information. Do you go to people who have a great deal of specific knowledge about each one of these institutions?

L: One of the things about writing these books is that you do learn so much on the way. Bob Priestly introduced us to a man whose profession is the organization of large sporting events. Well, when you stop to think about it, there are international track meets, Olympic meetings, all these things, which are just as complicated as a World's Fair, and there is a roving band of professionals whose entire careers, and they are very well paid careers, consist of going from here to there; they are specialists in all the varying aspects of getting athletes into competitions.

C: You've written about oil companies, short-order chains, professional sports franchises, trusts that wanted to take over church properties, and on and on. Is there any single institution you've left out?

H & L: Oh, lots, lots. Oh, yes.

L: There were two institutions that we decided not to touch. One is the university. That's been taken, by our betters and by our inferiors. And publishing houses.

C: Well, you couldn't do that, now. That would end the

careers of all of us, and of course no one would publish an interview naming the names behind the names, so all of us in this room would be sent away. This book's already dead in South Africa. Let's save the other 99 percent of the world for it.

L: Those two are safe. Everything else is up for grabs.

C: You know, I think there's a great deal of drama in business. A business professor once told me business was an exercise in ethics, and I laughed at him, being young and radical, but it probably is just that. It's where ethics — or a lack of ethics — functions on a day-to-day basis. There's a passage in *Going for the Gold* that I find worded more or less the same way in some of your other books. We're talking about Hathaway, the nasty guy who's been discovered shooting people from snow banks. "I think he was consumed by the goal of that half million beyond common sense, beyond prudence, and beyond humanity. No matter what the cost, he was unwilling to stop, and on the surface the murder seemed to accomplish its purpose." Then you go on to plot details. But that's really one of the themes of your books. There was a greedy doctor who had to murder to cover up.

H: When you write about the money world, yes. And all of our motives are essentially money, don't you think so?

L: I don't recall any lust, but it may be there somewhere.

H: Necessarily then, greed is an ongoing concern, but I think your point about ethics is very true. Business is an arena where decisions are made, and ethical ones. Some of our young people have very simplistic views about this, but once to every time and nation comes a big ethical decision. Like the Vietnam War. And then, perhaps, there's not another for a while; in the real world, individuals make big ethical decisions twice a day.

L: What is interesting is the end of the Vietnam sensitivity era. I think in many ways our time is coming, but I note with deep interest that as part of the women's movement there is the idea that women and money have a complicated relationship, and this never seemed to have occurred to anybody else before.

C: I know and I don't understand that, either.

L: But it's an awareness that there is something here, and it's exactly what you're saying — that this is where the litmus paper of responses to life can be seen — and this awareness is beginning to seep in as the Vietnam sensibility erodes.

C: That what you do to your neighbor, or your wholesaler, is more important than large, abstract moral issues, which you have to retire from anyway, since most of us never could *do* anything about the Vietnam War anyway. Even collectively, as it turns out.

L: I think so, I think so. It's a grand thing to sit around talking about, but . . .

C: You've mentioned women and the women's movement. Let's go into that. Sometimes women are heroes, sometimes they're terrible villains in your work and —

H: Are you seriously going to take the position that this isn't realistic?

C: No! Of course not! But if you read something by Robin Morgan or Marge Piercy or Jill Johnston, they'd all be heroes, pretty much on the Maoist model of the Detachment of Red Women.

H: They're not.

C: No, as most of us are not. I don't know if you want to get into this or not, but you mentioned that lust didn't operate as a motive in your novels. But you do write about sex in the way the nineteenth century was constrained to do, and it was very telling, very effective: that is, you see the beginnings of a sexual relationship and the aftermath of it.

L: You see the living aspects of it, as opposed to the dead aspects of it.

C: Right. And that's probably more important.

L: The social consequences, which are much more accessible to outside observers.

H: Well, for the most part, that's more interesting.

L: To the rest of us, yes.

C: And I guess one of the mistakes beginning writers make is that they think that sexual experience, the romps in the bedroom, can be transcribed so that they mean something to other people, and of course most of the time it means nothing, because that's all so private and they are all so dissimilar.

L: Pocketa, pocketa, three per pocketa. Do you remember the Dwight Macdonald review of James Gould Cozzens? Cozzens had the obligatory, labored descriptions of the act, and they weren't his best writing, and he wasn't a fluid writer, anyway. And it was Dwight Macdonald who described these people as uninspired and that in fact he was reminded of pocketa, pocketa, three per pocketa.

C: One of the things that is interesting to me is how economically, even stingily, you reveal the parts of John Putnam Thatcher's life — his wife, his children. Of course, his attitudes to Withers and Trinkam are obvious to all, but what was the purpose in slowly feeding us bits and pieces of Thatcher's life?

H: Well, first of all, the real Thatcher's in the office right there. He's spent most of his life there. That's him. Of course, there are other aspects, but those are the natural development of the real Thatcher.

C: Would it make any difference in the novels if he had a rampaging love life or an invalid grandmother somewhere, or liked to go down to the corner to play pool with the touts?

L: These books are not a portrait of Thatcher. We have not fallen in love with Thatcher and are not presenting every aspect of him, like his riffling through Bach while looking at rare books and having rose leaves fall on his Persian rugs. I suppose it's possible that he does all these things, but it doesn't seem probable to me. Well, there you are, you see. Dorothy Sayers really did a loving portrait of Wimsey and she thought that everything about him that she could imagine was so enchanting that she built page after page with those details. Our man is not that kind of figure and we're not doing that kind of study of him, a single man.

C: He's no less effective, though. To look at it another way, I hope differently: what part does characterization play in the novels? Do you worry about who the characters are going to be first, or do you pick out the institution first, or do you think of a good plot first?

H: I would say what we probably do first is think of the institution we'd like to do, then think of the people; then the work is coming up with some kind of plot that will credibly bring this institution and these people together in a murder mystery.

C: The institutions are never, with the possible exception of medicine, roundly condemned. You don't leave the institution a smoking ruin and walk away from it.

L: We are not instinctive Marxists. We are not anticapitalists.

H: Most of the institutions we deal with have a track record or, to put it another way, they have a batting average, and while God knows they aren't perfect . . .

L: Well, I can think of one institution we treated rather harshly, and, as it turns out, not harshly enough, and that was the American automotive industry.

H: That's right.

L: There we suggested that as an industry, quite apart from the individuals, there was much to be desired. Who knew then how much? But there, I think, we did criticize what was painfully criticizable.

H: We're dealing — or we try for the most part to deal — with the real world, in which everything has a cost.

C: Emotionally, legally, cost of the product?

H: I meant "cost" really in all the senses of the word. Take the Dominic novel about the nuclear reactor; energy has certain costs, financial, environmental, and you cannot simply condemn one source of energy.

C: Well, as you said, you're not anticapitalist.

H: Some of these people are more than anticapitalist. They're anti an industrial society.

C: Luddites, in fact.

L: Yes, yes.

H: In fact, they're really against urbanization. By no means are there classic Marxist-capitalist splits on these questions.

L: Small is beautiful.

C: But even Marx discusses "the anarchy of production," and says that finally certain manufacturing industries would have to be centralized and the countries most capable of producing those manufactures allowed to do that instead of every Third World country being given a grant by the World Bank to produce Chevrolets.

There's something else we can get into. In the detective and mystery field, which you find yourselves in, at least critically, rightly or wrongly — and I think wrongly on some counts — there is primitivism.

H: I think we're going to go back to that statement. Primitivism in the mystery as opposed to other forms of writing?

C: I mean the sort of writing that's uncomfortable with the Keynesian, or post–Keynesian world, whose protagonists want to get back to a simpler world where things were honest and pure and mothers had daughters, and so on.

H: I have a feeling those times weren't as attractive as most people think.

C: What was the statement that you wanted to go back to? About your being in the detective field rightly or wrongly?

L: Yes, I'd like to go back to that. What *did* you mean by that?

C: I think all good writing is good writing, and I don't like the way detective writing has been pigeonholed in America — although that's not so true in England — so that it's looked down on. One must get the question "When are you going to do a Serious Book?"

H: Oh, every now and then. As a matter of fact, more frequently now. For a long time we were spared this sort of thing simply because it was obvious that there was no place for narrative in the serious novel.

C: Yes, yes.

H: And if you were so misguided as to want narrative, you really had to be in one of the specialties. But narrative, I believe, is very slowly beginning to be a little more respectable.

C: Do you think that some of the best writers are going to find good examples of good fiction, or even works to look up to, in the detective field, because it is based on character rather than Oblomovian self-examination?

L: No, I don't think so. I don't think there is any such thing as American fiction. I think you really have to use the Chamberlinian categories of product differentiation. I think the different parts have very little to do with each other. I think you probably have ten slots and they do not have any horizontal relationship. I don't think the line from Jacqueline Susann to Judith Krantz has anything to do with the line of the mystery story or the line of the serious novels.

C: You don't think there's any crossing?

L: I don't think so. I think they're truly different product lines. They accidentally come together in a publishing house, in a bookstore or in a book club. A little like a supermarket: tea, coffee, and so on.

C: I'm sure there are people who read only mystery novels, but there must be people who read everything. Or do you think there is a hard-core detective novel readership that has nothing to do with poetry?

L: Of course there is. Certainly there is. That is to say, I would assume that there are a great many people who leave libraries with mysteries who have never heard of any of your Southern authors. I mean, don't you?

C: I think so.

L: Among other things, there are different levels of accessibility. You think of it from the writer's point of view. You're thinking of motive, aspiration, and technique, but the world of readers is just as fractionated. Some of them are quite capable of reading some things, but incapable of reading *with pleasure* anything else. And I think there's been insufficient study of that. We all know why Johnny can't read, but I think the distinctions —

C: Why Johnny reads Poe and not something else.

L: That's right. And I think it's much more complex than why they can't read.

C: Most publishers haven't done any market research worthy of the name, ever. When I ran an urban weekly, we knew how many thousands bought a book once a month, four times a month, three times a week, and where they were, in which social classes. We knew how many drank a six-pack a night and that, therefore, would give us the demographics for soliciting ads from beer companies. They say things like "The average reader wants you to ..." And newspapers know there isn't an average reader, although big magazines don't. They can't. They would be horrified at what the real state of affairs is.

L: No. No publishers have done any market research.

C: Did the fact that there was an audience help determine that you would begin writing detective stories?

H: Not only that there was a market there, but a market we knew very well from personal experience.

L: Yes, yes. And with which we felt comfortable.

H: You mentioned people telling you about the average readers. There's no doubt that from the first day we set pen to paper we knew more about the mystery reader market than certainly any editor we had in the first five years.

L: Yes, yes.

C: I was afraid you were going to say that. Now, you've done eighteen novels in twenty years, and because you wrote well and you did well, you were able to write full time. Would you like to keep on writing just as long as you enjoy the experience? Or do you have a cutoff point in your minds?

H: No, I don't have any. If you do, Mary Jane, will you tell me?

L: When I'm eighty years old, I can stop all this and start translating Dante.

C: Drop all this madness and write Anglican tracts.

L: You know, I read those Anglican tracts.

C: Not bad.

L: Odd.

C: Well, so are her [Dorothy Sayers's] translations of Dante.

L: I know, I know. No, I enjoy writing. The agony of writing, about which I read so much, may well exist, but I think when there are two of us we can, among other things, make little jokes. It's not for me a particularly painful process.

C: It must be a lot less painful when you're collaborating.

L: It doesn't have that feeling of "Oh God, when is this burden going to be taken from me?"

C: I've heard horror stories about collaboration and I have some rather uncomfortable memories about collaborating with Bill Kuhns on a short book about movies, mainly because we were so pressed for time. It is hard to collaborate.

H: It's easier if you do it year after year after year.

C: Is that the secret?

H: Well, certainly the work gets easier. I suppose if there's a fundamental personality conflict, that that will be exacerbated.

L: Oh, there are inevitabilities. Martha has no sense of humor and I'm brilliantly funny. Martha can plot a book, I can't. Martha insists on putting clothes in, I don't see . . .

H: Well, there's another thing. There's no doubt that if you've had a lot of personal experience under your belt, you're used to collaborating, and doing so without any nonsense about whether you get along or do you have the same ideas. That's part of being in business or being a lawyer. You have to work with others.

L: You forget your artistic sensibility.

H: And you have to turn out a written product with other people.

C: Whereas a young writer who's idiosyncratic and not used to being with other people would probably kill his collaborator.

H: It's perfectly possible to say "I don't think this is a very good way of putting it" without hurting someone else or in fact without thinking of anything other than whether it *is* a good way to put it or not. We had both heard this kind of thing a good deal from other people in different contexts and said it to other people.

C: And when you collaborate on fiction, the person who made the most compromises on the previous book may have comparative sales figures to demonstrate that the choices were wrong and that compromise ought to go the other way next time. Or does it work that way?

L: I think we have a sense of continuity. We can look back over our joint product and say that on *that* one we made a few errors of this sort. We feel it didn't work as well as it should have, so let's avoid those next time. I don't think we're that severely analytical, though. But it builds and we have a sense of the pitfalls.

H: Oh sure. And you remember all too well the pitfalls that you agreed to or that you proposed, and in chapter 7 you remember trying to retrieve what was wrong in chapter 3 and trying to correct all that.

C: Do you go through several drafts, one draft?

L: Generally speaking, we have our plot outline, we do our chapters, and then we get them all together. Then individual rewriting may be called for, then the two of us get together and look the whole thing over, together, and then just as we're preparing it for the typist, we take the opportunity to get a clean copy and go over it word by word. And now the clean copy for the typist is becoming less clean. *That* is a very important moment — when together we get everything and try to remember the mistakes we made.

C: Someone asked me to quiz everyone on what each of them had done for the American sentence.

L: We have reintroduced the colon, the semicolon, and the exclamation mark.

H: We were able to reintroduce the complex sentence. That is correct. It seems to me that the simple scheme of subject-verb-object has reigned long enough.

L: I can tell you with absolute certainty that we have contributed to the vocabulary of several publishers. I don't know about the general American public, but I can tell you with absolute certainty that nobody in American publishing knew what some of those words were.

C: I ran across a word early in *A Stitch in Time* of at least four syllables that I didn't think anybody outside of Willie Faulkner would use, and people were usually asleep when they got to his four-syllable words.

H: You can tell your friend the dialogue's not bad either. At least it has something to do with how the people actually sound.

C: Absolutely. There's a tone there and a level of diction that makes it funny stuff.

H: It's American — as spoken.

C: And I think good writers have always recognized and written American as she is spoke without trying to make it pseudo-British. Will you ever have female protagonists?

L: I like Safford and Thatcher.

C: I'm not asking for their replacement. And, of course, there is a wonderful California Republican congresswoman in the Dominic novels.

L: I don't think we've felt the need for yet another protagonist. And certainly there seem to be a great many female protagonists.

C: More so than ten years ago.

H: And there will be more. I should think they'd be choking up the weed patch.

L: One doesn't rule out our using a female protagonist. I just don't know.

C: Is there any reason not to use a female protagonist? For technical reasons? In other words, that it might not be believable if a female detective went into the slums and asked a wino what happened to the bank's missing traveler's checks?

H: As you have noticed, our protagonists tend to confine themselves to those of standard middle-class backgrounds. It's rare they have to protect themselves from somebody. And I doubt their competence to do so.

C: Why do women writers choose male protagonists?

H: Well, of course, with our background ... When we started off, those backgrounds were dominated by men.

C: Did women professionals, when you were starting out, have a harder time getting higher pay and promotions?

L: Did you just think these were fancies in someone's mind?

C: There's a rock over there I can crawl under. Maybe I should have said, "Here in the brave, liberal Northeast ...

H: Using a male protagonist was an accurate observation of the world as it existed. None of the vice-presidents of the Chase Manhattan were female.

L: The old law firms were certainly not exclusively female. No, it was the world as it was. And still is. It's changing, but it's still mostly the way it was. So it just seemed easier. We do not make a lot of statements in our books. They are a reasonably detached view of what is or could be as opposed to what should be. I know we have areas where we are, of course, unrealistic and sentimental, but we don't stretch them too far, except where we have to — somebody gets bonked on the head: plot and genre necessities — because we don't care to load the books with true improbabilities.

C: No editor said: "A male protagonist is what's wanted here"?

H: No editor ever said anything.

L: Oh Martha, you're being unjust. Someone said we must change "this" and therefore all "standbys" at American Airlines were changed to "bystanders," which gave it a sort of desultory flavor. You know how the lobbies at O'Hare are. People just drifting around. No, no one has ever made a comment about the protagonist's having to be male and oddly enough — forgive me, this isn't a criticism of your comment — I don't think it's a question that arises out of our work but rather out of the change in the world. Twenty years ago, that question never would have arisen.

C: Have the movies ever been interested in filming Emma Lathen or R. B. Dominic novels?

H: Well, we sold options constantly and they weren't picked up.

L: Hmm.

C: There's an industry you can deal with if they don't wise up.

DICK FRANCIS

Richard Stanley "Dick" Francis was born in Tenby, Pembrokeshire, Wales, on October 31, 1920, and was educated at Maidenhead County Boys' School, Berkshire. He grew up on the large Welsh farm of his grandfather, Willie Francis, who had been one of the best amateur steeplechase riders of his day. His father, Vincent Francis, a professional steeplechaser, became manager of W. J. Smith's Hunting Stables at Holyport.

Dick Francis served as a flying officer in the RAF from 1940 to 1945. In the autumn of 1946, when he was twenty-six and rather old to be a novice jockey, he began training. In 1947, he married Mary Benchley. He rode as an amateur from 1946 to 1948 and as a professional from 1948 to 1957. As he says in his autobiography, *The Sport of Queens*, "there were nine years and eight months between my first win on Wrenbury Tiger and my last on Crudwell." But, of course, he had thought of himself as a jockey for a long time. In his autobiography, he recalls his brother betting him sixpence that he couldn't get a donkey to jump over a fence while sitting on him backward. It helps to explain that the brother was nine and Dick was five. After a few attempts, he made the leap: "The sixpence was solemnly handed over and in this way I earned my first riding fee. In my heart, from that moment, I became a professional horseman."

And he was very good at it, but an awful loss at the height of his career is probably the reason the detective-fiction world came to be graced with his novels, two of which have won Edgars. It was March 1956, and Francis was riding the royal family's horse — more particularly, the Queen Mother's — in the Grand National, the *sine qua non* of steeplechasing. His horse was the famous Devon Loch and, as he says in his autobiography, "Devon Loch rose to the last fence confidently, and landed cleanly. Behind him lay more than four miles and the thirty fences of the Grand National Steeplechase, and in front, only a few hundred yards stretched to the winning post." Instead, "the calamity which overtook us was sudden, terrible, and completely without warning to either the horse or me. In one stride he was bounding smoothly along, a poem of controlled motion; in the next, his hind legs stiffened and refused to function. He fell flat on his belly, his limbs splayed out sideways and backwards in unnatural angles, and when he stood up he could hardly move." But a man who was National Hunt Champion in 1953–54 has no apologies to make for a decade in racing.

After he decided to retire from racing, he published his first book, the autobiography, and then became racing correspondent for the *Sunday Express*. His first novel was *Dead Cert*, published in 1962 by Michael Joseph, Ltd., for an advance to Francis of three hundred pounds. The publisher made his money back almost immediately and a book has come out almost every year (one year there were two) since then. Francis won the Silver Dagger of the Crime Writers' Association in 1965 and his first Edgar in 1969. He finally quit the newspaper scene and opened his own horse farm near Blewbury in Oxfordshire.

Almost everyone has been taken with the novels: his peers and the reading public and the critics. In his autobiography Francis credits his journalistic training: "Whatever I now know about writing I learnt from the discipline of working for a newspaper. There was a small space allowed so that every word had to be worth it, and a deadline to be met so it was no good turning in a masterpiece tomorrow."

The action in his stories usually takes place within the compass of a short time. The main (always male) character meets and usually falls in love with the heroine, who is always charming in the way that Southerners mean it: utterly competent, friendly, courteous, pleasant to be with. H.R.F. Keating has pointed out that a great deal of Francis's success comes from his exquisite ability to judge what a word will do, when a new fact should be put into the reader's head, when to step up the pace, and that Francis's heroes themselves have never shrunk from judging their fellow men and women.

Barry Brusha has said in the *Armchair Detective* article on Francis, "The whole point about Francis novels — indeed, about Mr. Francis himself — is that a person can do more than one thing well." And isn't this what is meant by English amateurism? Englishmen obviously have serious vocations, but their avocations — riding as amateurs in steeplechases, growing roses, playing cricket for the parish or Old Boys' team — are pursued just as seriously. The seriousness can in fact be daunting. Francis's heroes range from a toy maker to a suicidal secret agent to a racing correspondent to an ex-steeplechaser to a pilot and so on, but they are very, very good detectives, too.

This brings us to one of the objections, and all of them are rather mild, to Francis's work. He does tend to write about the aristocracy with great approbation. The villains with hyphenated names all tend to be *arrivistes*; certainly he never intended them to symbolize the aristocracy. And some of the pain the heroes must have inflicted on them is just a little too much. Past the gag limit at times. But, on the other hand, Francis's realism about violence can be refreshing. His kicked around heroes take the whole novel to recover from a good beating and that certainly adds, rather than detracts, if we are to have sympathy for them — and Francis's heroes uniquely command our sympathy. When Kelly Hughes's wife is killed in a wreck in *Enquiry*, when in *Forfeit* Tyrone's wife becomes an albatross around his neck because she's confined for life to an iron lung, and when Sid Halley loses his hand in *Odds Against*, Francis invariably enlarges the characters through their tribulations.

Francis's heroes now are less concerned with enduring pain and more concerned with becoming good and useful and loving men, and this development insures Francis of even greater success in the writing game. But what's most important is that they show us how to overcome our fears, how to conquer ourselves. This attitude, that one must first conquer oneself, is very English. Charm, courage, and competence are also very English, as the world knows. And that is probably the elusive factor in any analysis of Francis's success; what had not been noticed is that his heroes are metaphors for England.

Recommendations: The early work still appeals, and the best of these is probably *Odds Against*, which was the basis for the PBS TV "Mystery" program "The Racing Game." (The other "Mystery" program that was watched all over the United States was based on *Whip Hand*, set much later but also featuring Sid Halley.) *Bonecrack* is very fine, and so are *In the Frame* and *Whip Hand*, certainly one of his most ingenious books, almost like science fiction in its working out of a plot to destroy racehorses by infecting them with a disease never known to attack horses. *Reflex* is a fascinating look at the life of a photographic genius and at the grown-up survivors of the English sixties.

CARR: I've read Tim Fitzgeorge-Parker's book about racing, which mentions you prominently. Was he a friend of yours? Did you race for him?

FRANCIS: Yes, I rode two winners for him, and I see him quite often now. He goes racing. One of the racing press, really. He writes very well, but he does print things that people don't want, occasionally.

C: I was going to ask you why he called you Mother Francis. Or was that your nickname on the circuit?

F: No. I'd never heard it before it appeared in the book. He said I was called Mother Francis. I don't know why, unless it was because I sort of mothered the horses I was riding, looked after them.

C: Yes, he said you were not only a good rider but very careful of the horses, that, for instance, you wanted them to get close enough to the fences to launch off their hocks.

F: Yes, and that's probably why he called me that.

C: I must confess I thought it might be because you had a reputation on the circuit for not drinking, not smoking, and going to chapel every day.

F: No, I'm not a chapel man. I'm a Church of England man. I go to church Christmas and Easter; I drink and I eat.

C: I've read your autobiography and I know about the fluke accident — I suppose that's what it was — that robbed you of a certain win in the 1956 Grand National. Do you want to talk about that, or are you tired of talking about it?

F: I don't mind talking about it. If it hadn't happened, I might never have written a book, so really it was a blessing in disguise.

C: I saw a picture of Dave Dick, taken just as he is streaming past you, absolutely amazed, and the spectators there at the finish aren't looking at him but back at you, on the ground, I guess. Did you finally settle in your mind what happened?

F: The horse stuck his legs out in front of him. But I'm sure it was the crowd noise. There were 250,000 people in the stands and they were all cheering for the Queen Mother's (my) horse. In front of the stands the course gets very narrow. The Chair Jump is there and after that the Water Jump, which is narrow too, but it's just a few yards before you get to the winning post. We were galloping past it, as you do on the last leg, and the horse pricked up his ears. I've looked at the films of it a number of times. You see him prick up his ears, just having a look at this Water Jump, which was on the inside, probably thinking, "Well, I was here last time around." And as he pricked up his ears, the noise hit him; his hindquarters stopped working and he went down on his belly.

C: Was he an inexperienced horse?

F: No, no. Oh no, he was an experienced horse, but he hadn't heard — I doubt if anyone had heard — the sort of noise we heard on that particular day, and it is rattling. In fact, when Red Rum won his third Grand National, the chap who rode him said to me, "I know exactly what happened to your horse. The crowds were shouting me home" — there never had been a three-time winner of the Grand National — "and the noise was *fantastic*. I felt that my horse was going to do the same thing." And part of the trouble at Ainstree was that you finished riding right in a funnel. The stands were on one side and on the other they had motor coaches packed with people and the rest was open, so when you ran the finish into the neck of this funnel, the noise was terrific.

C: You rode seventy-six winners in the '53-'54 season.

F: Yes, the year I was champion jockey.

C: The champion jockey is the man who wins the most races?

F: Yes. And the Grand National is run every year, and the Gold Cup at Cheltenham, which is considered the most important race now, is run every year, weather permitting. There have been one or two years in the last fifteen when frost or sludge canceled it. It's run two weeks before the Grand National. They have the big Cheltenham Meeting and that's the high point.

C: The man who trained you, George Owen, was the 1939 winner of the Cheltenham. He also trained Stan Mellor and Tom Brookshaw.

F: That's right.

C: That must've been an interesting part of your life, being trained at what is a fairly late age for most jockeys. Aren't most jockeys trained earlier?

F: Yes, they are. I was late because of the war. I was in the RAF for six years. But Stan was very much younger; he started at about sixteen or seventeen. But when you say George Owen trained us ... He didn't really train us; he had the horses and gave us the opportunity to ride them.

C: There were no prolonged avuncular, mentor-pupil conversations about racing and that sort of thing?

F: He used to do a lot of the training of his own horses himself, schooling them, in effect, and you'd go with him and you'd see what he did, because he was a top jockey, and you tried to base your style on his.

C: And you eventually rode in your own style.

F: [*dryly*] No doubt I did improve quite a bit, but I'd ridden a lot before I got into racing. I was hunting; I learned all my racing when I hunted. We were hunting foxes. And the people who ride the horses follow them. There is no end of packs in this country that hunt foxes every year. The hunting proper starts at the end of November and finishes about the end of March. They also have cub hunting, which is trying to catch as many cubs as possible before they gallop over the fields, from about the last week in August until the beginning of November.

C: Are foxes really a problem in England?

F: They're quite a problem. If they're not controlled ... They could be controlled by shooting, but a hunting man hates the thought of a fox being shot (and farmers do shoot their foxes) because that means people can't hunt them. Lots of steeplechase horses get their basic training in the hunting field and no doubt it's the best school for teaching horses how to jump and how to gallop. They meet obstacles in all ways and all sorts of them. You see, England is a big farming country, and every farm and every field is divided by different hedges and you jump those. That's where steeplechasers learn their basic skills.

C: Did steeplechasing literally start when men raced from one steeple to another? The I-can-get-there-before-you sort of thing?

F: That's right.

C: And it's kind of regularized now?

F: Yes. Nearly all the point-to-points, as they call them, are over made courses, but they're soon going to have a certain number of these point-to-points of the old style, just going across the country.

C: To the horror of farmers and pedestrians in general, probably.

F: Probably, yes.

C: I love that story about the rider, Colonel Becher, who fell off twice in the 1839 Grand National, which earned him a creek named in his honor. I also loved his remarking how filthy water tasted without brandy in it. The course is 4 miles, 856 yards?

F: Twice round. The 4 miles, 856 yards is two circuits of the Grand National course; the race is always either the last Saturday in March or the first Sunday in April.

C: I know the Chair Jump is a ditch, but is it terribly difficult?

F: It's the biggest obstacle on the course and it looks bigger, too, because it's narrower than any of the other fences. The Liverpool fences, on the Ainstree course, are big, but they're very wide because they get a lot of runners and they don't seem so bad; but when you come round to the Chair, it's right in front of the stands, and the second time you don't jump it, you gallop around it to the winning post, and it's narrow to fit in there. It's called the Chair Jump because right on top of a wing, which is right to the side of it, there's situated a chair, where many, many years ago one of the stewards used to sit. It's about five feet, six inches high, three feet wide on top; the big, open ditch in front of it is six feet wide, and in front of the ditch is a pole about eighteen inches or two feet off the ground.

C: How far through the air does a horse have to fly to clear it in good style?

F: Oh, far. But you're traveling at thirty miles an hour and they push themselves off the ground and they've got to get high.

C: I wouldn't like to be on one of those big animals going through the air that fast.

F: Oh, it's great!

C: You've gotten hurt a number of times. I'm sure you haven't kept count, but have you broken everything there is to break without virtually disabling yourself?

F: I've — Touch wood. Is this table wood? Yes — never been stopped walking around. I've never broken my legs. I did break my back, or crush some vertebrae in my back, and I was kept lying down for two or three days. I remember when I was going over to America for the first time. I was going over to ride and I had this fall about the beginning of April. The fall was all right, but another horse fell on top of me. I knew something had gone. They took me off to hospital — Bristol Hospital — but they couldn't keep me there. They x-rayed me, but they couldn't keep me there because they were full up, so they sent me home by ambulance. I remember my wife being with me. They gave us the x-ray photographs they took and we rang up my specialist the next day, who lived in London (we had his private number). He said to Mary, my wife, "Get him up to London somehow tomorrow." This was on the Monday.

She got me up there. He took more x rays. I had apparently crushed three vertebrae. He put me in plaster from my chest down to my waist and on Thursday he cut it off. He was not a believer in plaster and I'm the same. I think you mustn't plaster things up; you must keep your muscles working.

C: But were the vertebrae wired?

F: No. They weren't actually broken; they were just

crushed. I said to him, "Now, am I going to be able to ride in America in three weeks' time?" So he got a webbing-and-steel brace made for me and I went over to America and rode.

C: You must have an extremely high pain threshold.

F: Well, that was the worst. But I did have a horse put his foot on my face and cut my nose and eye open (thirty-two stitches), but I did that on a Tuesday and I rode on Friday.

C: Nothing to it.

F: Collarbones — I've broken them six times on each side. Ribs you never count. They are a little bit more strict these days. If you have a fall, the doctor has to examine you closely, and if there's something wrong, you have to be off until you're better.

C: But when you were racing, if you felt you could go, you went.

F: Yeah.

C: I don't know anything about the casualty rate, but were there ever any deaths on the courses?

F: The average is about two a year. Horses fall on them, or they slide along and into another horse, or a horse jumps on a man and smashes his skull, which does happen. And of course it's not the horse's fault, and if he's a good horse he goes on and races for other people.

C: I saw all the Granada TV productions of your stories.

F: "The Racing Game."

C: With that wonderful young actor, Mike Gwilym.

F: Oh, he's a wonderful young actor, Shakespearean actor. He's busy at Stratford-on-Avon at the moment. A Welshman. As am I.

C: He has a wonderful accent, sort of cockney, I suppose.

F: Well, there are people who like to play up their Welsh accents. I can talk with a Welsh accent if I want to. Gwilym has the same Welsh accent I do, which is nil. Gwilym, being an actor, and a Shakespearean actor, has polished his speech up.

C: There's a scene in one of the programs in which a horse falls on a course. We see the horse quiver on camera. Now they can't teach horses to do that, can they?

F: In that case, they injected him with something, but it looked as if it were an accident.

C: But the horse was all right, really?

F: Yes.

C: When you began writing, had you read Edgar Wallace's *Calendar* and *Good Evans*?

F: Yes.

C: And you and John Wellcome edited anthologies of racing stories?

F: Three. We did *Best Racing and Chasing Stories I* and *II* and *The Racing Man's Bedside Book*.

C: I have this wonderful quotation from Harriet, Lady Ashburton: "Racing people seem to me to be the only people who hold together. I don't know why. It may be that each knows something that might hang the others."

F: That's very good.

C: American racing is rather crooked at the moment. In fact, they've just convicted a jockey in New Orleans of fixing races on a grand scale. But is English racing fairly clean, despite what we read in Dick Francis novels?

F: It is now, yes. Nowadays, since I gave it up, they've got a very, very high powered racecourse security service and they do a good job. There's always something going on. There's always someone who thinks he can beat the Establishment and he'll get up to some trick, but they don't last for very long. This security service is very good.

C: And you don't have organized crime over here like we do in America?

F: There are gangs around. Strong-arm people. That does go on, but as far as a syndicate fixing racing — no, I wouldn't say there was.

C: The Jockey Club is really the policing agency as well as an elite club.

F: They are the policemen and they are the organizers.

When I was riding, if they had someone in front of them at an enquiry, they were the defenders and the prosecutors at once. It was bad. When I was halfway through *Enquiry*, they decided the accused could be legally represented because they knew I was making quite a fuss about it in the book, and other people were making a fuss.

C: I think one of your most interesting books is *Bonecrack*. It's one of my favorites.

F: It was number ten. I've got them written down in a pocket secretary here.

C: In *Bonecrack*, there are contrasting sets of fathers and sons.

F: The trainer and his son, who takes over because his son is dying. Alessandro and his father ...

C: Your father was a professional rider.

F: Yes, before the First World War. He was a professional jockey. Between the wars, he was a professional horseman. He dealt in horses and bought a lot of horses and sold a lot of horses, showed horses.

C: Was some of that carried over into *Bonecrack*, your own relationship with your father? Your father was apparently rather stern, according to your autobiography. You'd come out after receiving a nice hand and he'd be a bit dampening.

F: Yes, he was stern. But he didn't knock you about or anything, although he did give me a good hiding once [*laughs*] and I never forgot it. But he wasn't one for giving credit unless it was — that is, at the time. People used to come up to me and say, "Oh, well done, Dick, you did great things," and Father would say, "Oh, you've got another one to do tomorrow."

C: Another interesting thing about your books, at least the early ones, is that the villains all had hyphenated names: Ellery-Penn in *Dead Cert*, the first one, Kemp-Lore in *Nerve*, Rous-Wheeler in *Flying Finish*, Carthy-Todd in *Rat Race*. But the heroes and protagonists all have sort of simple two-to-four-syllable names, and of course in the first book, the villain is truly villainous. Was there any sort of plan in having all the villains bear aristocratic last names and the heroes plain names?

F: I suppose there was a sort of plan, really, when you look at it that way, because I like my heroes to have an ordinary name. I don't want them to stand out, and if you give the villains aristocratic names, people don't immediately have suspicions about them.

C: I was thinking you gave them hyphenated names as an indirect criticism of the aristocracy.

F: No. I haven't any criticism of the aristocracy. I'm quite conservative-thinking about that. I think if you give them names like Lord So-and-so, people don't suspect. The name is sort of a red herring.

C: You know, one of the things people like about your books, and I think this has probably been brought up before in reviews, is that they really are sweet, in the sense that most Shakespearean early comedies really are sweet: they really are about love and courage. And that doesn't seem to be a very dark view of the world, even though some of your heroes don't *feel* particularly cheerful. One had a wife who was in an iron lung. One was a suicidal secret agent.

F: Well, now, as for the wife in the iron lung, that was fairly autobiographical. My wife was in an iron lung for five weeks. She had polio in 1949. She got over it, although she can't get both her hands up above her head, and that's why we've got an apartment in Fort Lauderdale, because she can't stand the cold weather. Her chest muscles are all gone. There were a lot dying here of polio, but she was just lucky. She was determined not to die if she could, and she was pregnant at the time. She wanted the child. She was given the opportunity to have him ... taken away from her, but she wanted the baby because we thought we might never have another one.

C: This is not a term of condescension, or at least I don't see it that way, and I certainly agree with the assessment: a reviewer in the *Times* said that your books are adult fairy tales in that the hero wins, and the beautiful woman is won, or at least redeemed, by the hero's attentions. Did you self-consciously want to create a classic fairy tale in modern dress?

F: No, I didn't want to do that. It's just come about like that, I suppose.

C: Because of who you are?

F: It's very satisfying to me when you say something like that.

C: Well, after all, the fairy tale — the myth — is the oldest form of literature and still one of the most appealing.

F: Yes. Yes. The children are the ones who love fairy tales and it stays with them forever. It's surprising the number of children who read my books. They love them. I get no end of letters — not really from small children — but I do get letters from thirteen- and fourteen-year-olds, and they are children, aren't they?

C: Seems so from the viewpoint of forty years. But it's pointed out to me, and I think it's true, that the world's greatest novels — not poems or plays or short stories, but novels — have been the ones that children could read.

F: Yes.

C: It's not fashionable anymore, but I love Scott and Dickens.

F: Absolutely, yes. I found it hard work, reading Shakespeare, and before we were married my wife took me to see *Hamlet*. There's a lot one can enjoy about that sort of thing, but I didn't read much Shakespeare in school (no more than I could get out of doing). Shakespeare, Dickens, and Scott — they're all such great writers, aren't they? I read all of Edgar Wallace's books I could get my hands on when I was younger. He wrote so easily. People could follow him and I hope they can follow what I write.

C: Your writing is wonderfully Plain Style. It's crystal clear. Not many people could or should write like William Faulkner, after all.

F: No.

C: You know, it seemed to me at times that your style is almost American in its plainness and simplicity, in the way you're able to point it up and make it solid. English writing is sometimes criticized in the United States for being a little "fancy dancy" at times.

F: The writers who are members of the Crime Writers' Association don't write in a fancy way. They write so that the ordinary reader can follow it as you would an everyday discussion.

C: Peter Dickinson, whom I admire very much, writes in the High Style. It's elegant. Yours also has elegance, in its simplicity. Besides the classics and Wallace, did you read anyone else particularly?

F: I read the Bulldog Drummond stories a lot. Nowadays I don't read as much as I did when I was race riding. At that time, I didn't have to think about stories. I'd do my day's racing and relax with a book in the evening.

C: Did you read a lot when you were riding all those years? Was that kind of your recreation?

F: I don't say I read a lot, but on Sunday afternoons when I was racing, I'd read a book. But in recent years, when I've been writing myself, I've found I don't read as much as I should read, because reading other people helps your own style. An American author whom I like reading is Ed McBain. We correspond, send each other books, and we've met at these gatherings. Another crime writer I enjoy, whom you probably don't know, is Desmond Bagley. I saw him last night; he's over in this country for the moment. He lives in Jersey now. They had a dinner last night in London of the Detection Club, which is different from the Crime Writers' Association. You have to be invited to join the Detection Club. If you've written a book or crime articles, you can apply to join the Crime Writers' Association. I had a letter from Hilary Waugh of the Mystery Writers of America recently because I won an Edgar [for *Whip Hand*]. But I wasn't even told — I'd been changing publishers. I didn't even know I was on the short list. The first thing I knew about it was when someone came up to me at Ascot Races in June and said, "Oh, congratulations." I asked what for and they told me I'd won the Edgar. I said, "You must be thinking about *Forfeit*," because I'd won it for that and even went over to collect it that time and had a lovely time. Oh no. And I immediately came back and got on to my agent and he got on to my agent in New York and found yes, it was so. I wrote to Hilary Waugh saying how pleased I was and how disappointed I was — am — that I didn't know about it, because I would have gone and received it or written a note. He wrote back saying, "Why aren't you a member of the MWA?" He said if I'd been a member, I would've known.

C: I wanted to talk to you about *Dead Cert*. It was published in 1962. When was it composed, actually?

F: About 1961. Yes, it really was '61, because it was published over here in March 1962.

C: Is there a season over here, by the way?

F: No, there isn't. Books come out all the year, but publishers don't like books coming out in midsummer. There are quite a lot of books published in the spring, but if you are thought worthy, they try to get you onto the Christmas list, that's October. They made me work very hard in 1965. I submitted my third book, *For Kicks,* for fall publication in 1965 and they said, "Come on, now. We want you to do another one in the fall. Two books this year." And I said, "Keep *For Kicks* until the autumn." They said, "Oh no, the people have seen your books coming out in the spring, and they'll be expecting another one." So that was a very hard year. And I had the newspaper work as well to do.

C: As racing correspondent for the *Sunday Express.*

F: It's the same company as the weekly *Express,* but different editorial staffs. Quite a lot of the people write for both editions of a paper. John Oatsey, who's a noted writer, does his article every week for the *Sunday Telegraph,* but he also does one, if he's got something, during the week for one of the daily papers. They had two of us writing on racing — they've still got one of them, Tom Forrest, who covered the flat-racing scene. I covered the steeplechasing scene as much as I could, although when steeplechasing wasn't on, they expected me to go to flat racing and do an article about the Derby and so on.

C: Do you like flat racing?

F: [*smiles*] I like it more now than I used to.

C: A diplomatic answer.

F: It's more of a business. Steeplechasing and hurdle racing is still a sport.

C: Because amateurs can still do steeplechasing?

F: Amateurs can, but amateurs can ride on the flat in a few races. You don't get the amateur jockeys mixing with the professionals on the flat. In steeplechasing, they're in the same dressing room, they're chatting, they're changing next door to one another. Amateurs are well accepted in steeplechasing.

C: The steeplechase horse is a different horse too, isn't it?

F: Nowadays not so much.

C: But Irish mares used to be the dams of so many.

F: That's where all the good steeplechasers came from, and they still do, a lot of them, but nowadays horses that just miss it for being good flat-race horses try their luck at jumping. They don't have to go so fast and the fences today aren't so formidable as they were fifty years ago. Most horses can get over them.

C: In the late twenties, the fences were —

F: Oh, they were bigger.

C: And the horses were bigger, too, weren't they? If they were out of Irish mares.

F: Since I gave up riding, the Grand National fences have been altered. At one time, when I was riding, they were straight up, you know. You'd get in the bottom, and you couldn't get out. But now you can't get too close to them. You take off at the bottom of the apron and you get over all right.

C: Did anyone ever smash the fences?

F: Oh, they do, but there'd be a great hole there and the horse would never get over it if he smashed it that much. But they take off the top of the fence sometimes.

C: You were moved to write at least one novel because the owners of the track were going to obliterate an English race-track. Did that really happen? Was it plowed under?

F: It was the Birmingham track. Yes, that's been completely built over now. The one I wrote about was Hurst Park, in *Odds Against*. It was down on the side of the Thames, not far from London, and the ground was worth a fortune for building land. In *Odds Against*, all sorts of things were done to make the racecourse lose money and they had to sell in the end. Most of my stories are based on something that has happened.

C: Even some of the most awful dirty tricks in your books?

F: Yes. They probably haven't been as bad as they were in the books, but there's a grain of truth in all the stories.

C: When did you start writing for the *Sunday Express*? When you were still riding?

F: When I announced my retirement in January 1957, I was interviewed by the press, the radio, and they all said, "What do you want to do, Dick?" I had started writing my autobiography before this. My author's agent persuaded me to do it and I'd done about half of it. Then I had to give up riding and I said, "No, I don't know. I don't particularly want to train horses." So I decided to see what developed. Well, the publisher of the *Sunday Express* had decided I could put one or two sentences together and he asked if I'd write half a dozen articles for him on the racing scene. I learned a lot from writing for the *Sunday Express*.

C: How different is English journalism from American? There's a chapter of your autobiography that describes your going to — was it Saratoga?

F: No. I rode at Belmont and at the hunt at Radnor, Pennsylvania.

C: I don't remember the exact wording, but you felt that the American press was to be treated like the English press and it seemed as if the English riders and the English racing press had a sort of adversary relationship.

F: Yes. The riders and trainers are more hostile to the press now than they once were because the press only has to get a *hint* of something and they will blow it up and make mountains out of moleheaps, as you might say. But they also now realize that the press does racing a lot of good, brings it into every man's sitting room, and therefore they've got to sort of play ball with the press.

C: But in America they were always sort of playing ball, weren't they?

F: The American press are, I think, more accepted by the racing fraternity than are the press over here, although over here I like to think that I did a lot of good for the press. I used to go round to stables, writing articles about the stables, and a lot of trainers didn't like the press going round.

C: Didn't want you on the premises?

F: Didn't want me on the premises. Although, being an ex-jockey, they always said to me, "You know what riding's like, you come round." Now they've got round to thinking that the press do do them good, so the press are made much more welcome now than when I was riding.

C: Some of your protagonists are in the press, and some secondary characters, too. Bert Checkov, a murder victim . . . He's a wonderful creation. Even the name is funny because obviously he's not the great writer that the Russian doctor was.

F: Well, I didn't know anyone who did the same thing: throw himself out of the window. They're still there, on Fleet Street, and if you wander down there, you'll see the Telegraph Building, the Express Building, Reuters, the Press Association; they're all down there.

C: How did you like being a journalist for twelve years?

F: I got used to it.

C: Another diplomatic answer.

F: I can't say I really liked it because I hated — If you picked up a little bit of news that wasn't quite proper and if you could use it, editors, quite rightly so, expected you to use it, but I hated to print anything in the paper that would give the people I was writing about a black name, a dirty name.

C: Is that traditional in the English press, to write gossipy stuff?

F: Oh, very much so, especially in papers like the *News of the World* and *Sun*.

C: I was surprised to see in the *Standard*'s rugby article yesterday that the writer lapsed into first person right in the middle of a news story. In about the second paragraph he said, "And I thought the coach should have" et cetera. Do they use the first person? This article was supposed to be straight news, the reporting of a match.

F: Oh yes. The writer is giving his personal opinion.

C: An American writer might put that in a column, or request a column in which to state his opinion.

F: Oh no, they do give opinions while reporting over here.

C: Here's a quote from one of your novels. Alan York in *Dead Cert* says: "One can be too secure. Adventure is good for the soul, especially for someone like me." Is that the way you have always felt? Is this your personal belief?

F: Yes. As you know, the books are all written in the first person. I'm afraid that the first person protagonist always thinks along very similar lines to myself. I wish I were as tough as some of them.

C: I think you need have no fears on that score. Six broken collarbones, a horse stepping on your face. Nobody in American detective fiction, much less a writer of American detective fiction, ever had a horse step on his face.

F: Well, probably that's why people say to me that my books are rather sadistic. They're not sadistic, really; I'm just trying to get injury and pain into the lives of the characters, the kind of injury and pain I've received myself, but in a different way from how I received it.

C: That fellow whose dislocated shoulder popped out occasionally — that was painful to read about.

F: Well, that happened to me. I go to bed now every night with my arm strapped down, and every time I ride a horse, I have it strapped down. My right shoulder used to do it all the time, but I had it operated on. They can operate on those things, but it's a nasty operation. I was in hospital ten days with it when they did this right one, and after I'd done it, I said to the surgeon, "Do I need to wear the strap?" He said, "I should if I were you; it'll give you a little comfort." And I did until about six months after, when I had a fall and the left one went out. So I took the strap off one and put it on the other and haven't had a bit of trouble since. But rather than have it operated on, I gave up racing.

C: Would you say your books were masochistic? Poor old Sid Halley. I'll tell you, when they started whacking on his mutilated hand, that went past the gag level for me.

F: That probably was a little bit masochistic.

C: Another interesting thing about Halley is that he's the only one who's carried over into another book.

F: He was carried over because York Television started basing the series "The Racing Game" on Sid Halley in *Odds Against*. I saw a lot of it being made, saw a lot of the scenes being shot. The producer talked to me a lot about it and he used to send me the scripts to see if they were all right before they started shooting. All the scripts were my ideas; they were my story lines. I gave story lines to a scriptwriter.

C: Story lines were different between the novels and the teleplays, I guess, because of the need to compress all that action into an hour's show.

F: Actually only one novel came into it: *Odds Against*. I wrote *Whip Hand* because after seeing these episodes shot with Mike Gwilym in them, Mike and I became friends and he came and stayed with us a number of times. It was just like Sid Halley coming in and sitting down with us at home. And I must say that's how I started out putting Sid Halley in another book. And I had to start it off by giving him a false hand because in *Odds Against* he loses the use of his hand, so I went to the orthopedic place here and did quite a lot of research there.

C: You know, I really know very little about English society, but would people really have been as nasty to Halley as those people were at that country weekend party? That was more than mere verbal abuse.

F: Probably not. But there are different characters about. Latin characters come over here and some Mediterraneans can be very nasty.

C: But English people would be a bit more polite?

F: Yeah, I think so.

C: Halley and some of your other protagonists are rather Hemingwayesque. Halley says, "You had to hide what you felt about it, had to keep it locked up inside. Silly, really, but there it was."

F: Yes. But as a matter of fact, I thought Hemingway was a little bit morbid. We went to see his house down in Key West last month. The wife and I were out there. I couldn't have written under those conditions, although some of the books he wrote were wonderful, weren't they? But, no, I wouldn't say I was an addict of Hemingway.

C: Your female characters are all fully developed, more so than many other women in English fiction. That I found surprising coming from someone who was involved so long in something as macho as steeplechasing.

F: Well, the jockeys' wives and the trainers' wives are not a bad lot of women.

C: I'll bet not, and they're around all the time too, aren't they?

F: Yes, they are. Oh, yes. We spend a lot of time with them. In fact, my wife used to come with me more than a lot of other jockeys' wives because we were lucky in one way: we weren't well off. But after our son was born, she couldn't pick him up and bathe him — she'd lost the use of her arms — so we had to have a nanny all the time and she could go with me when I went racing, and if I had one of my bangs, she could drive me home. A lot of jockeys' wives never go racing because they've got children and they've got to nurse them at home.

C: Is it harder to be a wife on the circuit? Is there always a fear on the wife's part that her husband might fall off and be hurt or God knows what?

F: I think it's worse for them, much worse than for the jockeys. When my son was riding a bit, I used to hate watching him go round, because I knew what it called for. And I knew that there could be accidents.

C: Did he ride long?

F: He only rode as an amateur. He was hoping to follow in my footsteps and turn professional, but he got too big.

C: How big is too big in steeplechasing?

F: Well, he's over six feet and he's quite robust. Dave Dick, who won the 1956 Grand National, is six feet and he had great trouble throughout his career keeping his weight down. Brian Marshall had trouble keeping his weight down and had to retire.

C: Back to Sid Halley for a moment. Did your publisher, or a publisher, ever come to you and ask you to write several novels built around a series character? It's thought that those are more reliable, attractive, profitable and so on.

F: I don't know if any publisher has asked a writer to do that over here, but I wouldn't want my publisher to do that. I've always felt that writing wasn't my first way of life, you know, and writing is hard work. If I had the same character in every book, I don't think the books would be long enough because I couldn't write enough about the characters.

C: Would it bore you to do the same man over and over?

F: It would, yes. I used Sid Halley twice and I didn't get bored, but it's a bit worrying to think about it. That was fifteen, sixteen years ago and it's difficult trying to remember what you were thinking then.

C: Why did you pick first person? I thought on the other side of the Atlantic it might be a reaction against objective journalism and the inverted pyramid format in journalism, et cetera, but that's obviously not true in England.

F: I think I did it because my first book was in the first person — my autobiography — and therefore I thought, "Why can't I put myself in Alan York's shoes?" Probably it's easier, and I don't want to change. The most difficult thing I'm doing, or have done ever, is writing Lester Piggott's biography. I've been doing that for the last six or seven years.

C: He's a contemporary of yours.

F: Yes, I rode against him. He doesn't want his biography to come out until after he gives up riding. It's very hard work, writing about that, because I'm not writing as Lester Piggott but from the outside looking in.

C: Lucky old Lester Piggott. All your fans will run out and buy his biography because it's by you.

F: Well, he's an astute man. I didn't want to do it, but he'd just come back from the West Indies one year and rang me up and said, "Would you write my life story?" And I said, "No, Lester." He said, "Come on, your books are doing so well all over the world. I want you to do it." And that's one of the reasons he asked me: my books are selling well. Oh, he's a very brainy chap.

C: But you were doing a lot of research before putting that on your plate. I mean, for all your novels. *Reflex*, just to cite one example, has more photographic lore in it than most other novels I know anything about, including an aside to the manufacturers of English photo supplies for not printing instructions on the bottle as we do in America. And in *Whip Hand* you did a hell of a lot of research in coming up with a new application, if that's the word, of erysipelas.

F: Mary does that. My wife loves doing research on a novel. After *Reflex* she's a first-class photographer now.

C: And she flies, too, doesn't she?

F: I asked her to go and do a bit of flying for *Flying Finish* and she got bitten by the bug, so both of us set up a little air travel business. She couldn't fly for hire, so we have two professional pilots do the flying and she runs it.

C: You really get involved.

F: Oh, we get involved in everything! *Twice Shy* is written in two halves. One brother writes the first half and the other brother the second, both in the first person. Some of this research had to do with computers. We had to get a computer in order to write about them, and now we might even add a word processor to it so I can use it in composing the novels.

C: Your recent novels stress psychological pain more than physical pain. Is that because the farther you get from your racing days, the more you've been able to work out the physical pain that entered into the first six books? You've experienced a catharsis in writing about it, in other words?

F: I think probably I'm not so aware of it these days as when I was writing the first books. The pain was closer to me then, wasn't it? But now one has to think back more.

C: Psychological traumas are a little more complex, too. Not as easily overlooked.

F: Yes, and in a lot of novels nowadays you get psychological problems, don't you? Not in my novels, but in some people's. And I think I am using psychological pain instead of using physical pain.

C: How have you been able to develop so rapidly as a writer?

F: I don't know. But I've got twenty years' experience behind me and one learns as one goes along, doesn't one?

RUTH RENDELL

Ruth Rendell was born in London, on February 17, 1930, and educated at Loughton High School, Essex. She was a reporter and subeditor with the *Express* and *Independent* papers in West Essex from 1948 to 1952, and is the mother of one child, a son.

She has been hailed as the new Agatha Christie, an epithet she despises, but the more discerning among her readers are able to see immediately that she functions as a real novelist.

There is no doubt that the very large reputation of Ruth Rendell has been built upon her considerable gifts of characterization; many of her character studies are of the psychotic, the sociopathic, the murderous, the warped, and the loveless who plague, distress, and — more often than not — murder those of us who would rather count ourselves among the sane.

Most of the novels are about Detective Chief Inspector Reginald Wexford of Kingsmarkham and his assistant, the often vexed Michael Burden. Those are her series characters and they have appeared in an even dozen of her mysteries. But some of the most memorable of her novels have nothing to do with the (rather mild mannered) English police procedural.

The premier example of that is *A Demon in My View*, in which mere coincidence — a shared first initial *and* last name — drag a young scholar into the world of one of the most repugnant yet pitiable psychotics in all of English literature, Arthur Johnson, whose sexual obsession brings death and misery to his fellows in a London apartment house (Rendell knows intimately the topography of what she calls "bedsit land," the Royal Borough of Kensington and Chelsea). *A Judgement in Stone* opens by saying that on such and such a date, an English family was murdered by their illiterate domestic and this is, then, how it happened. This takes courage, a trust in the audience, and great confidence in one's ability to tell a story.

The audience's trust is justified and the author's confidence vindicated. This is a great book for those totally unacquainted with Rendell's work. The suspense is maintained, and pity and terror, to use the Aristotelian formula, are built up by such details as showing how a reference number left by the woman applying for the job of maid could have been answered by one of the sleazy denizens of her rooming house, which would have ruined everything, for the pretense is that it is the number of the woman's very satisfied referee (as a reference is called in England). The lie is told and a lethal chain of events is set in motion.

Wolf to the Slaughter is about sexual fetishism and its terrible consequences. This is an Inspector Wexford and one of the outstanding detective mysteries of the post–World War II period. It is one of the few examples of the author playing fair with the reader and still outwitting him or her; the whole book is right there in a carefully drafted opening scene, which reveals everything without seeming to do so and lets our prejudices lead us down the wrong path. *Death Notes* is about a murder that Wexford has to solve by chasing the clues to California and then back. The solution of it depends upon a linguistic clue. *One Across, Two Down* is not a Wexford, and Rendell now does not like it, but it's still a gem of characterization; although the satire of the English petite bourgeoisie is biting, there are some very funny moments as the book moves smartly along.

One could go on. Her production has been continuous and very even, which is to say always at a high standard. Also available in this country are two collections of short stories: *The Fallen Curtain and Other Stories* and *Means of Evil and Other Stories.*

CARR: Let's set the record straight. An important reference work has apparently confused the record of your awards.

RENDELL: I won the Mystery Writers of America Edgar Allan Poe Award in 1974 for "The Fallen Curtain" and the Gold Dagger from the Crime Writers' Association for *A Demon in My View* in 1975.

C: Good. That sets it straight.

R: But I want to tell you about my latest award. I'm so proud of my awards, you see. And I won an award in 1981, which is my best award: the Arts Council of Great Britain's Award for a genre novel. It's my nicest award, and apart from everything else, it was seven thousand pounds.

C: And they say there's no money in British publishing. It must've been for *The Lake of Darkness,* which is a good, good novel.

R: Yes. There were three awards made: one to a "straight" novel, one to a genre novel, and one to a work of nonfiction.

C: What do they regard as a genre novel?

R: Oh, it would be crime. You know, we don't use the term "mystery" here. I'm very accustomed to it, but we don't use it.

C: Do you ever resent being called a genre novelist? Does it ever make you angry?

R: Not being called a genre novelist. Some things I don't like. I don't like being compared to Agatha Christie; I think that's a bit much. I don't like a condescending, patronizing tone, but I don't particularly mind being called a genre novelist because I've found that if I write a book that is good and is literate and critics like it, it gets raised above the genre anyway in reviews and in the way it is treated, so it doesn't really matter very much.

C: That's what happened to John D. MacDonald.

R: Yes, you can do it, you see, yourself.

C: But over here detective novels and suspense novels are reviewed on a regular basis in the *Times Literary Supplement.*

R: Oh yes, they are. In fact, the *TLS* devoted a whole issue to crime to coincide with the Crime Writers' International Congress in Stockholm in 1981. It was very nice. I had a very nice article written about me. But, anyway, I don't mind being called a genre novelist because I think that if one can transcend it, that transcendence will be recognized, shall we say. There's an awful lot of very bad crime and mystery writing. Their English is terrible, but then a lot of "straight" novelists write pretty terrible English [*laughs*]. But it isn't just that, it's also that it's very dull, very pedestrian. There are a set of cardboard characters who are sort of waiting in the wings when you finish this one, and it's been done since 1920, and it's still going on. I've got a novel here in Norwegian. My mother was Swedish, so I thought I'd brush it up — Swedish and Norwegian are much the same, aren't they? But, you know, I can't get through it. It's so boring. Of course, if it were in English or French, it wouldn't matter, I could skip, but I'm not up to skipping in Norwegian and I cannot get through that kind of thing where the sentence is left suspended. You know: "She looks, she falters. She said, 'I meant to say . . .' " And then, of course, somebody comes in with a gun.

C: You know what Raymond Chandler said about having someone come into the room with a gun in his hand.

R: Oh yes, indeed I do.

C: I was thinking that maybe one of the reasons people

compare you to Christie, aside from the fact you're both brilliant, is that, like Christie, your clues are linguistic more often than not.

R: A lot of my clues are linguistic, and I think if you're writing detective stories, and my Wexfords are classic detective stories, what else can you do? You have those sorts of things. The plot of some of my earlier non-Wexfords — there's one called *The Secret House of Death*, in which a lot of the plot hangs on whether the ascender in the figure 7 has a tick across it or not. We don't do that in England; it's European.

C: In America, Anglophiles cross their sevens. But back to linguistic clues: in *Death Notes*, the German family name Fassbender can be translated as "cooper." Now, in the beginning of the novel a man named Cooper lifts some silver. He's trotted in very fast and then whisked off stage. But someone named Fassbender continues to appear. But I never would've thought to look up the name Fassbender or its components in a German dictionary.

R: Well, of course, I relied on that.

C: You *do* rely on that — that people will not consult a dictionary when reading?

R: And they don't. Even critics don't. In another book of mine, called *A Sleeping Life*, the solution depends on the word "eonism," a word meaning "transvestism" that Havelock Ellis coined after reading the biography of a man named the Chevalier D'Eon, who dressed himself as a woman for about forty years and went undetected until he died. Well, I used this word because the principal character is a transvestite and nobody knows whether the person is a man or a woman.

C: Did anyone ever accuse you of writing down because of your dependence on linguistic clues?

R: Surely if I were writing down, my readership, my audience, would be looking these things up. The thing is, they do not. Various reviewers said, "I would have known the answer to this if I had looked up 'eonism' on page 50."

C: But of course they didn't. Well, most people when they read a book just read a book. They don't treat it like a puzzle.

R: But I would look it up. But then I'm into that.

C: I wouldn't until the end, and then only if it bugged me, but in your defense I must say there are coincidences that really work out kind of wonderfully because it's the kind of thing I think really must happen. In *No More Dying Then* that poor man, Scott, murders this little child, Stella Rivers, the stepdaughter of Swan, who when he was a younger man had let one of Scott's relatives drown. In Swan's case it was an act of omission, really. He didn't commit an unlawful act, but he was morally responsible. I don't think that murder was mere coincidence. Here's a man who sees a chance to do in a split second what would be a satisfying act of revenge. He's rather old and he's dying, too. And there's the motive and the opportunity, and the method is fairly straightforward. So you just do it.

R: Well, of course, talking about solutions: people want not to know. That's part of it. To be able to say at the last: "Why didn't I think of that?" It's fun. That's why I really prefer writing the other kind of book, because I get tired of plotting.

C: And a novel like that, which is heavily plotted, is really a superstructure built on the structure of another novel, one below it or one that happened before it that you haven't written down, only composed mentally. The skin of it is there and the bones, and then you smash it and show it to us bone by bone, but not in the real order or in such a way that we can put the parts back together to make the structure plain. It's tough; it's writing two novels.

R: Yes, that's why I like to write the other kind, which isn't like that and hasn't got this intricate plotting thing. I mean, it's like a honeycomb, isn't it?

C: But you always play fair. The solution is adumbrated, or foreshadowed, or whatever critical word you like best, right there in the beginning.

R: Oh yes.

C: And you have to play fair, don't you?

R: Yes, you do.

C: Raymond Chandler once said it was impossible to play fair, and I think the context of that statement was a criticism of Agatha Christie [in "Casual Notes on the Mystery Novel"]. I think he was miffed at her.

R: Impossible to play fair? No, it isn't. The reader knows that there is intent to deceive.

C: And the reader should be on his or her guard. Some people read detective fiction for the action and the characterizations, though. Have you run across readers who don't really care for the plot? They're glad it's there and they're pleasantly surprised, but it's the characters that matter more to them.

R: Yes, but that's because my readers fall into two categories: those who like the psychological novels and others who like the detective stories.

C: There really are two categories of readers of your novels?

R: There are. They overlap, but you find that almost everyone has a preference. Of course, there are some who like to read them all.

C: One vote here for that faction.

R: But most of the psychological thriller people will say, "Why do you write those Wexford books? Why don't you write more books like *A Judgement in Stone*?" And then the Wexford people will say, "I liked your last book, but I long for another Wexford." Those are the reactions.

C: I've read the American pioneers of the psychological thriller — James M. Cain was one — and I've read the English writers of the twenties and thirties — John Dickson Carr, who was an American but belongs in with the English, Ngaio Marsh, Margery Allingham — but who were the pioneers of the psychological thriller in England?

R: It's going to be post–World War II, really, before you find psychological thrillers. And some people, notably Julian

Symons, have said that it's really quite a new genre with a lot of potential waiting to be developed.

C: Have you ever written a novel you thought might be more easily understood by Americans rather than Englishmen?

R: No, I've never written anything on purpose. I've never written a formula novel and I've never set out to write a novel that I thought people would want. Not because of high-mindedness. It's just the way I am. If I didn't do what I wanted, I couldn't do it at all. It's just that I find it very hard to write anything I'm asked to write. I did write that short story for *Ellery Queen's Mystery Magazine* when I was asked, but since then . . .

C: And the editor gave you leeway, didn't he? He didn't say we want it about —

R: Oh no, no. He gave me absolute freedom, except that it had to be a mystery story. But I have been asked since then to write stories for magazines and I've done one or two and they've been rejected. It's impossible for me to do it. It's no good my saying to myself, "You will sit down and you will write this. You will have people of this age, this sort of appearance, this racial type, in this sort of setting because that will be most appreciated in the United States." If I do that, I know it will fail. The only thing for me to do is to write what I would like to read; that is my best guide.

C: Did you start with short stories?

R: No, no, I didn't. Well, I wrote a lot of short stories before I had a novel published and they were all rejected, so I didn't write any more for years. Then *EQMM* asked me if I'd write one for them and I did. That was in a collection, and it's called "Venus' Fly-trap." Now I write four or five short stories a year.

C: Only sixteen have been anthologized?

R: Yes, but I've written about forty-two and I have a new collection coming out called *Fever Tree*.

C: You know, most novelists in the United States don't also, as a regular thing, and certainly not up to the number forty-two, write short stories. Sometimes a brilliant short story writer like O'Hara or Hemingway or Cheever will write a novel, but I always turn back with some relief to their anthologies of short stories, particularly Hemingway's. And there's a whole subculture of people, usually academics, who write nothing but short stories aimed at the little magazines.

R: The whole thing is so different on the two sides of the Atlantic. We tend to think that it isn't because we speak the same language, but it is, isn't it? It's very different. The cultures are very different. Novelists write short stories here. I would be hard put to think of a novelist who didn't sometimes write short stories. I think writing short stories is good for me. I write them because I used to find economy very difficult. I overwrite — a great spate of words comes out — so I thought it would be good for me, and I think it has been good for me.

C: Yes, one of the things I like about your novels is that they're not padded. So many so-called detective novels really could be boiled down, without much effort at all, to about thirty thousand words. The extra twenty thousand words come with *longeurs* about the state of the world economy, devoted old friends, great lays of the past, et cetera.

R: I was fortunate in my editor, my late editor; he taught me about that. He was the sort of man who would've had *War and Peace* down by a third.

C: It might not have hurt it a lot. If I had to choose two short stories, the two I like best are "Almost Human" and "The Fallen Curtain." "Almost Human" was particularly attractive because the bad guy was made so sympathetic and because his motivation, or lack of it, came from such a bizarre source.

R: That has been a very popular story. I've had a lot of letters from people who ask me to write a novel around that character. But what would you do? He can't refuse to kill people who have dogs. It's a one-off, isn't it? But it has been very successful, that story.

C: That's not, as far as I'm concerned, a genre story. It's just a great short story, as is the other one.

R: But then a lot of my short stories are not genre stories.

C: "The Fallen Curtain" has such scope for such a short story: three generations of men, counting the protagonist-when-young as one of the characters, all of whom come face to face with a cleverly vague but absolutely traumatic experience, the major component of which is this aching need on the part of a lonely man to communicate with a little boy. We'll move on: where is Kingsmarkham?

R: It's in Sussex. It's entirely fictional, as you know, but I lived for a while, as a child, in a town in Sussex called Midhurst, and when I wrote the first Wexford, *From Doon with Death*, I based Kingsmarkham on what I remembered of Midhurst. I've never been back to Midhurst, but I've been to various places in Sussex. I rather regretted that I'd made it Sussex afterward, because I know other counties better.

C: Does each county have its unique personality?

R: Yes, I think, to an English person.

C: Different dialects and so forth?

R: Well, of course, Sussex doesn't have much dialect. It's one of the Home Counties and there isn't much dialect. If I had chosen north Essex or Suffolk, which I now wish I had done, there would be plenty of dialect, and, in fact, the house where I lived in the country — it's four hundred years old — is in a district where the people speak a dialect so strong that I doubt if you could understand it. I can't always.

C: It'd be even.

R: No, it wouldn't. I can't tell you how strong it is. And that is very individual and sort of interesting, and I rather wish I'd taken that county or area as the location, but too late now. *A Judgement in Stone* is about that part of the world.

C: Let me give you a quote from *Wolf to the Slaughter*. The quote is: "It distressed him [Wexford] to know that passion could exist and grief beside it, that they could twist in a man's bones and not show in his face." That's really one of the great motifs in your books. What are your own views on normality and abnormality? Burden in *No More Dying Then* —

R: That's when he loses his first wife.

C: Yes, and he's about to go crazy. It's really almost the chief interest in the novel. Do you think that most people have a little grain of abnormality in them and it just takes a little pressure to bring it out?

R: Yes, I do. I do think that. I think I know a lot of people who are mad. They are mad. I think there's much more of it about than we think. We do have these things in our souls. It's not a rare thing, as one might suppose, and it can be triggered by shock, grief, stress, whatever it may be. I see it happening to people a lot.

C: You once mentioned that you knew two women who were widows and had been somewhat repressed all their lives, and now they didn't know how to deal with grief.

R: Yes, yes, I certainly do know such people, and I feel that that's just one of many instances of these things that happen to people. You can see it in people's faces: repression and suppression and grinding things down and not showing their feelings, all coming out in very strange ways, ways that are very disquieting and frightening to other people.

C: Is English society more repressed than American society?

R: It's certainly more reserved than American society.

C: But that doesn't always mean repressed.

R: I don't know if it's more repressed. I would say that our society is quite repressed, especially among older people in this country, and that the older you are, the more likely you are to be repressed. It is said that the thirties were the most repressive time in recent history since the Victorian era.

C: Why?

R: I don't know. But you can consider those people who were in their teens or twenties in the thirties to be in a very repressed state, and those are the people I'm thinking of. I was born in 1930, so therefore I think I escaped it. Of course, I had a rather unrepressed childhood with highly emotional parents who were always fighting and generally expressing their feelings, bursting into tears and so on, which, though hazardous at the time, I think didn't do me any harm. But I know a lot of people who are my age or older who suffer from an inability to express anything except a kind of cheerful, dogged continuation of life.

C: Stiff upper lip.

R: Yes, yes. That has not come my way personally, but I see it a lot in others.

C: Were you chapel or C of E?

R: C of E.

C: I asked because someone made a disapproving comment in *Death Notes*. Someone said, "It must have been a Baptist." And also because I understand chapel society can be rather repressed.

R: My husband's grandfather was a Methodist lay preacher, and although I see very little of my husband's elderly relatives, such as remain, I have done in the past. They were perhaps my prototypes, although they're splendid North Country Methodists — unbelievably fine.

C: There's a phrase that occurs in your work a hundred times if it occurs once, and it's in the mouths of some people in America: "keep yourself to yourself."

R: Oh yes, that's very English, and it's something that respectable lower-middle-class or working-class mothers might say to their children. I think people still say it today.

C: Mind your own business.

R: Yes. Don't lay yourself open, don't make yourself vulnerable, don't give people an advantage over you, keep yourself to yourself, shut yourself in, keep your defenses up.

C: And, of course, England has about sixty million people and is just two thousand square miles bigger than Mississippi, which has only two million people in it, so it must be socially useful to keep yourself to yourself at times. I don't know where you put them all. Mississippi now seems crowded to one who grew up there and we only have 3 percent of your population.

R: Walk down the Old Brompton Road or the Cromwell Road. It's awful really the way we've crammed people into the cities. But I can go into the country where I live at the weekends and go for a walk and walk for miles and see no one, not even a passing car.

C: At some point you said, "My victims are victims by accident, normally." But the woman Arthur kills in *A Demon in My View* is known to him; she's married to the drunk in that apartment building. She's known to him, really.

R: But he doesn't know it, does he?

C: Well, I kept thinking that perhaps subconsciously, or unconsciously, there was something he recognized about her footfall, her shape.

R: It may be so, but *I* don't know it. Does Arthur know it? Well, I think that it's chance; it's accident. She happened to be there, but anyone else would have done.

C: And Camargue's daughter is certainly killed by someone she knows.

R: Yes, it isn't invariably true.

C: And in *Wolf to the Slaughter*, that wonderful young policeman's girl friend, who has murdered —

R: But again, that's not on purpose — as far as I know. That's an early novel of mine and I don't think I've reread it. She kills that man who is her lover, doesn't she? Isn't he a sadist?

C: He's a sadist and a knife is important in his little sexual game, and she really reacts to the stimulus and jabs him with it.

R: That's right.

C: And then she helps him out of that tragic woman's apartment house, which he uses for the assignation. And speaking of coincidence, and linguistic clues, there are two Anns in the book. Ann Anstey, who's been divorced by the sadist, and Ann Margolis, Rupert Margolis's sister, who manages to go to Italy during the confusion, providing us with a red herring.

R: It's a common name, of course — Ann. Common here, anyway.

C: Chance and coincidence play a large part, extremely large part — is that fair to say? — in your work.

R: I'm very interested in them in the Jungian sense and I like to read about coincidence; it fascinates me. I collect coincidences in people's lives. So, yes, I like to write about chance, the kind of chance that makes you go left instead of right and the whole course of things is changed.

C: Just blind chance.

R: Yes, that interests me a great deal.

C: Speaking of *A Demon in My View*, didn't you find a mannequin in an apartment you had rented?

R: Yes, I was living in this flat that had a garden. There was a shed in the garden, as far as I remember, and I found this torso. It had a head and that started me off. Also, I was sharing this flat with my cousin, who now lives in Philadelphia, and his name is Richards. There was somebody else in this house, in another flat, called Richards, and their mail got mixed up, so you see these two things contributed to the making of that novel.

C: Everything really comes together in that novel — your reading in psychology and your own experience.

R: Most of my novels are like that. But that one, yes. I set out to write about a psychopath and Simon, my son, found a lot of literature on psychopaths for me at the time. I think he must have been doing something about it specially at the time and that's why I really went into it. There's a whole mass of stuff listed in that.

C: You say in one place, "Criminology is very unsound." What do you have against criminology? I don't have a bone to pick either way; I was just interested to see that you didn't think it was terribly sound.

R: I suppose I find criminology boring.

C: You mean police science?

R: Yes, I do. And I avoid it.

C: The textbooks advising the future lieutenant of a precinct how the watches should be spaced and what technology is available for identifying corpses?

R: Yes. There are periodicals and magazines, semiprivately circulated magazines, all very innocent and earnest, instructing crime writers on the latest developments in criminology. I just find them rather boring.

C: Well, your work really doesn't need it.

R: Look at what used to be around as criminology: the Bertillon system of classification of criminal types, that sort of thing. Such amazing nonsense.

C: I can't help thinking that some parts of our so-called science of crime are more amazing nonsense, particularly the FBI's profile of the typical skyjacker. And abnormal psychology doesn't seem to get at the etiology of abnormality, or its cure, which ought to be the acid test of a so-called science: whether or not its results can be replicated. Couldn't we spot crazies a lot sooner if it worked?

R: Yes, you could. You could. Another thing: it is supposed to be of enormous significance how a baby is treated the first six months of its life. But we know that it isn't. We see examples around us of people who had the most monstrous, atrocious childhoods. Bertrand Russell's childhood was pretty dreadful. He was terribly neglected and so on; he was not loved, cuddled, the whole bit, but, well ... And there were large numbers of the aristocracy in this country who were far closer to their nannies than to their mothers, but did they not love their mothers? And were they not perfectly good children? And they grew up into responsible people. The theory doesn't work out, but it's interesting to read about, just the same. And to speculate about. I wouldn't dismiss abnormal psychology the way I'll dismiss criminology because I find one interesting and the other boring, I guess. Of course, P. D. James does that sort of thing very well.

C: Yes, she does, and she was a cop — or at least high up in the bureaucracy of the Home Office.

R: And people like it and she does it very well. I don't like it and I would do it very badly, and that pretty well finishes what I feel about it.

C: You've said about Eunice in *A Judgement in Stone* that "Eunice is not a killer by chance. She was going to kill somebody and has already killed her father — with me it's the killer who's the most interesting and not the victim." But, of course, it would be another kind of novel if you did a victim novel, wouldn't it? I don't know how you could write a victim novel. Don't critics always say, "Well, the real hero here is the killer." But what else could you do?

R: Oh, you could do it. I can see that because there is a kind of person — and I'm sure this has been very carefully dealt with in psychiatry, probably by Freud — who's a born victim, who attracts a killer.

C: All his life, or just at a particular junction in his life, when the time and the place and the mind of the times come together?

R: Oh, I should think so, yes.

C: The junction — or juncture — of these things?

R: Yes.

C: Zoologists who've followed wolf packs say the wolves only pick out the members of the herd who seem to be inviting attack by the wolves. It's almost as if, according to the scientists, what takes place is not a traumatic act but a transaction that redounds to the good of the forest. The wolves don't like to attack a healthy, scrappy caribou, and the herd really can't stop for the stragglers.

R: Yes. If you are in a game preserve I think you can see the impala, for instance, standing and you can see the leopard or lion lying in the grass there. They know. There is an awareness. But on being a victim: it's only perhaps an extension of the kind of patterns that recur in life. You see, for instance, a woman who will marry three times. She is successful, speedy, go ahead, but every time she marries some complete idiot, and people will say, "Oh, she's done it again. Doesn't she ever learn?" But this is what she wants, this is what she's attracted to, it's what she draws to her.

C: Or she may continue to marry men who abuse her physically, so that it seems to be at least masochistic.

R: It may take that form, yes. Or a man will marry a silly, nagging, girlish creature and then spend ten years of his life trying to get rid of her, and when he gets rid of her, he immediately falls in love with another one.

C: That's deeply rooted in the unconscious, I think: the real reason we choose to marry whom we do.

R: I think it is, too. I think we don't have very much choice.

C: Are you more deterministic than not at this point?

R: I think things happen to us because of what we are. So I think it's useless to say "If only I had not driven off in my car at that moment; if only I had gone into that shop or gone in to see that person and waited ten minutes, then the accident would not have happened." I don't think we can say that. I think we did it because of what we are. What we are is what we are and we can't go back and change that. Well, I dare say deep analysis would change one, but we won't go into that.

C: Is that different from soldiers who've been up front too long and who will smoke a cigarette even though someone's using it to zero in on them? Is it foxhole fatalism: "If my number isn't up today, I can do anything?"

R: I think they don't take cover because of what they are.

C: I think they're tired beyond self-preservation. I never will forget a description I read of street fighting in Jerusalem in 1948. This platoon of Jewish young people was supposed to cross an alley and storm a building, but they were so tired they went to sleep in the building between setting up the attack and actually storming the building, and it was just a matter of minutes. Adrenalin failure, if you will, but they just fell out instead of firing.

R: I don't know. I think that they are just tired because they are that sort of people, whereas there are other people who, yes, will never get tired of self-preservation or the desire to live. You are what you are. So I do believe in determinism and I believe in destiny and I believe in fate, but I also believe in choice and chance. They go together.

C: How do you reconcile that mix?

R: You can do that, you can do that. You are what you are. If you didn't do it, it would be because your nature was changing.

C: Does that happen, though? Does one's nature change?

R: Yes, I think it does change with some people. It changes very slowly. We are not what we were twenty or thirty years ago.

C: You've also said, "Even if guilt doesn't seem to have been brought into people's lives, they make it for themselves." Do you think people are still, even in this post–Freudian era, still making up a lot of guilt for themselves?

R: Yes, I do, and I think even very young people are. For example, I tried very hard to bring up my own son without feelings of guilt. It's impossible, but I did my best, especially in trying to squelch those feelings of obligation toward parents, and I think in a way I was successful. But I still see signs in him of feeling that he ought to have those feelings. So although he has never, never been reproached for going off around the world, not coming home, doing this and that, he will manufacture guilt feelings himself, so that there will be a kind of "I'm terribly sorry I didn't write" or "I assure you I will come over and see you next week," although no pressure has been put on him and we don't even particularly want to see him. That is perhaps the point — I didn't even want to see him. I'd be perfectly happy without him, but it's caught from other people, I suppose. It's infectious, or reading establishes it, or something.

C: Christian training.

R: Yes, there it is. As if he were saying, "I ought to go see my mother and father because if I do not I will feel really guilty. I am obliged to do this. I am a child and therefore I owe this to my parents. They have never told me so; they have never implied it, but ..." And I'm pretty sure that's true. Easy to say, but I think so.

C: Was there a sense of guilt fostered by the C of E?

R: I wouldn't think nearly to the degree that it would be fostered by the nonconformists. No, it's not the church. And I think that I am subject to very strong feelings of guilt. I think it has something to do with the times and the age in which I was brought up and the people among whom I was brought up. I feel guilt. I know that I feel it. I know why I feel it and I can do something about it, but it's still there; it may even be a source of some amusement to see that it's there, but there it is. I see it in people all around me, and I put it into my books because I think it's so important in people's lives. How they're always apologizing —

C: I'm sorry. I'm so sorry. I'm sorry for this, I'm sorry for that.

R: Yes.

C: Do you believe in original sin? Or that there is some sort of evil agency in the world, à la the most fundamentalist Catholic teachings about the devil?

R: No, I don't. I don't. No, I don't believe that. I believe in good. I believe in an ideal good. I suppose in a sort of way I believe in God. I do, really, but I don't believe in the devil or any force; I don't quite know what that is, anyway.

C: P. M. Hubbard, who died in 1980, was one of my favorite writers and he says in that odd, dark last book, *Kill Claudio*, and in other books that it's impossible to live in a city without being deformed in some way. Do you think that's true? I think city life in England is very civilized, let me say that. You should live in New Orleans in the Carrollton section, where it's impossible to walk at night without a gun or a big dog or both. But even living in London, do you find that city life has deformed a great many people psychologically?

R: Yes, I do think so.

C: English writers all flee to the country, don't they?

R: Yes, yes, I think so. Perhaps it's just noise and stress more than violence, although we are becoming more violent here. But we still haven't got to the levels found in American cities. I feel we will — it's horrible, really.

C: Oh, I don't think you possibly could. But speaking of psychopaths, do you believe, as naturalistic writers like Zola and Dreiser did, that people are made into psychopaths by a combination of circumstance and heredity or other forces?

R: I don't think so, although it is not known how psychopaths are made. There's no accounting for it. You can delve back into the childhoods of such people as that girl, Mary Bell. I don't know if you've ever heard of Mary Bell. Mary Bell is our child murderer. She's confined in an institution now, but she killed a baby when she was herself a little girl. They were unable to find any particular reason.

C: Along the same lines, one of the most disgusting scenes, and most disquieting in the spiritual sense, I've ever read in Anglo-American literature was in *A Demon in My View*, when Arthur as a child sticks a pin in a baby's abdomen and the blood bubbles up.

R: It upset a lot of other people, too.

C: I can't think of a worse scene. There's a lot of animal cruelty in American literature, which I despise —

R: I hate it.

C: And American movies are going back to animal cruelty.

R: Yes, I really don't like it. But of course when I wrote that, I knew that it would be horrible, but I very carefully had the child survive. Nothing more happens to that child.

C: He probably would've survived.

R: He does, anyway. He does [*laughs*]. Am I not God?

C: Are you not a novelist? But talking about psychopaths, one of the things they've found out is that almost all criminals and many cops have child abuse in their backgrounds. And yet one group, which in itself doesn't account for the majority of children who were abused, grows up to rob banks and murder people for what's in their wallets, and the other, perhaps smaller, group grows up to wear uniforms and arrest them. They aren't above beating holy hell out of the crooks when they catch them, but they're on the "right side."

R: I think that's been discovered here, too. The cops have become very close to the criminals. They've become very close to each other. A very good and successful policeman will be very much like the person he catches. He has that mentality, comes to have it more and more, and he understands that mentality. It's very disquieting. And child abuse is very much on the increase here, and I'm always very prejudiced — my son deals with it all the time; he's a children's officer.

C: Have you ever actually observed the court scene here in Britain — gone to court and listened to criminal trials?

R: Yes. I used to cover a court when I was a journalist. I've been to the Old Bailey since as a visitor, although not recently. I'm going to go and give evidence in a court case in a month's time. Somebody wrecked my car. I'm not looking forward to it, but some experience may come out of it.

C: Have you ever driven around with the police in their panda cars?

R: No. I'm not really interested in the police themselves, you see. My readers don't want that. If they want that, they read somebody else. No policeman is really like Wexford. No policeman can be like Burden. Because anyone who's been a policeman so long will be so hardened that that prudishness won't exist anymore. I doubt if any policeman in Wexford's position would be as sensitive as he is.

C: I thought that might be true, but then I don't know what police work is like over here, except through reading *Spike Island*. It's dreadful in America. The leading cause of death among policemen is suicide, and it's far ahead of the second cause: being shot while answering a domestic disturbance call. The husband's beating hell out of the wife and the cop comes in and knocks him down to put the cuffs on him and the wife shoots the cop dead.

R: Well, I think it's getting pretty bad over here. It is said that the riots we had back in the spring of 1981, which were not race riots but rather riots over unemployment and various things, were principally caused by police attitudes. Well, Wexford's not like that. Although I try not to make errors in my descriptions of police work, I accomplish that largely by leaving it out.

C: I think it's a good choice on your part.

R: And as far as forensics go, it gets more and more complex because more advanced techniques are always being discovered. There are all these analyses of tissues, of hair, of fingerprints, of bits of skin, and of almost everything else that can be done, but it doesn't interest me.

C: There's one thing I noticed about all your novels, Wexford and non-Wexford. I hope I don't embarrass you by saying this.

R: I'm not easily embarrassed.

C: There's more sexuality in your novels than in almost any others in this somewhat narrow field, with the exception of certain American police procedurals, but there it sounds like a bunch of boys talking dirty. It's not sexuality, as it is in yours.

R: Yes. Yes. In fact, Julian Symons has said that all my novels are about sex — not so much the Wexford ones, but the psychological mysteries. And I say, "What's the matter with my psychopathic sex?" No, I really think so. I'm very interested in sex. I think it's a fascinating subject and I've never been able to come to terms with people who think that it isn't very nice to be interested in sex. I like sex. I'm interested in it. I like reading about it and I like writing about it. People like reading about it, too, don't they? I don't have much explicit sex in my books, though, not very many sex scenes, because I'm really not interested in doing that.

C: No, that wanders into cliché.

R: Too much of it today. I don't disagree with it because I think it's a very false argument when people say that these things should be only hinted at. But it's just not me.

C: Some people write about it well, others don't.

R: If you do it well, that's fine. I can think of people, like Simon Raven, who do it so well that I just don't feel like competing. Kingsley Amis does it quite well, and so that's fine. I'm not into that. But I like a lot of sex in books. I like the interesting byways and little anecdotes and things that have been discovered and oddities.

C: Have you done a lot of reading in the psychology of sex or abnormal psychology?

R: I read an enormous lot, you know. I've always read a lot.

C: Five books a week, you once said.

R: Yes, and I read everything and I've done so now for, I suppose, getting on forty years. And I've got a good memory, so of course there is a lot lying about there and I still read a lot. I read everything, any old thing.

C: Does it all kind of come up unbidden later, when you need it?

R: Yes. It's a good associative process, although I've run out of quotations for the Wexfords. That used to come, and come beautifully, out of the unconscious and something else would link on, but it's a bit heavy now. Of course, the whole Wexford writing is growing heavy for me.

C: A burden — so to speak? That's one of the perils of doing a series, isn't it?

R: Oh yes. He's very popular. I get a lot of fan mail about him. People seem to think that there is no reason why I shouldn't be producing two or three Wexfords a year, and of course I'll do it and I am very fond of the man in a way, but I've almost had enough of him.

C: You've said that Wexford is sort of you and sort of your father, too. Were you an only child? Is that what I can infer from that?

R: I was, yes. I didn't really know about Wexford's being my father until one day my son, who was doing a psychology course — I was sitting up in bed reading — came wandering in eating a plateful of chicken and chips, and said, "Mother, I hope you don't mind my saying this, but has it ever occurred to you that Wexford is your father?" Then I thought about it and said, "Yes. Yes, he is."

C: Your father wasn't a policeman, I suppose?

R: No, no. My father was a teacher of mathematics.

C: Did you inherit any of his ability?

R: No. I reacted the other way.

C: Here's a quote: "I would have thought that most people would say that intense sexual relationships led to pain and unhappiness rather than to happiness and fruition." Is that always true in your books? Poor old Michael Burden was having terrible experiences all the way through *No More Dying Then* with Gemma and with Grace, the woman who was home, and he was thinking about his dead wife. There seems to be a lot of bad luck with sex all the way through your novels.

R: I suppose that I believe that there is a great deal of bad luck involved with sex, and I think that if people have very fraught, intense, passionate relationships, they do lead to a lot of grief. Of course, sometimes these relationships become softened or are mitigated by becoming steady or regular, or people get married, and that's something else. But, yes, in my novels that's true, and I've always thought that was true to life.

C: *One Across, Two Down* — to get off the subject of sex — is one of my favorites. I've read it three times.

R: Really? It's one of my least favorite books.

C: Oops.

R: It's rather a cliché book. I could have done it much

better — could do it much better today. It's a good idea, but it isn't very well done.

C: It was almost a play. The settings were all houses except for that scene by the canal.

R: Yes, I think so, too. Except that it's not very suitable for the stage or the screen because of all that crossword puzzle stuff.

C: Yes. It would be hard to present dramatically the guy getting those excruciating headaches and retreating into his crosswords.

R: It could have been done in the thirties.

C: That was a good observation or series of observations of the English social scene, though.

R: It was crossword puzzles, too. I'd been doing the *Daily Telegraph* crossword puzzles since I was a child. My father always did it and he was like Stanley Manning in that. He was not like Stanley Manning in any other way.

C: I should hope not.

R: But he used to travel up to East London in the tube and he used to see if he could do the puzzle between stations. Sometimes he could do it in ten minutes, which I think was his record. I used to sort of do it with him, and then I did it every day and that gave me the idea. It cured me of crossword puzzles. I didn't do another one for years after I'd written that book. I sometimes do them now.

C: You did a nice job of fabricating American talk in *Death Notes*. When I got to the section of the novel that takes place in America, I thought to myself, "Oh God, here it comes." But when you did the California section, it was great.

R: Thank you.

C: You even got that thing people have always done — of referring to the neighbors as people at 711 or 713, instead of using their names or saying "the blue house." It's not so true in New Orleans, where people all know each other, but I've noticed it in other parts of America.

R: I have a friend who teaches English at Indiana State University in Terre Haute, and I sent the relevant chapters to her and asked her if she would correct them for me. She put the thing right round the whole faculty.

C: They all had a hand?

R: They picked things out. She sent it back. Janie's very very meticulous, and everything that was wrong I removed. I wasn't going to make a mess of that, you know. I've read too many American novelists who've come over here and made a hash of English later.

C: Some of it pretty dreadful even to my ears. I suppose there are age dialects as well as regional dialects — people who are older using slang young people would never use.

R: Oh yes.

C: We're still having foisted off on us the stage Englishman of the fifties, and they all sound like Edith Sitwell.

R: But I was very careful not to have too much American talk. The talking is by expatriate English people.

C: It is with almost palpable relief that you turn to these two English people in California.

R: Yes, but you have to be careful about that sort of thing. It's much more difficult than taking people into Europe. It's very, very, very difficult.

C: Writing American talk is not easy even in America. A friend of mine, Sylvia Wilkinson, wrote a wonderful novel about growing up in the back country of North Carolina, and her editor in New York wanted to rewrite her Southern dialect for her. She was horrified. It was awful.

R: I would never attempt a Southern dialect or anything like that. I know my limitations. It can't be done. I wouldn't even attempt to do a West Country dialect or Scots. I do Yorkshire because I know that and I do my own county of Suffolk — I live there over the weekends — I can do that dialect. But I think one should be very careful. In *Tom Jones*, I think, Fielding says that an author should be very wary of anything that is liable to raise a horse laugh in the reader. I always remember that.

C: I didn't exactly know what you meant by California police. It could be the California Highway Patrol or the San Francisco Police Department or the CID of some county sheriff's force.

R: I think that's just Wexford seeing it that way. A bit sweeping, I suppose, but an English person sees it like that.

C: You have said you always start with an idea and it usually comes from something someone's told you.

R: Yes.

C: Do you ever sit around and think, "Wow! What kind of puzzle can I put together?"

R: No, I don't. There's always something there that's waiting to be used in that way. There are usually two or three things, you see, that I've been told or read that come together. It was very clear in *A Demon in My View*. And I think in, say, *The Lake of Darkness* there would be — I wanted to write something about a housing problem, about the steps that are indeed taken in London, and probably in other large cities, by people who wish to be rid of their tenants. Sometimes the means are very desperate indeed, especially in England, where the rent laws are very strict. If you've got a tenancy here, unless your landlord murders you, there isn't any way he can get rid of you. I wanted to do something about a man like the Greek who owns property that could be sold at a very high, inflated price, but that could scarcely be sold at all or sold only for a pittance if that woman continued to live in the flat. Then, of course, I have my psychopaths and I wanted to do a little bit of magic stuff in it — not that I believe in it at all — but I find that sort of Alistair Crowley business rather interesting.

C: You have said that you're superstitious, that you almost believe in the occult, that if you step on a crack you break your mother's back, that sort of thing.

R: Yes. I do have some sort of belief in that sort of thing. If

you live where I do in the country, you start off not believing
in the supernatural and you end up to some extent believing
in ghosts. We have such a haunted countryside that I do
have a sort of belief, but it's quite a vague and yet subtle
belief in these things. I do not believe in the witchcraft, black
magic stuff, that appears in *The Lake of Darkness*. Most em-
phatically not. I'm writing now another novel that has a lot
of magic in it, but there again it's not in any way an *Omen* or
Exorcist novel. It's really showing how gullible people can be
about this sort of thing and how in the end it all amounts to
practically nothing.

C: We were talking about rereading.

R: I do reread my own books sometimes.

C: Thinking "What wonderful stuff!" as Disraeli is supposed to have done.

R: Well, sometimes I have to reread. I don't keep any kind
of record or chart of these things, so I have to check up on
them.

C: You mean that when you're working, you don't keep a
chart?

R: I don't. For instance, when Wexford's grandchildren
were born or when his daughters were married or things like
that about him — I have held them in my memory, but if
there's a doubt, I have to read back.

C: Is it easy or is it difficult to make a modest living writing detective stories in Great Britain?

R: I don't know [*laughs*].

C: Do you know many people who are able to make a living doing it?

R: Let me tell you — this is England. People would rather
tell me the intimate details of their sex lives than tell me
what money they have. I know a great many writers and I
know some of them quite well. I have for the most part no
idea whether they only write or have other jobs or have private incomes. I do not know. I'm English [*laughs*]. Do they
know mine? No, no. I'm being perfectly open with you. I see

that people who write may be teaching in college, and after a time I see their books succeeding and I see them quitting their jobs, so I assume that they are now making enough out of their writing to stop teaching people how to write English or whatever it is they do.

C: What's the normal press run of an English hardback?

R: Five thousand? I don't know about these things, presumably because I'm an author and not a publisher, and I'm not very interested in figures.

C: Some English writers depend on the American market because they have a lot of sales in America.

R: Three-quarters of my income — more — comes from the United States. Oh yes, at least. My advance from Pantheon — how could it compare? — it's enormous compared to my advance from Hutchinson; it must be five times as much. The English sales, I suppose you might say, include Canadian, Australian, New Zealand, and South African sales, but it's the American market that matters to me, especially the American paperback market.

C: Some of your American paperback covers have been pretty bad, unfortunately.

R: My English paperback covers are infinitely worse than anything that any American publishing house has ever done to me. They are so appalling. They're absolutely unbelievable and they have caused a lot of derision from critics, and in fact I think my paperback publishers here feel bad about it now, but it was really dreadful.

C: Do English writers need an agent to get manuscripts through the initial line of resistance to a publisher?

R: I never had an agent until this summer. Well, I did have an agent in New York for my short stories, but that's largely because he was my publisher's American agent. Then my friend with Hutchinson died in July. He was a very close friend of mine also, and I depended on him so much and I felt that while he was alive it would be all right, but I immediately got an agent after he died.

C: Gerald Austin, to whom you dedicated *A Judgement in Stone?*

R: Yes.

C: I love that quip you made that your books are going to come out in May forever because of the remark by a critic (perhaps now you feel it was unfortunate) that "Ruth Rendell books are like a breath of springtime."

R: Yes, that's right. Well, it is so. My next novel is coming out April 5.

C: Do you wish that would change, or is that the season over here?

R: No, there is not really a season in publishing here, but I don't think the remark was unfortunate and I don't wish to break the pattern. It suits me very well. I do sometimes bring out a volume of short stories in the autumn as well. A publisher with a difficult book, though, say a volume of short stories — as you know, they're harder to sell — might bring those out in November, for Christmas presents, and mine have always come out in November. But I don't like, speaking of America, this divergence in titles. It is not a very good thing.

C: Let me just ask you what you'd tell a young person who wanted to write detective stories or thrillers or whatever we shall call them.

R: "Don't," I suppose [*laughs*]. That's the classic reply, isn't it? To start with, I would feel very wary if somebody came and asked me what to do. They do give me manuscripts to read every now and then, and they might be any kind of fiction. I feel that a writer who's really going to be a writer will write, and almost in secret, in a compulsive sort of way, too, and will find an agent — it's very easy — and will find a publisher, and will not be wanting my encouragement, my approval.

C: Wouldn't need it?

R: What are they doing? Are they trying to write, or are they trying to do something else? Are they trying to impress, to make it the easy way? That, I think, would trouble me, yes. Also, there's no joy in advising people because on the whole they don't want to know. On the whole, they want to be told they're wonderful, with one or two notable exceptions, and those notable exceptions are probably going to be very good novelists.

PETER LOVESEY

Peter Lovesey was born in Whitton, Middlesex, on September 10, 1936, and educated at Hampton Grammar School and the University of Reading, where he received a B.A. Honours in English in 1958. He married Jacqueline Ruth Lewis in 1959; they have one daughter and one son. He won a Crime Writers' Association Silver Dagger in 1979 and his first novel, *Wobble to Death,* received the Panther-Macmillan prize in 1970.

Lovesey and his wife now live near Bradford-on-Avon, high in the lower part of the Cotswold Range, on a ridge where the magpies fly from spur to spur and the patient watcher can see the badgers emerge from their setts at night. But he was a London boy and one of the first joggers. He has been interested all his life in sports and became interested in the Victorian era through researches into the life of an American Indian who was a famous runner in England at that time.

Readers can be grateful. His books are certainly some of the most interesting and most amusing detective novels ever published and they depend for their success on Lovesey's laconic, witty style, his knowledge of special developments of the period (not just sport), and the fascination of the Victorian era, which Lovesey knows thoroughly. He has read, for instance, all of the Victorian sporting papers — and there were a great many — and researched the great criminal cases of the age.

"For atmosphere," Lovesey says in his essay "The Historian: Once upon a Crime," published in 1977, "the counterpoise of teacups and terror, cosiness and crime, the Victorian mystery is supreme. The architects of the popular detective story — Poe, Dickens, Wilkie Collins and Conan Doyle — built citadels of suspense that still dominate the scene."

After his first novel, which he says "drew on my amusement at a curious endurance contest held in Victorian London in 1879," and which was seen on PBS TV's "Mystery" series, Lovesey published *The Detective Wore Silk Drawers*, about the fight game, and *Abracadaver*, a fascinating study of the atmosphere and personnel of the music halls that continued to play a large part in English life right into the 1920s. *Invitation to a Dynamite Party* (also published as *The Tick of Death* in the United States) has shrewd insights into the Irish terrorists of that era; it holds the interest of the Lovesey fan to an even greater degree because in this novel Sergeant Cribb of Scotland Yard's Criminal Investigation Department is forced to doubt the loyalty of Constable Thackeray. Is he in sympathy with the Irish? The heroine, of sorts, Rossanna, is a fully developed character and though she too is guilty of treason, Cribb lets her off, no doubt because they've had a brief roll in the hay. Lovesey said later: "It intrigued me to see if I could manage to create a situation in which my rather staid Victorian sergeant would actually get into bed with a lady, and he managed to achieve it in that book. He did it for Queen and Country, of course."

A Case of Spirits explores the world of the art collector, another cultural development that grew to unexpected dimensions in the Victorian era. His last Sergeant Cribb mystery is *Waxwork*, which revolves around one of the most ingenious and diabolical murder plots ever described in detective fiction. A woman murders someone and then arranges to be convicted, but on grounds that will surely be found to be insufficient. She knows that once the insubstantiality of the proof (which she planted) is proved, she will be pardoned. She cannot be tried again, under the double jeopardy rule, and so the discovery of the proof will be an exercise in futility. Sergeant Cribb's discovery of the real proof before the Queen can pardon her and she can leave the country is one of Lovesey's most fascinating exercises.

Nor should Lovesey's other writing be neglected: he has published *Golden Girl* as Peter Lear, which was made into a movie starring Susan Anton, and he and his wife have written six television plays based on the Sergeant Cribb mysteries. In addition, he wrote *The Official Centenary History of the Amateur Athletic Association* and *The Kings of Distance: A Study of Five Great Runners.*

CARR: You got the Crime Writers' Association Silver Dagger in 1979.

LOVESEY: Right, for *Waxwork*, the last of the detective novels that I wrote, actually.

C: Yes, people have been complaining about that. They want you to write more.

L: I've been doing other things. Jackie and I got on to television. They wanted some stories just written for television, so Jackie and I collaborated on six scripts, just for TV. Most of them have been seen here. They were based on the character of Sergeant Cribb.

C: I thought *Waxwork* was good as a novel and as an adaptation, too.

L: They gave it more time on television, which was nice. They gave it ninety minutes, instead of the fifty-one minutes that they gave for the others. The books that have been adapted for television have been perhaps less successful than plays that are tailor-made for television, because I've been trying to adapt fairly complex plots. In a whodunit you have so many suspects and so on that it's fairly difficult to condense that into fifty minutes.

C: I loved the premise that the guilty woman would let herself be convicted on evidence so flawed that any decent investigator would say "Hold on! There's been a miscarriage of justice!" and set the wheels in motion to have her set free, after which she could never be tried again because she would be placed in double jeopardy by a new trial. That was wonderful. At first you "know" she's the murderer, but at the end you *know*. And the actress who was given that part was wonderful. The scene at the end, which I'm sure was due to your writing, that shows her abandoning the passivity she'd been able to indulge in because she thought her scheme would work is especially strong. She confronts the idea of her death really for the first time and comes unglued.

L: That was Carol Rodd. She's gone on to very good things since. She's working for the Royal Shakespeare and had some very good parts. I think they captured the atmosphere of the prison very well, too.

C: Have you ever been in an English prison? Visiting, I mean.

L: No, I haven't. But obviously I studied everything I could about Newgate, which was the prison Miriam Cromer was supposed to have been in.

C: And now the Old Bailey is built on the site.

L: Right. They tore down Newgate in the early years of this century. I think they simply needed a new site for the courts building. Madame Tussaud's went along and bought up a lot of the items from Newgate at that time, and if you go along to the Chamber of Horrors on Marylebone Road, you can see quite a lot of the original brickwork. They've reconstructed cells from Newgate. In *Waxwork*, you know, I used the memoirs of James Berry, who was the actual executioner and was the man who starts and finishes the book. I wanted to try to show that the executioner was a man who did a job of work and who saw it in very much those terms, who has a wife and eats a meal.

C: Didn't you once receive a letter from an old hangman?

L: Yes. He offered to give me a certificate. He said that if I would go and stand in his cellar, where he had a gallows set up, and stand on the trap with a noose around my neck, he would be very glad to give me a certificate saying that I had stood there with the last official hangman, or something to that effect. It was pretty gruesome. But, after reading about Berry, I went to the British Museum and found the memoirs of the longest-serving hangman. His tenure lasted from the beginning of the nineteenth century until about the 1870s, and he was hanging them when they were hanging in public outside Newgate Prison. That was Calcraft, who actually served from 1828 to 1871 and was the City executioner. Those hangings were quite terrifying, terrible.

C: Another Victorian spectator sport, really.

L: They were, yes. Sometimes mass hangings were done, several of them on the gallows together, but the business of dispatching these unfortunate people was quite horrible and it was very slow.

C: Kellow Chesney in *The Anti-Society* says that Calcraft was not "particularly proficient at his trade."

L: In effect, they were being strangled. He didn't do it right, so to help them out he would jump on their backs and swing with them on the rope to try to speed it up. And the thought of this grotesque little man in his seventies or eighties climbing up on the hanging man is really quite —

C: They didn't know how to snap the neck?

L: They didn't. The theory about the length of the drop and the weights and all that sort of thing was a more recent innovation that came up with a man called Marwood. And then James Berry was rather scientific. Between them, they seem to have worked out the scientific approach to hanging, but they still made mistakes. James Berry went to hang a man called John Lee and three times the trap wouldn't open. It was a very famous sort of case because it was considered that perhaps the man was innocent — you know, that God was trying to tell us something. The whole procedure of hanging was a ritualized thing. The condemned were told it would be at a certain time in the morning and very often the executioner would visit the prisoner the evening before and talk to him and try to sort of reassure him — tell him that if he was cooperative it wouldn't be painful for him. I've no doubt that when they had a nervous prisoner, they would have to sort of grab him and hustle him along. But I don't think it was done unexpectedly. I think they had a very clear idea of when it was going to happen.

C: Did they really put on the little black cap when passing judgment?

L: Oh yes, and I used the wording of Florence Mabrick's death sentence for the sentencing of Miriam Cromer in *Waxwork*.

C: Why did you choose the Victorian era rather than another? You could have chosen anything that was easy to research.

L: Yes, it's interesting. I think it goes back to my school days, really, and my interest in sport. I would have loved to have been a good athlete in running and jumping, high jumping, that sort of thing. I saw the Olympic games in 1948 when they came to London. That was very exciting. I saw the Flying Dutchwoman, Fanny Blankers, and the great Czech runner Zátopek, and after that, when I was a little older, I was one of the first joggers, I suppose, trotting around the streets of suburban London, imagining either that I was holding the Olympic flame in my hand or else that I was the Human Locomotive, but the trouble was that after two hundred yards I was breathless, and I suffered from stitch. In those days, if you were out running the streets, you really had to be a good runner to get away with it. You couldn't just sort of jog along quietly.

C: The neighbors must've thought you were crazy.

L: They did, I think, but I was only a kid, and I soon found out that it wasn't for me, really. I persisted for quite a long time, but it was borne in on me that I was only going to enjoy sport vicariously, through taking an interest in the achievements of other great runners of the time. I did, but I still felt I wanted to participate in some way, so I began to write about it. I used to send in articles to athletics magazines. They didn't pay, but . . .

C: So there's a whole backlog of Peter Lovesey sports journalism?

L: That's right. So I began to find a little corner of the sport that hadn't been written about very much. Everybody was interested in the future of the sport — who was going to win the next Olympics, that sort of thing. They were not interested in the past, and not at all interested in the remote past. So I began to dig out amusing character pieces about runners who had been long since forgotten. I read just about everything I could, and out of that came a book on long distance running back in 1968 called *The Kings of Distance*. St. Martin's Press has just brought out a new edition to fit in with the jogging enthusiasm that's big over here right now. But that was my first — and, I thought, my only — book. It was a study of five runners over a period of a hundred years. About every twenty years a great runner crops up. The first one was Deerfoot, an American Indian who came over here in 1861.

C: He was mentioned in *Wobble to Death*.

L: He was somebody I sort of discovered, really, and wrote about quite a lot, and I decided I would like to feature him in a book. But to get him into a book, I had to write about more modern runners as well, so I came up to date with Zátopek, who was the modern runner, with others in between, like Nurmi and W. B. George, who was a great English runner of the 1880s. But *Wobble to Death*, which got me on to the Victorian thing, was written in response to an advert for a first crime novel. There was a thousand-pound prize. I saw the advert in the *Times* and decided that I'd like to try.

C: You blew them out of the water with that one.

L: Well, I remembered that there had been these descriptions of six-day endurance competitions, which I'd seen when I was researching for the first book, and I wondered whether I might be able to use that as a background and write a whodunit around that sort of idea.

C: Did guys like Chadwick and Darryl actually make a good living as long as they won?

L: Yes, they did. The top runners of the time could sort of tour the world, making enough money to get by. There was a lot of betting, too.

C: Like Chadwick putting eleven thousand pounds on himself?

L: Yes. If they were sensible in their betting, they could back themselves to either win or lose and reckon on making money that way; that way there was something to be made from it. I think there were a lot of people who were exploited and I think if anything, if there's any common theme in my books about the Victorian period, it's exploitation.

C: And in at least one case, self-exploitation, like the Reed brother in *Wobble to Death* who's ruining himself because his brother, who's also his trainer, is egging him on. It was really kind of touching when he said he'd trained by running five hundred yards a day in preparation for a six-day run. What possessed the Victorians to stage such killing events? Did people attend out of the same motive that sends a lot of people in America to stock car races: the hope that someone will really hurt himself?

L: I think so, and the same motives that prompted people to go along and see the dance marathons of the twenties and thirties, see those poor devils who were driven to that sort of thing.

C: Were there a lot of unemployed men at those wobbles who hoped to make a strike?

L: People who came in off the streets, saw a poster, thought, "I'll try this. I might make a few pounds this way. I can keep going. I might as well be tramping around a small track indoors as tramping the streets of London." Some of them did make money at it and did find that they were quite successful at it.

C: So there were some working-class boys who achieved some temporary respite from poverty by doing this?

L: Yes.

C: Instead of people like Chadwick, who was already in condition.

L: There were one or two. There was a catsmeat salesman who certainly got to be quite famous and went to America and did the same event at Madison Square Garden and was quite successful over there.

C: What is a catsmeat salesman?

L: He sold horseflesh to people for their cats.

C: Cats were treated that well in Victorian times?

L: I doubt that they all ate horse meat. But they had their barrows and their cries. We had all these criers in London, you know.

C: Without doing a solo, what did the catsmeat salesmen cry?

L: I couldn't tell you.

C: According to a recent book, the Victorian era was one of the worst since the seventeenth century for crime. Today, it seems such a desperate era. There was unemployment, those murders in the Whitechapel district, the rookeries. What was happening?

L: One of the things is that there was a pretty incompetent police force, which I think counted for quite a lot of it; certainly there were many blunders in the Jack the Ripper case. The people who were at the top of the police force had very little understanding of what the work of a policeman on the beat was. They were very often military men who had retired from the army and gotten good jobs, well-paid jobs, on the police force, but had very little idea of what the man on the beat was doing. This was one of the things I tried to bring out in my novels: that somebody at the level of sergeant or detective constable was probably as honest and thoroughgoing a policeman as he could be, but of course he had limitations if he wasn't getting the support of the men on top, or understanding and direction from them.

C: Yes. Cribb is fighting that idiot inspector every foot of the way. The criminals, being criminals, aren't terribly complex; they can be at last figured out. But then Cribb's inspector puts hobbles on him and, as you pointed out once, they didn't have a lot of crime-fighting technology. There was no fingerprint system, for instance.

L: But they were very good practical psychologists. They had to be.

C: Cribb is wonderful in *Invitation to a Dynamite Party*. He does pretty much what a modern policeman would do. He infiltrates the enemy, he splits them up, then he is given a position of authority where he can really hinder their efforts, but in a negative, preventive way, unlike some American *agents provocateurs*. It's all very believable. Were there policemen who left memoirs behind that you read?

L: Yes. I based a lot of the story on the memoirs of a man called Henri Le Caron, who was not in fact a policeman, but who wrote a book called *Twenty Years in the Secret Service*, which contained accounts of infiltrating the English dynamiters in much the same way Cribb does. He was an agent of the police, paid to report back to them.

C: With God knows how much completeness. Probably both sides of the fence were played in a situation like that.

L: Oh yes, yes.

C: Where did men like Thackeray come from? Who were the London policemen in those days?

L: They would probably start as young lads from school who gave signs of being right for it. I think it was a job that was given to boys who showed some sort of intelligence. They started at the age of twelve or thirteen.

C: That young?

L: Oh yes, that was quite common. My father, back in 1911, 1912, left school at thirteen, so back in Victorian times it was certainly common enough.

C: What could these boys expect out of life? It was a secure job, I guess. Was there a pension?

L: A pension was introduced, I think, in the 1880s. It was a pitifully small thing, but it was the beginnings of a pension scheme. And the conditions of work in the police force were really quite harsh. If they were ill, it wasn't long before they just got no pay at all. There was very little sick pay.

C: Because their superiors thought it might be connected to alcoholism, or just weren't going to pay them if they were sick?

L: No, I think perhaps this was standard throughout probably all forms of work at that time. I don't know that it was necessarily just typical of the police.

C: But they couldn't use weapons. I don't know much about English culture and society, but why were policemen in what was a fairly dangerous and tumultuous time not allowed to carry pistols?

L: I don't know. There isn't any answer to that, really. It was probably because there was a great mistrust of the police by the public. Only grudgingly would the public accept a police force at all. They didn't regard them as their protectors in any way. The country had managed perfectly well for centuries without an established police force. They were laughed at and they were figures of fun in *Punch* magazine. There were poems and there were stories about them and there was a song in the music halls called "If You Want to Know the Time, Ask a Policeman."

C: Because he'd stolen someone's watch?

L: Right. That sort of thing was just a stock joke, so I think to have handed them guns would have been regarded as a tremendous betrayal by the authorities. The police had to work hard to establish themselves, to get themselves regarded as respectable. But they didn't do very well at it for many years and there were tremendous cases of corruption.

C: Yes, you mentioned that in *Dynamite Party*.

L: That's right. There was a scandal out of which came a new detective department, the Criminal Investigation Department, and even after that there were cases where things were handled very, very badly, including that big rally of the unemployed in Trafalgar Square. The police chief simply organized troops, who were in the street with drawn swords. This wasn't back in the seventeenth century; this was a hundred years ago, and they just sort of put down this riot ruthlessly.

C: So the working class really resented the police.

L: Tremendously.

C: Although most policemen probably came from the working class.

L: They did, yes. Before all this, we had a system of constables, which was rather different from the police constables. There were local justices of the peace and things went along fairly happily as far as most people were concerned until, I think, the Industrial Revolution. It was the growth of the great urban centers that made police necessary.

C: Displaced peasants and yeomen, some unemployable in a city, who began stealing and robbing and breaking into houses.

L: Yes. Masses of people required supervision.

C: There must have been a time when Bath was a small town sleeping by the river. Also Bristol. And Manchester.

L: Yes, yes, yes. And there were slums and occasions of public disorder, but I suppose they were more the exception.

C: Yes, and it was rational. If the corn tax rises and food is dear, there'll be theft and mugging. Today it's degenerated into something entirely random, or so it seems. But let's talk about the depiction of those conditions. What did your publishers say to encourage you to do a second book?

L: I think I was probably keener than they were. No, really. Having written one and had some success with it — because it won the prize and a thousand pounds was more than my annual salary as a teacher, so it was a marvelous boost — having tasted that, I thought I'd better try another. I'm a very safe sort of person. I play it safe. I kept in the same period, I kept with sport, and I kept the same detectives as my characters.

C: You're not the only one who keeps the same characters.

L: Right. But I suppose if I'd been more adventurous, I might have turned to another period. I didn't feel that I was an expert in the period at that time, but I knew Victorian sport — well, athletics. I didn't want to write another one about athletics. I didn't think there was another whodunit to be written at that time about Victorian athletics. But it seemed to me that the clandestine sport of prize fighting . . . Bare-knuckle fighting had been banned by Parliament. There had been some very bloody fights and people had been either killed or left as idiots. It was a very brutal form of sport. And the rules didn't say just fight fifteen rounds. You fought until the other man was senseless and just couldn't get up anymore. And the rounds wouldn't last just three minutes. A round would go on until somebody fell down or was sensible enough to put his knee on the ground and demand a rest. It could last fifteen seconds, if someone was knocked down, or it could last for six minutes.

But I think sport has tended to become safer and more civilized for the most part. I think what is uncivilized is what it's doing to people who want to excel at sports these days, to these kids who are turned into monsters, really, by drugs and by delaying their puberty, in order to compete, with steroid shots and all those things.

C: Was rugby or soccer played professionally in those days?

L: No. They were both fairly new sports and the rules were only just beginning to be standardized. They'd been developed in the public schools and now they needed their own rules. The Football Association was only formed about a hundred years ago.

C: How long did it take for some sort of professionalism to creep in?

L: It came in pretty soon. Soon towns were forming their own sides and paying them. Football was a much more professional sport than athletics — perhaps I'm mistaken there in thinking this about it — but there was a strong professional element in athletics that was quite different from the amateur side. The amateur tradition took in the public schools, Oxford and the universities, and they were sort of trueblue. They wouldn't take a bribe and they wouldn't hire a coach who was professional, whereas the professionals were runners who made a living at it and it was the subject of heavy betting. Really heavy betting, very much involved with the public houses.

C: I know there were people who probably fiddled the bets, but was there ever an organized criminal element that tried to manipulate sporting events so that their bets would or wouldn't come in?

L: Oh yes. The most famous stadium in London in the nineteenth century was a place called Lily Bridge, in the Fulham area of London. It was burned down in 1887 by partisans of two sprinters, Harry Hotchkins and Harry Jett. They were marvelous. They were very fast runners, and they had never lost and never been matched against each other. One gang supported Jett and one supported Hotchkins. They went into the stands before the race and — the place was full, but before the race was due to start — they tried to decide who would lose. Each gang was betting his own man to *lose* the race.

But Jett and Hotchkins couldn't agree. They both wanted to win for the sake of their reputations and the gangs who were backing them wanted them to throw, and there was a tremendous argument. In the end, Hotchkins and Jett were taken out of the stadium by an underground route to the station and got away. The crowd was still in the arena and they were so angry about the whole thing they just set fire to the place, and that was the end of Lily Bridge. It was sort of the Los Angeles Coliseum of its day. And the brawling was so frightening. They got to West Brompton Station and the stationmaster there had a heart attack and died on the spot when he saw them.

But as far as other sports go, in the Victorian era Wimbledon was just beginning. It didn't get popular until the Edwardian era. The big thing with Oxford and Cambridge was the boat race, the interuniversity boat race. Thousands lined the riverside to watch that until fairly recent times, when television began to show it much more effectively than you could ever see it by watching from the side.

C: What were the big spectator sports?

L: Boxing, horse racing, walking, or running. Rowing, of course, was well supported, but those were the main things.

C: What does it say about the English national character that they turned out, at least then, to watch individuals rather than sides.

L: Part of it was the fact that they were wonderful opportunities for betting, and people then were great bettors. Clearly, if there's an afternoon that is made up of a whole series of contests between individuals, there are many opportunities for betting. If it's a football game, there's only one result.

C: Had there been, before the 1870s and 1880s, that emphasis on sport in a person's life, other than for people who were actually sportsmen? Did the people in the little villages or even in London turn out to watch rowing, racing, and walking in the 1850s and 1860s?

L: No. Sport before 1850 was really confined to special holidays, in a village like Bradford-on-Avon here. They might have a special thing on May Day and everybody would turn out and take part, in running or a little bit of fist fighting.

C: Fist fighting? You mean, in a ring?

L: Yes. And there'd be a bit of rowing if they had a river near by, but it was on a sort of essentially rural basis. But horse racing goes back much farther.

C: To the eighteenth century.

L: And when I was talking earlier about spectator sports, I

didn't say much about cricket, which of course has a long history and goes back before the eighteenth century. And it was popular as a spectator sport as well.

C: Are you ever going to write a novel about cricket in the Victorian age? Or rugby?

L: No, probably not. I don't think they quite lend themselves to it in the way that these other sports did because . . . I think I covered the two sports that I could — long distance running and boxing — and then I moved on to other things, but they were all strong enthusiasms of the Victorian public. Things like the music hall and spiritualism and the river and the seaside.

C: I loved *Swing, Swing Together* and the idea of basing a detective novel on Jerome K. Jerome's *Three Men in a Boat*. Cribb uses that book to follow the trail of the alleged murderers, who turn out to be a bunch of real loonies. I loved it when the police find those three in the hold of a boat with three naked ladies.

L: Yes. Jerome's book really was the best seller of the day. And after that, everybody wanted a trip up the river. There really were groups of three people with a dog going up the river in a boat. So it seemed to me quite conceivable and quite amusing that we would have two bunches, two sets of people, who appeared to be suspects making their way up the river in that way. The chance to actually do the trip place by place was quite amusing and I had some fun myself. I walked up the riverbank and called in at the pubs and so on and got to know the route. In many cases they were the same pubs mentioned by Jerome a century ago.

C: The pub is an enduring English institution, isn't it?

L: Oh, it is.

C: There's always a scene or two in a pub in each of your books. And they're all different.

L: Right, yes, yes. The pub in the country would probably have a rather different character from the places in town.

C: *Abracadaver* is my favorite punning title in English fiction. Did they really have houses for down-and-out artists, run by eccentric old parties?

L: You still do. There are still variety artists' homes, where old people live who back in the thirties were well known on the stage and who are now seeing out their days in convalescent homes. The homes are supported either by their guild or by public subscription. They have a flag day or something like that for them.

C: There is a startling variety of acts in *Abracadaver*. Was that the Victorian music hall repertoire? Dancing bears, operatic singers, dagger throwers, clowns?

L: Oh yes, the lot. And I think it must have been very colorful and very entertaining, like your vaudeville. Certainly it was a very popular form of entertainment. They still have some revivals and there's a place in Leeds called the City of Varieties, where they have a regular music hall. Everybody dresses up in the old Victorian costumes, the audience, too. I've seen it on TV. But that's quite a thing. I don't think it's anything like the real atmosphere. During the Victorian era, I think they were very coarse and ribald.

C: There were whores there.

L: Yeah, right.

C: People were spitting on the floor. And there were banks of cigar smoke.

L: And I mean they were busy. They were having meals and they were drinking and all the rest of it. This City of Varieties is just simply considered a theater where people are sitting in their seats watching what's going on in their nice clothes. In the old music halls, the songs were full of innuendo. I saw a film not long ago that seemed as if it were straight out of the music hall, starring Goldie Hawn. She was singing a song about won't you buy my plums? The music hall comediennes were very risqué indeed. Our music hall contributed to your vaudeville quite a lot. I think the people who started in the early films with Mack Sennett and some of Chaplin's group were from the music halls. Those

early comedies, the things done about the time of the Keystone Kops films, I don't think have been surpassed.

C: And there were pantos, of course. I saw the Dick Whit-
tington panto in Richmond, Virginia.

L: Yes. They go back quite a long way and they're still
popular. They still put them on — every little town has its
pantomime and in London there are usually three or four.
Sometimes, they put on a panto-on-ice, that sort of thing. It's
a treat for every child after Christmas to be taken to the
pantomime. Usually it gives them a lift after the disappoint-
ment of the presents' having been opened and the Christmas
pudding's having been eaten: at least you've got the panto in
a day or two.

C: Why was there such a need — and I'm not denying
there's always a need — for so much entertainment in the
Victorian era?

L: I think it was because their lives were so circumscribed,
so dull otherwise. It was hard and they were trapped, many
of them, in their situations, in their class. One class couldn't
really communicate with another, but you could go into a
music hall and laugh at another class. It was escapism,
really.

C: You have talked before about murderers and said it
was almost easier to knock off your wife than get a divorce.

L: Yes. There was a stigma, wasn't there, about divorce?
You were a social outcast if you were divorced. It was even
more true among chapel people than C of E people; they
were even more strict about things like that.

C: And, of course, the Anglican church had strictures
against divorce.

L: The Church of England accounts for by far the greatest
number of people in England. I don't know what the present
count is — I don't go to church myself now — but I think
the C of E has always accounted for perhaps three-quarters
of the country's church population. Divorce was regarded as
something that one didn't do. It wasn't so much, I think, the

church. The form of the marriage service was that it was till death do us part, but I think perhaps the strictures came more from society than anything else.

C: Here's something I've thought about. I'm not sure anyone can answer it, but I feel bound to ask: would there have been the repressive social and cultural climate without Queen Victoria, or was this fated to happen because of economic and cultural factors that swept on regardless of who sat on the throne?

L: That's a tricky question. I have the feeling that a certain amount of it came from Victoria herself, but I don't think she had such a tremendous influence personally. I think for a lot of the time she just didn't want to know. She doted on Albert until he died and then she mourned him. Occasionally she'd express her disapproval of, for example, the women's movement or something like that. I don't think too much was done about it. It's possible that a more active and enlightened queen or king might have influenced things for the better. I think perhaps there was a lifting of the tension when Edward was crowned.

C: The Playboy King.

L: Yes, that's right. At least for the people at the top of the tree things got gayer and more exciting.

C: And yet there was an underside to Victorian life. Chesney and others have written about it.

L: Well, yes. I suppose it's only in the last twenty years that people have really begun to discover the underside of Victorian life and the books have begun to appear: Frank Harris's memoirs and so on.

C: Have you ever read that pornographic anthology called *The Pearl*?

L: I haven't read it.

C: It's not something you sit down with and read straight through, but those stories were being published somewhere in somebody's shop in that era and apparently the police never stopped it.

L: There were whole streets that dealt in nothing but that kind of thing. In *Waxwork* I had a reference to a street where there was nothing but shops with dirty post cards and books and so on. Or walk around Soho today. Although we've just passed a new law controlling pornography, I don't think it's going to make a lot of difference, really, in practical terms. The police don't have any definition of pornography. Nobody's been able to give them a clear definition of what is or is not indecent. So you get a little magistrate somewhere who thinks he knows and he's disgusted and sends someone away to prison for six months. In the next town, the magistrate will dismiss the case. So there's no consistency about it at all, and never has been.

C: That crazy Oxford don who was suspected in *Waxwork* of being Jack the Ripper — why did you place him at Merton? Is there somebody at Merton on your hit list?

L: Somebody I like, actually. Have you heard of a crime writer named Anthony Price?

C: Yes, particularly *The Labyrinth Makers*.

L: Yes. He's well known here. He writes crime novels that have a strong historical background. He wrote one called *Our Man in Camelot,* which somehow in a very ingenious way managed to involve King Arthur and the CIA. He wrote one called *Other Paths to Glory*, which won the Gold Dagger of the Crime Writers' Association, about the First World War. Anyway, he's good and he's a friend and he happens to be the editor of the *Oxford Times*, which is sort of the main newspaper in Oxford. Well, I was researching *Swing, Swing Together* and he asked me to go to Oxford and walk around with him, and Merton happens to be his old college, so I had the opportunity of looking around and that locale worked out.

C: Did you have a chance to review the Jack the Ripper dossier in the Home Office files?

L: No, I didn't go that deeply into it. I didn't feel that was necessary to my story, and so many other people have spent thousands of hours doing the research and getting the material. It's readily available in books like Donald Rumbelow's, so I had an idea of what had been done before. And I would've had to start getting official permission to look at those things.

C: And I suppose really brutal murders don't interest you; you try to maintain a lighter tone in your books.

L: No, it does interest me. I've always been interested in the Ripper case.

C: Rumbelow in his book indicates that the officer in charge of the investigation had kept private notes, stating that he thought the Ripper was that man who'd been to both law and medical school and who drowned himself after the fifth murder.

L: Montague Druitt.

C: Right. His family had accused him.

L: Yes, that's right.

C: Do you think he was probably the one?

L: I think he's the likeliest suspect except for the fact that somebody found a cricket roster for a match in Kent the morning after a murder, which does seem to sort of tell against that theory, but in most respects the Druitt theory seems to fit in pretty closely with the crimes. I think it much more likely than those theories about it being one of the royal family or somebody like that.

C: I saw pictures of the last victim, Mary Kelly. Really savage.

L: Yes, it was horrid.

C: Was that, as well as other cases like it, the result of Victorian repression and sentimentality and religious enthusiasm? "Sexual insanity" is a phrase that keeps cropping up in Rumbelow's book. And the crimes became more and more savage. About the only thing left was to saw some poor creature in two, things had been so savage.

L: One of the things that interests me too about the whole thing are the letters. Whether they were all penned by Jack the Ripper is very doubtful. I talked to Rumbelow and he's very doubtful. I believe he thinks that only one was actually written by the man himself, which is a shame because whoever wrote several of those letters was a jolly good crime writer himself. Imagine someone who could think of "From Hell" when he wrote the return address. I think that was incredible.

C: There's another murderer you talk about in your work: Charles Peace.

L: In the end, he was hanged, but he was always escaping. He was a very skillful burglar. The public sort of tended to take him to their hearts in a way that they never did Jack the Ripper. He was a figure they tended to side with because he was so clever at getting away from the police. He used various ingenious things like a collapsible stepladder that he could carry around with him. He was a small man, very athletic, though, who could climb into tiny spaces. He carried out some very dexterous burglaries and committed a couple of murders in the course of these. In the end, he was caught by the police and everybody felt rather sorry that he had to be. But he was being transported, I think, from one jail to another, and managed to escape the police and jump out a train window. He was at liberty again. In the meantime, a man had been brought to justice for a murder and the judge had been lenient and given him time in prison. But then Peace was caught and found guilty of another murder and finally confessed to the murder this other man was serving time for.

C: Makes you wonder, doesn't it?

L: I think the whole question of conviction for murder is a horrifying one, much more so when capital punishment was the thing here.

C: Do you imagine that probably some innocent people were hanged in those days?

L: Yes, I think some innocent people were. It's quite possible that it happened and has happened in this century, too.

280/THE CRAFT OF CRIME

C: The machinery is almost irreversible once they get an indictment.

L: As far as capital punishment is concerned, I've always been an abolitionist, and in this country that's fashionable; the hang-'em-flog-'em crowd in this country would like to have the rope back. I haven't pushed that in the books. I regard the books primarily as entertainment, except that I want to treat the subjects as realistically as I can.

C: The heroine in *Dynamite Party* gets away with murder, but she's beautiful and she's slept with Cribb, so how could you punish her?

L: Right. It just didn't seem right at the end of that book.

C: One of the stereotypes, or rather two I suppose, about crime in England versus crime in America is that the American criminal will hole up somewhere with a Thompson .45 and when the cops arrive, yell down, "You'll never take me alive, copper!" whereas the English criminal confronted by a tactful police constable knocking on his door will begin to weep and say, "Yuss, I done it," and the kindly but firm bobby will say, "Right. Come along naow." In fact, this stereotype was helped along by Alistair Cooke a few years ago when he was introducing a PBS TV show of one of those marvelous films starring Ian Carmichael based on the Lord Peter Wimsey series. And there's a grain of truth in that. Did the criminal class feel less sure of themselves in England during the Victorian period? Did religious sentiment and the growth of chapel Christianity and the official piety make them feel a little more inclined to walk the straight and narrow?

L: The motives for crime were so powerful and so compelling that I doubt whether it made a lot of difference, and I think anyway that it was primarily the middle class, the shopkeeper and the small businessmen who were churchgoing people, who were the patsies for the criminals. The poorest class didn't belong to churches and didn't have these conventions to think about.

C: Yes. One of the touching things about Rumbelow's book on the Ripper murders is that section on the struggles of an Anglican rector in the Whitechapel area to do something for the people. He couldn't do much and they appreciated it even less. But it's also true, isn't it, that if you were raised in one of those rookeries, you were predestined for a life of crime?

L: No, no.

C: So it was not a one-on-one equation — poverty, filth, squalor, therefore vicious crime?

L: No, I don't think it was. I think there were a lot of people leading upright lives who were doing as well as they could in those conditions. But sometimes something happened that did involve religion and crime; somehow the two wires crossed, as they did in the Adelaide Bartlett case. She supposedly had a nonconformist preacher as her lover and she was alleged to have been a poisoner. It was one of the famous cases of the time. She was one of the Victorian women poisoners — or in her case an alleged poisoner. There must have been about half a dozen of them in the period. They were marvelous celebrated cases and are wonderful reading now. But the Bartlett case caused a tremendous outcry. She had as a lover a local preacher and that added a lot of interest to the case.

C: Why were there so many women poisoners in the Victorian era?

L: I think it was the best way to dispatch a man, really.

C: Strictly from the viewpoint of efficiency?

L: Yes. I don't think women either could get a pistol or knew how to use one. I think it was the obvious way to do things. They could get all the various kinds of poisons, most of them, and they could get flypapers.

C: Flypapers?

L: If you boil them down, you can get arsenic — or you could then. I think that's the method Bartlett was alleged to have used.

C: In *Wobble to Death* you have one of the trainers going around to different chemists in London buying strychnine, and it was that man's practice to do that.

L: Yes. You could get small amounts of strychnine. In small amounts it was used to affect athletic performances. The Olympic marathon was won in 1904 by a man named Thomas Hicks Lewis, and his trainer said quite openly in a book written later that he had given him small amounts of strychnine. A lot of people took laudanum to help them sleep.

C: Wilkie Collins apparently took so much he was nocturnally assaulted by a monster as he went upstairs to bed.

L: And there was chloral. And then, of course, you had doctors committing crimes, as several of them did, such as Dr. Crippen in the twentieth century.

C: Is poisoning uniquely English?

L: Florence Mabrick was an American woman.

C: But she came over here.

L: Yes.

C: She was infected, talking to the old dearies down at the pub.

L: She was trapped in a marriage to a brute of a husband in Liverpool and she poisoned him and she was found guilty and sentenced to death, but her sentence was commuted to a long term.

C: Let's talk about Cribb. In the first book, he almost can't speak in complete sentences. He grabs someone and is going to shake the truth out of him. But he gets mellower and funnier as he goes along.

L: Yes, he must develop, I suppose, as a character. Cribb was brought into that book halfway through to solve the crime. For me, the main thing in that book was establishing the atmosphere of the race and getting my characters and getting the crime under way. Cribb was brought in simply to be a working Victorian policeman of the time, quite different from a Sherlock Holmes character. I wanted to have somebody who was as close to what I conceived of a Victorian detective as being. Maybe he does alter a bit in the books, but not too much. I try to keep his rough style of language pretty much.

C: He becomes more human; he's sleeping with some Irish terrorist.

L: Well, essentially he was doing that for Queen and Country.

C: Ah, the distasteful things one must do for one's sovereign!

L: I think it's quite a tribute to the quality of my writing that I've written eight crime novels and I don't think I've shown a couple in bed in any of them. I've had quite a few cases of nudity. Cribb actually got into bed and she wasn't there. They got close to it, but . . .

C: Shucks. Is it hard to keep on working with the same characters?

L: No, it's too easy.

C: Is it hard to be original with the same three guys all the time?

L: I enjoy them. It didn't get to be a bore. I think in a way — I may have said this to other people — each is a different aspect of my own personality. Thackeray is me when I feel I'm rather put upon and exploited, when I'm working in the garden, which I hate. If I suddenly have a bit of success or feel that I'm getting through or my organization is beginning to work, that's Cribb.

C: And I come on like Chief Inspector Jowett. "What does this *mean?*"

L: Not at all. No. Jowett is based upon someone I once worked with. You could say an academic boss. I'd better not identify him any more closely than that. He was full of new ideas without actually being able to see how they could possibly be put into practice, but we've all had bosses like that, bosses who are sort of wanting to impress all the time. They're very good on paper, very good at sitting at a desk.

C: But Jowett's bosses think he's a fool, too.

L: Yes, right.

C: But there he is and there's a class difference between Cribb and Jowett that Cribb could never hope to overcome.

L: No, I don't think so. When the CID was set up, most of the detectives who were allocated to the various divisions were inspectors. There were, I think, two or three sergeants, and when I read that I wondered what must these sergeants have felt, having been given a job that was just as responsible as the inspectors' and having been stuck with all the work because they had to talk to the criminals. But there it was and so Cribb remained a sergeant and probably always will.

C: Usually a cop or a newspaperman is only as good as the information he can buy, extort, or trade for. Did Victorian police work proceed along those lines?

L: They went mainly on tips, but it doesn't make very interesting reading, so that's one of the real fictions in the fiction itself. You have to have a detective who sort of ferrets out all the information himself. He does get information, he sees the right people, but he has to work out for himself who the likely murderer is.

C: To me the intuitive approach is just as valid as the technological approach that's used almost to the exclusion of intuition now. Because after all, and the homicide manuals used in police academies stress this, the equipment is no better than those who run it, and even in twentieth-century America a lot of p.d.'s don't have that much equipment, particularly poorer departments.

L: There wasn't much in the Victorian era. They could make plaster casts of footprints. I've got something called *The Police Code of Criminal Law*, which was written by Sir Harold Vincent, who set up the CID. It's a training manual for Victorian policemen and the hints and tips he could give them on investigating crime were really sort of laughable.

C: "Beware of the dark-skinned foreigners."

L: Yes, almost. It was at a very elementary level and Sherlock Holmes was another world entirely. Conan Doyle had a great sense of humor, I think. They were very amusing books and they were meant to be. Somebody walks into the office and Holmes says, "Apart from the fact that you're a Freemason and you were married to an Irish woman, I know absolutely nothing about you." It was marvelous. I love those stories and yet Doyle was right up to date in his knowledge of the forensic science of that time, and I think the majority of things that Holmes was using in order to assist his investigations were based on real things. But this was in the nineties, when things were beginning to move. My books are set in the early eighties, most of them.

C: Is it inevitable when looking back on an era or in writing about an era that we create a whole set of people more like us than the people of that far-off time?

L: What you said just sparked something off. I read an account by Ross Macdonald of what he regarded as the typical American detective hero. He said that one of the things about the hero was that he speaks for our common humanity. Another was that he was intolerant of hypocrisy. I remember thinking as I read it that these were things I would claim for my detective as well, even though he was working in Victorian times, and I wondered whether I had simply written a modern man into a Victorian story. I think the essential things, the human qualities, go back, though. I don't think I have written a modern man back into the 1880s. When you read the Victorian novel, you do come across people who would fit the set of characteristics I've given Cribb. I think Cribb is plausible and I think he has this in common with Lew Archer.

C: Did you and Jackie enjoy working together when you did the six TV scripts?

L: Very much, because we've always been involved together in the writing of the novels. She reads far more whodunits than I do and she's always read them at the rate of two or three a week. She's reading a Stanley Ellin at the mo-

286/THE CRAFT OF CRIME

ment and liking it a lot. When I came to write my first novel,
I'd read Agatha Christie and I think I'd read the Sherlock
Holmes stories, not much else at all, but she was able to en-
courage me to work out a plot.

C: Red herrings and so on?

L: Yes, that's right. And she tells me which pitfalls to
avoid. If I suddenly say I've got a marvelous idea, you know,
I'll write it from the point of view of the narrator and he'll
turn out to be the murderer in the end, she'll point out that
Agatha Christie's already done that. So she's able to sort of
give me a lot of advice and help, but when it came to the
writing of the television series, they wanted them very rapidly, as they always do in television. The books take me
about six to eight months to write with a bit of time for research included. But these scripts had to be done quickly —
six of them in six months.

C: Well, it was your material, but, still, one script ground
out a month . . .

L: The only way I could think of doing the assignment in
six months' time was by asking Jackie if she'd do three of
them. So she did three set mostly in the country, the bucolic
scripts.

C: Have you ever had movie offers for these?

L: At the beginning, there was some interest from Carl
Foreman, the writer of *High Noon.* He was intrigued with
Wobble to Death and would have liked to have made a film of
that. He kept an option running for some time, but in the
end it lapsed. Since then I've had a movie called *Golden Girl,*
starring Susan Anton, which I wrote under another name.

C: Why did you write under the name of Peter Lear? Just
wanted to try another genre?

L: Yes. When I became a full-time writer — I'd been a
teacher and decided, I think, in 1975, that the time had
come to take the plunge and drop the job and write full
time — I thought then I couldn't carry on with Sergeant
Cribb indefinitely, that I ought to try to widen my range. It

was sensible to look for a rather different market and write an up-to-date book, and I didn't think that my Cribb readers would particularly appreciate a book about the modern Olympic games.

C: They might have, who knows? Let me ask you general question number three. Why do detective and suspense writers not start until their late thirties in most cases?

L: I think this particular genre makes very strong demands on organization and structure, and I think that the type of novel that is written by a younger man has a rather looser structure. I think this is much more of a craft, shall we say, that you learn and perhaps you have to have knocked around in the world a little longer and seen a little more and thought a little more about what you might do.

C: And be less engrossed in your own personality.

L: Well, it's right to write from experience, I think, but certainly as far as crime writing is concerned, that's my answer to your question.

C: Any last messages?

L: Let me tell you about my next novel, *The False Inspector Dew*. I've come into the twenties. It takes the famous Dr. Crippen case of 1910, the case of the doctor who murdered his wife and tried to escape to Canada with his mistress, Ethel Nead. They found the body in the cellar and the captain of the ship recognized Crippen; Ethel was dressed as a boy. The captain sent the message back and Inspector Dew, who was the Scotland Yard inspector on the case, managed to get a faster ship and went to Toronto. He was waiting for Crippen and arrested the poor man. Everybody felt sorry for him because his wife was a grotesque sort of figure who gave him a terrible time. They all felt she deserved what she got. Crippen was hanged and Ethel was found not guilty and went off and lived in obscurity after that. I decided it would be rather more interesting to rework the story, so I have a dentist whose patient falls in love with him and has very romantic ideas. Between them, they get to talking about the

Crippen case while she's in the chair. A bit of romance develops between them and he tells her about the tough time he has with his wife. They decide to murder the wife and do what Crippen did without making the mistakes Crippen made.

C: Because they could work off that story, as could you.

L: Yes. The story is set mainly on the *Mauretania* and the question is whether they can get away with it, get to the other side and escape.

C: I love races.

L: I hope it'll succeed. People who've read it so far rather like it. For me, it was a refreshing thing to get away from the Victorian period after all those television plays done in a very short period of time. I just wanted a change, and the twenties is a very invigorating era to work in, I found, with this sort of naive release that they had after the First World War, when suddenly they were dancing and they could go to cinemas. And it was an innocent time. There was this feeling that at least they could begin to enjoy themselves. Girls' skirts started year by year getting shorter and fashion changed; they cut their hair shorter and they began to wear make-up, so it was a lot of fun to turn to something like that.

JANWILLEM
VAN DE WETERING

Janwillem van de Wetering was born in 1931 in Rotterdam, the Netherlands, "into a family that was upper middle class"; he is the son of a successful businessman, the last of five kids. He "grew up alone" and "felt very uncomfortable at home." It didn't help that he grew up in the city the Nazis bombed when he was eight, although the Dutch had declared it an open city and ceased resistance. His wartime experiences no doubt made a deep impression on him and led him to ask "Why do I live?" — the question that eventually drove him to a Zen monastery in Kyoto after he had gone around the world working for his father's company. This led to his first book, *The Empty Mirror: Experiences in a Japanese Zen Monastery.* In the monastery he underwent rigorous spiritual training, which has shaped his life and certainly informs his books; furthermore, it gave him a few insights into human nature, which, he discovered, subsumed both masters and mystics as well as the ordinary, unreligious people of the world: "In Japan I suspected, and later reflection made the suspicion grow, that mystics have a double personality. The everyday personality, the act which is played, continues. The adept never really loses his identity or his habits. The old Japanese master liked going to the cinema to see films on Africa, he watched baseball on T.V., he didn't like going to the dentist and he tried to avoid middle-aged ladies who came to ask questions. He preferred gardening to washing dishes. He liked some of the cartoons in the daily newspaper ... He enjoyed eating sour plums and drinking a special type of green tea ... He also had the master personality. He was a rare man, he knew, he knew his own face, the face which he had had long before his parents were born."

His life as a Buddhist later brought him to America, to a community in Maine led by Peter, whom he'd known in Japan, and his second book on Zen, *A Glimpse of Nothingness*. Besides some amusing comments on American Buddhists, this book contains van de Wetering's personal credo:

> Emptiness, the core of Buddhism, Emptiness, the great goal which is to be reached by losing everything there is to lose. Emptiness, the great danger. If you have nothing to do, you run a lot of risks and the training frowns on you. Yet the final goal is to have nothing more to do, to be nameless, to be stripped of the last aggression, the last defense. When Bodhidharma, the Indian Zen master who took Zen to China, was invited by the emperor, the meeting immediately became a display of vanity on the emperor's part. He told the master about the many monasteries and temples he, the emperor of China, the son of heaven, had originated and financed ... He asked the master what this important display meant and Bodhidharma said, "It means nothing, a great emptiness."
>
> And when the emperor, stupefied, asked the master who he, this messenger giving this weird reply, really was, the Bodhidharma said, "Don't know," turned on his heels and left the court.

Van de Wetering's first detective novel, published when he was forty-four, was written in English. It was dedicated to his wife, Juanita, whom he met in South America, and launched a career without precedent either in the United States or in Holland, where he is also a best seller and, of course, doesn't have to face that nemesis of writers, the unknown translator. In fact, he is very hot news in Holland, where he is treated as a mainstream writer.

This first novel, *Outsider in Amsterdam*, introduces van de Wetering's trinity of unusual cops (starting with the lowest in rank): Sergeant Rinus de Gier, a tall blond young man who wears a scarf and custom-made suits; Adjutant H. F. Grijpstra, who is stout, growly, favors boring, rumpled off-the-rack clothes and is the archetypical *homme sensuele*, subvariety Dutch; and the Commissaris, whose first name we are permitted to know at length — it is Jan — and whose religious views are clearly Zen. He enjoys sitting in his garden and easing his arthritis while he talks to his turtle. The first novel is about the drug trade (many of van de Wetering's novels are) and the involvement in it of certain members of the Hindist Society, semihippies who have taken over an old seventeenth-century gabled house on one of the canals in the Old City. It should be reiterated that these novels are composed in English; van de Wetering's writing is an advertisement for the Dutch educational system.

Van de Wetering spent a number of years on the Amsterdam police force doing his national service, so he knows the people, the cops, and the city. But his police procedurals are rather unique in that each policeman has dreams and visions that are as important to him, ultimately, as the "real" world through which he moves. Grijpstra dreams of a world of sensual memories and fantasies, de Gier sees visions that are symbolic and indirectly solve the mysteries he's working on, and the old Commissaris has thoughts that soar above ethics and even above religion into the emptiness that van de Wetering himself found in the Zen monasteries he lived in.

Tumbleweed has an overtly religious theme. Maria van Buren, a lady of the evening, or certainly an inhabitant of the more elegant precincts of the demimonde, is found dead on her houseboat and her collection of plants and potions suggest she's a witch. De Gier is the first to put a name to it and the rest of the novel is devoted to finding her murderer, who it turns out is another witch. This novel sets the pattern that van de Wetering usually adheres to: the justice in these finely rendered, vivid novels is usually poetic rather than statutory.

The Japanese Corpse is probably his best novel before the current crop and has to do, again, with the smuggling of drugs into Holland, this time from Japan by the *yakusa*, a society of gangsters that has functioned (indeed, flourished) in Japan since the end of their middle ages. The book, aside from its suspense and mystery and chilling bits of murder and mayhem, is a meditation on Zen and on Japan.

One of the latest novels is *The Maine Massacre*, set in the mythical town of Jameson, Maine. Van de Wetering lives in fact near Ellsworth, Maine, way up the coast, almost on the edge of the cliffs of Maine, in a wooden house he built himself. The flavor of rural Maine is captured perfectly in this book, which features the unraveling of the mystery of Cape Orca by de Gier and the Commissaris (who has come over to help liquidate the estate of his brother-in-law, who died in an "accident" outside his home on the Cape). Grijpstra never gets to go on these jaunts; perhaps he is the presiding genius of the Amsterdam police and cannot travel. Regardless of the setting, however, those who have never read van de Wetering are in for a treat.

CARR: How was it to grow up as a preadolescent and I guess adolescent in the war? I guess the war was very much with you, wasn't it? You were always afraid. Were you actually bombed?

VAN DE WETERING: Oh yeah. Although not our house; they stopped just a street away from us. We were never hit. I never starved. But I was in a school that was almost exclusively Jewish. Little kids. Every single one of them was killed, but they left me. So I developed a neurosis. Why not me? Why everybody else? Sounds ridiculous but it may be even more nasty. It always bothered me. It still bothers me.

C: Let's go through your confused biography, which is not readily available because the reference work that won the Edgar last year doesn't mention you or van Gulik, but of course throws in a number of "straight" writers who wrote one pseudodetective novel. We've gotten you to age thirteen in the Netherlands, with World War II over.

vdW: I was born in Rotterdam into a family that was upper middle class. They weren't into reading, looking at paintings, listening to music, or thinking about anything; they were just career-minded people, it seemed to me. They wanted me to have a career, and I was going to have a career, but then when the war ended, I realized that I wasn't really interested. I just wanted to know why all this had happened, to cure my mental wounds, I think. The hippie complex. So I deliberately selected a training that would get me out of Holland as soon as possible, to get away from the whole thing. I really wanted to travel. I collected stamps. Immediately after the war I went to England; I traveled all over Europe as a kid, took any chance offered me to be abroad — France and Scandinavia. I always avoided Germany, but I've been to Germany, too, and Italy.

C: So you went to a technical college?

vdW: No. I went to a business college. First, to a mathematical high school. I really had an excellent training in mathematics, which would compare to college training here, but we already had it in high school. After that, I went away. For a year I worked on this and that, I worked on farms, because my father wanted me to go in for his career, but I didn't want to have anything to do with it. Finally they traced me through an emergency call on the radio. The farmer realized they were looking for me and made me contact them. Then I went to business college (it was only two years), and after that I went to Africa. I worked for a while in South Africa in one of my father's projects, but then he had me transferred because I was doing well. That is, he gave me a promotion and transferred me out of Cape Town, which is where I wanted to be. So I refused and he fired me through several intermediaries, but ultimately *he* fired me. Then I did any old thing. I drove with a mobile library around Cape Province and then I worked as a salesman here and there. I had a bad motorcycle accident with a lot of insurance paid out, so that gave me a year off. I read a lot. I had vague ideas about becoming a writer, but I couldn't get it together.

C: Did you try to write "straight" fiction when you were that age?

vdW: Yes, but they were all very abortive attempts and I got mixed up with a group that I described in *The Maine Massacre* called the Bad Motherfucking Gang, a motorcycle gang of intellectuals. I had a lot of fun with that and that was modeled on Dostoyevsky's *Devils*. It was a deliberate effort. We had a mentor who was a very strange guy who had a strange war record. He deserted from three Allied armies, went all over the world, and every time he didn't like it, he would desert. He finished up as a cook in the British merchant navy, hiding from all the military police who were looking for him. When he came out of that, he had to run for his life because they were still after him. He became the disciple of a black bush doctor in Natal, South Africa, and he picked up a little interesting stuff there, but it was mostly evil; it was real black magic. I became his disciple, but I didn't like the badness of it. I liked the insight part of it, but I didn't really want to inflict suffering on anyone, certainly not deliberately, so I broke away from him. But, looking back now, I realize I really picked up a lot of knowledge, a lot of trickery, which I've used many times, but not the way it was designed. I never used it for evil because I thought that was a waste of time.

C: It's hard to imagine you as a sorcerer's apprentice after reading your books on Zen.

vdW: Yes, but in a way that prepared the way. It was very useful, although I didn't see it at the time. It was all part of the Bad Motherfucking Gang, of which *he* was never a member, which was very strange.

C: And just to keep the record straight, this guy was white.

vdW: Yes, white Jewish. I stayed six years in South Africa, then I went to London, intending to study philosophy, which I did at University College of London University. I tried to write my first novel, which I did in Cornwall, and I managed to finish it, but it was a useless document; it was just good for discipline.

C: What was it about?

vdW: About me, of course, about my life in South Africa, trying to figure out what had happened to me, and I invented characters.

C: Did you have any contact with the Afrikaner community?

vdW: I never liked them.

C: They speak a sort of Dutch, don't they?

vdW: It's pure Dutch, archaic Dutch.

C: Seventeenth-century Dutch?

vdW: Yes, pure Dutch, very easy to follow. They can't follow us because Dutch developed back in Europe, but they reminded me of Germans. Very fascist people, and an example of the stupidity of intense Protestant faith. My father shopped around in religion and he took me to just about every church that's ever been in Holland. His main interest was Buddhist and Hindu philosophy, but he never got into it. He just read them. So I was never formally in any church.

C: In one of your books, the Zen master points out the difference between those who are shopping around or looking for thrills and those who are looking for enlightenment.

vdW: Well, he was shopping around. I don't think he was looking for thrills. He was looking for explanations, as I was. But he was also a big businessman, so it all sort of conflicted. He wasn't a happy man, but he was a very good man, clean, pleasant, and I have very good memories of him.

C: Did you go to Cambridge?

vdW: I went to Cambridge to get my proficiency certificate in English. They gave me a degree with some title that

I've forgotten, but I did get a paper. I passed the exam, oral and written.

C: Where did you first study English? Holland?

vdW: Yes. I started reading English when I was fourteen, outside school. At school I wasn't doing too well with the real course, but I was reading English as a kid and I taught it to myself. When I went to England, I picked up the spoken language fairly easily and I seemed to recognize England, everything about it was very familiar to me.

C: From the literature?

vdW: No, as though I'd been there before. I felt the same thing with China later, but Japan I never recognized; South Africa I didn't recognize, but I recognized the British colonial influence, so maybe there was some previous life when I was British. I must have been Chinese, because when I got to China the whole thing looked very familiar.

C: And then after England, you went to Colombia?

vdW: To Japan. And after Japan I went to Colombia and became a businessman again and did very well.

C: What were you doing?

vdW: I was running a big Dutch chemical agency, importing chemicals and distributing them locally. We were really doing fantastically. But after my contract was up, after three years, I could see the way we were going: we were all going to become millionaires — there were three of us. The guys that stayed are millionaires now; they own their own Lear jets and they are well up on the Onassis way. But I didn't want to go that way, so I went to Peru. For some reason, Peru looked like adventure. By that time I was married and I had a kid and in Peru the company almost went bankrupt. In fact, it was liquidated. I had a little bad luck there. So I went to Australia and I spent a year and a half there.

Then an uncle who was running a little wholesale textile company in the Old City in Holland died and I thought, "That's it, that's just what I want." So a partner and I built that company and it's become a very big company. Again, we were on the way. We had a huge boat on the Inland Sea, and we were sipping gin at eleven o'clock in the morning, talking to all these big shots and being big shots ourselves. Meanwhile I was in the police because I had dodged the draft.

When I came back, I had to either join the army or do something else to serve the Queen, so I joined the police in my free time.

C: How many weeks did you actually put in?

vdW: Well, the first two years I was there all the time, all on my free time, to become a cop, but they were strange hours: weekends, holidays. Then I had to spend two years as an active duty cop, again in my free time, and I rode a cop car in the center of Amsterdam.

C: What do they call free time? Ten hours a week? Twenty hours a week?

vdW: Well, a minimum, I think, of four hours, but you could do more and I always did more because I became a sergeant and then an inspector.

C: You became an inspector?

vdW: Well, I was going to be commissioned, but then I left for America. But I passed the exams and that was the best time: as a student officer I could go right through the night, stick my nose into anything I liked, ask questions and get answers, look at the files, and that's really where I got all the material for my books.

C: How many murders are there in Amsterdam per week?

vdW: Five a year. But then we have a different definition of it from what you have. Murder with us is premeditated. Anything else is manslaughter and a lot of murders somehow become manslaughter.

C: Through reduction of charges?

vdW: Yeah. And the squad de Gier and Grijpstra belong to is not called the Murder Brigade; it's called the Brigade of Heavy Crime, but that didn't sound good for my books. And that brigade isn't even in continuous operation. They only set it up when there is a murder — a real good murder — to solve.

C: Holland must be a nice country. But I guess guys are always getting killed in bar fights, which you would call manslaughter.

vdW: Never.

C: Never?

vdW: No. The Dutch don't fight in bars. They eat a little. They make a lot of noise, maybe, but they're not a vicious people.

C: They must not be if Amsterdam only has five murders a year.

vdW: It would be less in other places. But the Brigade of Heavy Crime also gets into a lot of other stuff, real bad stuff like the prostitution of minors and big drug stuff. They work together with the Drug Squad, and they're supposed to be the best we have in Amsterdam on the police force.

C: You've ridden, I know, with the sheriff of this county in Maine and the police in Durham, North Carolina, and probably you've seen policemen all across the world. What's the difference between the attitude an American cop has toward his society and the attitude a Dutch cop has toward his society?

vdW: Here there seems to be an emphasis on violence, while we just try to get away from violence. We never showed our guns. They were hidden under the coat. You never went for them. When you stopped a car, you wished them the time of day, you introduced yourselves. Here, a cop will walk to a car with his hand on his gun and any movement the guy makes inside the car is a dangerous move — the cop will pull the gun. For any shit the guy gives the cop he's arrested. We don't do that. We just smooth it down because we figure that if the cop is violent, if his attitude is violent, he provokes violence. And we've gotten away with that for many hundreds of years, but maybe Americans are more violent people.

C: I think we probably are. But was the Netherlands ever a place where the police had a problem in maintaining public order?

vdW: Now they have a problem.

C: Now?

vdW: Because of heroin. The junky's got to get his three hundred dollars a day and he'll do anything. They cause terrific problems.

C: A friend of mine went to Amsterdam in '68 and wound up on heroin.

vdW: Because Amsterdam is the magic city, you see. Only Amsterdam was a magic city. The rest of Holland is straight. The stuff the hippies were getting away with in Amsterdam . . . If they'd done a tenth of that in Rotterdam, they'd have been arrested and deported straight away.

C: And Groningen?

vdW: Yes, that's all very strict country. Amsterdam has always been a tolerant place. When the hippies came, we opened up the parks and they could sleep anywhere they liked. The police were helpful, a lot of them. That was the time I was working there and the number of hippies I dragged out of houseboats . . . They were dying, and a lot of them did die.

C: Like that girl in *Outsider in Amsterdam.*

vdW: Yes. That happened to me just the way I wrote it down there. But that was just one of a hundred cases. But that's all over now. It's not a hippie town now.

C: Didn't the Dutch ever get sick and tired of all that? Did they figure it was not worth the effort to clean it up?

vdW: Well, that's not the Amsterdam attitude. They don't get sick and tired of things. If they just open up to it, tolerate it, it'll go away by itself, they believe. And sure enough, it always does. They know it's a wave; it won't last forever. But there was a big crackdown on heroin. Much to our regret, we had to deport every illegal Chinese in the Netherlands.

C: How many were there?

vdW: Oh, lots, and they ran all the little restaurants, all the cheap restaurants, and they were marvelous restaurants. But the Singapore Chinese got in there and used that setup of all the restaurants as a distribution system. They terrorized the local Chinese into cooperating with them, so what we finally did was to arrest every single one of them. No paper, away with them. We flew them at our own expense to either Hong Kong or Singapore and did away with that side of the problem.

C: You came to America in '75, and straight to Maine?

vdW: Yes, straight here. I've lived in this house ever since.

C: What attracted you?

vdW: I had friends here because of the monastery. They asked me to come up and then I went once a year for ten years, from '65 to '75. By that time I was getting tired again of being a businessman and I had a feeling that my books would sell very well, although they hadn't even come out yet, except *The Empty Mirror*. But I was convinced they would sell well, so I thought I'd just live off my writing and live in America, which is much more comfortable than Holland.

C: Another myth gone.

vdW: Well, Holland has fourteen million people in half the size of Maine. There are nine hundred Dutchmen to the square mile and the only way to live there is to figure out what everybody's going to do and then do the exact opposite.

C: So you won't run into them.

vdW: Yes. My mother has a house in the country and when she wants to see me, I say I'll have breakfast with her at 6:00 A.M. so that I can drive out there on an empty road. If it was a beautiful weekend and I knew everybody would go to the beach, I'd go to the Sea. I even changed my sleeping times, but that becomes a nuisance after a while. You don't have to do *that* here.

C: No, if you got into trouble where you live, you'd have to send up a flare.

vdW: Yeah, it's great.

C: Let's take the whole Buddhist thing from beginning to end. You arrived in Kyoto, which had been left alone by American bombers.

vdW: Well, there was a deal, you know. The B-29s regrouped off Kyoto, and in return for the Japanese not bothering them with either fighters or antiaircraft fire, the Americans promised not to bomb Kyoto.

C: We declared it an open city, probably.

vdW: The only guy who ever strafed Kyoto is a guy who lives up the road here, and he did it by mistake. His instruments went haywire over the mountains by Kobe and he thought he was taking Osaka and he was really taking Kyoto. By the time he came back, the Japanese had complained to the Swedish ambassador and he had gone to the Americans and they had got to the air force and told them that when this bugger gets off the plane, smash his head, and they certainly did. He was cleaning airplane wheels for a while.

C: Anyway, when you arrived at Kyoto, it was as if your whole life had pointed you there, hadn't it?

vdW: Yes. Yes. And what caught me was that there were a lot of masters there, available, who would see me, I was assured. And they did.

C: How had you been assured? Over the grapevine?

vdW: Books on Japan. And by people who had been there, but not Buddhists. I had a feeling that it would work out.

C: A serendipitous experience, wasn't it, when you arrived and everything was waiting for you? You didn't know where you were going; you just wandered over to the first temple and there it was.

vdW: Yeah. Yeah. I didn't even know that it was a Zen monastery. I knew about Buddhism, but I'd never heard of Zen. Everybody thought I was just like the Americans who came there, the hippies and the guys like Gary Snyder. Gary Snyder was in the same monastery I was in at the same time I was there.

C: You called him Gerald, didn't you?

vdW: Yes. But they'd come there because of Zen. They'd heard about Zen. Well, I never knew what Zen was.

C: There was a paperback book about Zen, by D. T. Suzuki, that swept America about that time. The more adventurous read that and some of those took off for Japan.

vdW: I read that in Japan. I couldn't make heads or tails of it. It didn't seem to conform to reality at all. There are lots of different Buddhist sects in Japan, but I got into the Zen sect and that seemed where I should be.

C: Pure serendipity. You came to a place you'd only read about, went to a temple you'd never seen, and were taken in by a religion you really knew very little about.

vdW: Yes.

C: You spent two years there?

vdW: Yes.

C: A Vietnamese priest once told me that he could teach me Vietnamese in two years if I behaved myself, but that it would take me at least six years to learn Japanese.

vdW: Oh yeah. It didn't take me long to figure out questions in Japanese, but I could never get the answer although I could understand every word that they'd use. It's a different mental attitude altogether. They can't say no. Negativity is rude, so everything is phrased positively, but the meaning is negative and I could never figure that out. That's the reason I was able to get through that heavy meditation week.

C: Your description of that made me hurt. It was incredible what demands they made on themselves — and on you, of course.

vdW: But, you see, I thought, because I couldn't understand Japanese, that they were going to throw me out if I didn't get through it. And really they were just telling me I could leave any time because the exercise was beyond me; they didn't expect me to do it. I lived with that constant misunderstanding all the while I was there.

C: Did you have the feeling sometimes that you weren't

getting all of it exactly the way a Japanese would have gotten it?

vdW: Well, I had direct contact with the teacher. The teacher had a very good idea of my mind, I think, and he made this direct contact in which there was no trouble about negative and positive. Anyway, he didn't care about all of this. He tried to go beyond that. He was beyond there and he appealed to the part of me that was beyond it, a part that everybody has, the Buddha nature that everyone supposedly has. Although at the time I thought it was a complete flop and I had wasted my time and his time and everybody's time, I realized when I got out of there how much I'd changed.

C: There's one scene, a very moving scene I think, when you realize they're going to drown all those kittens.

vdW: Yes.

C: And there's nothing you can really do about it.

vdW: No.

C: You can't keep them, the monks are sure not going to keep them, but these people would leave these small animals, I suppose most of them were cats, with little ribbons around their necks.

vdW: And they'd starve to death and get maggots all over them, wandering around in the temple gardens under the Buddha's care. The poor little things were suffering to death.

C: And that really cracked you at that point.

vdW: There was a lot of cruelty in Japan and a lot of stupidity. The neurotic behavior of the Japanese even to a Dutchman is amazing to watch. But it's also a beautiful place. Their artistic sense is so highly developed and their subtlety is certainly more developed than ours.

C: I thought part of your sadness was because it was so ironic that these innocent little animals, to whom the Buddha is supposed to pay more attention than Christ, were all going to be drowned by the priests of Buddha.

vdW: After at first having suffered as long as possible.

C: Drowned only when they were in imminent danger of death?

vdW: When they really became rotten with disease, they were drowned.

C: Were their souls supposed to be in Buddha's care after death?

vdW: I think nobody cared about them. They were just a nuisance. And the pomp of Buddhism always annoyed me, too, even in the Zen sect, where you all had to have different colored robes, indicating different degrees of insight. This guy's temple is more important than that guy's. All this politics and the power struggles. I thought, "What has this got to do with what they are supposedly looking for and certainly what I'm looking for?" I just wanted to figure out why it all started anyway, to find real religious insight.

C: I loved your comment, which all the Japanese delighted in, too. Some English lady kept pestering you about Buddhism and you finally said, "Bullshit, lady, I'm just here for enlightenment."

vdW: Oh, I had a good time, too. I had plenty of days off. I would go into the prostitution quarter there, which was very artfully designed. And I did a lot of drinking and fucking there, too. I never had anything against that side of life. A lot of that got into *The Japanese Corpse*. All that stuff I couldn't use in *The Empty Mirror* because it would have gotten away from the point, I kept and used in *The Japanese Corpse*.

C: Do you not want to tell what your *koan* is? Is that strictly forbidden and was it impolite of me to ask?

vdW: Well, I won't tell you what it was because that's sort of against tradition, but there are three main *koans*. They're basically all the same. One is the *mu koan*. The student asks, "Does the little dog have the Buddha nature?" And the master says *mu*, which means no. Then later he says *u*, which means yes, and you're supposed to meditate on *mu*, which is complete nothingness, like *om*. You start to struggle with it and eventually it supposedly breaks you open. And the other big *koan* is for the teacher to ask, "What is the sound of one hand clapping?" And there's another, but they're all the same, in a way. If you really solve them, you're there, you're going to see it all.

C: Can you decide on your own that you've solved it?

vdW: No.

C: The master has to see something in your face, or hear something in your answer?

vdW: Perhaps the teacher can't either, but he gets bored with you, I think, after a while, and if you have some little insight he'll pass you. That is a very dangerous point in a boy's training because he thinks he understands it all now, and then the teacher will give him satellite *koans*. They're all pretty easy. Some of them you could spot straight away, but some of them give you a lot of trouble because they open up the hidden part of your mind.

C: There really is not a straight, always infallible answer, is there? Or is there? Is there an agreed upon answer?

vdW: Yes. I have a book of *koan* answers here, and as far as I could check the book against *koans* I've had, the book gives all the correct *koan* answers. But that's all nonsense. It's theoretical study. A true teacher will tell you to *show* the answer in the way you *are*.

C: You had a nonverbal answer, didn't you? Your answer was one of those that couldn't be expressed.

vdW: Yeah.

C: In mere language. But there are books that have been printed since about 1400 that have a list of the traditional *koans*?

vdW: And the traditional answers. There's a very good book, one that I studied, that was really excellent. It's somewhere lying around the house. There was once a Zen student who passed all the *koans* and was declared by his teacher to be there. He could start teaching, the master said. The student said, "I still know nothing. This has all been highly theoretical training and I need a lot more training before I can start teaching." The master said, "No, I'm the authority and you are now ordained." So the guy went home and wrote down all the *koans* he'd been asked, with all the answers, and then he told his teacher he was going to publish them all. The master said, "You do that and I'll kill you." All the Zen teachers got together and really harassed this fellow, but he published it. The Zen masters sent their students out to buy every copy available, so the publisher had a great time — and published it again and again and again and finally it went all over Japan. It was translated. He really cuts through bullshit.

I met a lot of so-called advanced Zen students, and they're so full of pride. They have their robes and their dignity and they're there and you're not. They have the correct way. It's the old religious trap again.

C: I don't want you to tell on your friends or tell any more about Gerald than you told in your book, but did you meet a lot of Americans who thought they were really Zen masters?

vdW: Yeah. Future Zen masters. I split from that group. I did five years of it and then I just couldn't take it anymore. I never got into it for that anyway, to be a member of a group, to be an advanced Zen student, to do lecture trips. The Rockefeller Foundation phoned me and asked me if I wanted to do a lecture tour on Zen Buddhism, but I don't, and I said in that last sentence of *A Glimpse of Nothingness* that I would never write about it again. I never have. I just want to know why those Jewish kids were killed. Why, for God's sake ... The universe was created, but what's beyond the universe? And what happens when you draw two parallel lines forever? Those are basic questions I want to understand, but I don't want to be an advanced student or have any advanced status.

C: To be technically proficient in a theology?

vdW: Yeah. Who cares? I just want those answers and it probably will take a long time. The guy who, since my Zen studies, has impressed me the most is Jung. But I couldn't have enjoyed Jung so much if I hadn't had that training.

C: Yes, because he synthesizes things that are not so Western or Christian with the things that are. Did you find that your fascination with things Oriental actually survived being there?

vdW: Oh yes, yes. I'm an avid collector of anything translated from Japanese literature and I created a guy called Inspector Sito and I write a series of short stories that are published by *Alfred Hitchcock's Mystery Magazine*, but I do those under a pen name.

C: What is it?

vdW: Le Gru. I've become very interested in the life of van Gulik [creator of the Judge Dee mysteries], and I did a lot of work on that. I had him republished in Holland. I did introductions to each of the seventeen books.

C: They were probably in print in English when they weren't in Dutch.

vdW: Yes, he wrote most of them in English.

C: Did you have to retranslate?

vdW: I translated one into Dutch.

C: He's fascinating.

vdW: Absolutely. I have his collected works. In fact, I wanted to write the eighteenth Judge Dee, or *Judge Dee in Conflict with Lady Woo*, because that's a historical case, but his heirs didn't want me to do that. He has two sons. They think I wouldn't do it on the level their father had done the others on, maybe take away from his image, or whatever their reason is. I'm not doing it now.

C: You probably could do it anyway. Look at all the Sherlock Holmes pastiches and the Joe Gores pastiche drawing on the Dashiell Hammett novels. Van Gulik was a lifelong Dutch diplomat, wasn't he?

vdW: He was our ambassador to Japan. I have a fairly good collection of his non–Judge Dee books. He wrote a lot of scientific stuff. He wrote a book on sex life in ancient

China, which I have, and a book on how to mount scrolls. He drew in a Ming dynasty fashion, played the seven snail loop, and was a collector of gibbon apes. He wrote a book on gibbons, which I have, and he did translations of erotic, almost pornographic, books and he wrote in Chinese. Some of his books were written in Chinese and published by him in China and Singapore. I think van Gulik is very good proof of the reincarnation theory: he was collecting Chinese characters when he was four years old and drawing them in the sand.

C: Does he have a biographer?

vdW: I'm supposed to do it, but again there are some problems with the heirs.

C: Were you influenced by any other Dutch detective writers besides van Gulik?

vdW: No, there never were any. We have some local detective writers, but they never caught on beyond the fringes, and they never really caught on in the Netherlands. But I had such success with my books that now there are several people who are doing pretty well now, because I got it out of a slump. *Detectifs* in Holland were books that were published very cheaply. I made a deal with my publisher that he would publish my books in expensive paperback size, which he did. So they're paying as much for a *detectif* as for a regular novel and it was a great success. The guys who came after me are doing the same thing, and finally that whole type of literature is accepted now in the Netherlands as a legitimate way of expression.

C: You've done for your country what Raymond Chandler did for his.

vdW: Raymond Chandler I studied. I write a column for *NRC* in Holland (which is our best paper), an art column on American art, and I can do anything I like, so for one issue I wrote an essay on Chandler.

C: Just to get back to the Zen books for a moment, Peter was a real person, rather than a composite character.

vdW: He was real, yes.

C: The others were composite.

vdW: Yeah. The Master was a composite of two people because I really had two teachers there. I tried to put that in the book, but it took away from it rather than adding to it.

C: I liked the part of your second book that is really a flashback to the time and place of the first book: you and another man, a younger Japanese fellow, went up into the mountains and knocked on the door of a monastery that practiced another sort of Buddhism than Zen. The master there told you the story that, I guess, furnishes the title. A noble lady was anxious to get spiritual enlightenment and the master told her to line her room with mirrors and to look in them, which she did. Finally, she reported, "I see nothing," and to you that was the answer.

vdW: There's nothing there. That was the ultimate answer, you see. Intellectually, that's fairly easy to grasp. But the whole thing is completely illusionary, and out of all these reflexes you get mirrors, meaning nothing. That's *mu*. The purpose of the *mu koan* is to bring you in contact with that nothingness that underlies it all, but you can break it up pretty cleverly with your brain without really completely understanding it.

C: Do you think you have a spiritual understanding of that?

vdW: No. No, no. But, tough shit.

C: If it ever sank in, it would probably destroy you, wouldn't it?

vdW: That touch is the reason for the success of my books. It's in all my books because it's in the Commissaris. That's why he can jump free from any situation and that's why people identify with him, because he's such a crazy old bird, but he does do a very good job and at the same time it never touches him. He sits in his garden and talks with his turtle. And here is this disciple, de Gier, trying to follow him and he has this heavy Dutch conscience: what to do, what not to do, the superego in Freudian terms. But the Commissaris is ego; he moves. But because I've got that touch in there, and I saw some of it . . . That's my basic inspiration.

C: I love the Commissaris. He's a nice old fellow besides being an unusual fictional character.

vdW: I'm writing about him now, and he always makes me feel excellent.

C: When you write about him?

vdW: Yes.

C: Did you know a Dutch policeman like that?

vdW: Yes. The Commissaris was inspired by a certain cop I knew, but when I got to know him better, of course, he wasn't this way, but he had some of that. It goes back in Holland to a statesman of ours called Thorbeck, who created Dutch law after we'd been using the Napoleonic Code. He really understood that very well.

C: The nothingness concept?

vdW: Yes.

C: Thorbeck's code also set the tone for police work, didn't it?

vdW: Yeah. You create an order in which everyone can do what he thinks and that's your main purpose, your only purpose — to maintain that order with as little fuss as possible. An old cop told me, "All you have to do is be correctly dressed and be in a trouble spot, or in a potential trouble spot, and look at the civil population." He said, "Don't look aggressively at the civil population, at any one person, because you might as well be pulling your gun. But your gaze sweeps over the crowd and you're unruffled." The British bobby used to do that, but they have big problems now.

C: A couple of months ago all of that disintegrated.

vdW: We were there. They were breaking windows in the streets next to us.

C: But what would happen if an American cop tried what your old mentor told you to do in Holland?

vdW: Probably get murdered.

C: In fact, while you were doing research for *The Maine Massacre*, you got in a cruiser to ride around and pretty soon they'd handed you a riot gun and you had trained it on three people.

vdW: Yeah, just after I'd gotten in the car. You know how the sheriff checked me? I went into the station and said, "I'm a writer, here's my book, my photograph's on the back. I'm a cop — or I used to be a cop. I'd like to ride in your cruiser for a few nights because I want to write a book on Maine." He said, "Oh, is that so? Really?" And he looked at the photograph. He said, "Oh, by the way, what do you think of this gun?" He gave me a pistol.

C: Just gave it to you?

vdW: Gave it to me and I took it, took it in the flat of my hand. I immediately opened it — it was an auto — to see if there was a cartridge in it and there was and it was stuck. He'd just put it in. So I popped it out and got the clip out of it, and then of course it's harmless, and he said, "Right, you're a cop." Because it's automatic, you know: those are the movements you make automatically with any gun.

C: To see if it's loaded, right.

vdW: And your finger never gets on the trigger and you never point it at anyone. You point it at the floor. That's what they did at exams at the police school: they give you the gun and if you make one mistake, your whole year's gone; you have to start again. They're very famous for that. And if you ever draw your weapon, you have to fire it. I drew it once and didn't fire it, but you're supposed to give one warning shot and then the second shot is in the guy's leg.

C: What had the guy done to make you pull your weapon?

vdW: It was this crazy case. It was late at night, we were very tired. We'd been driving around all night, gotten into several bar fights and stuff. I was very exhausted and I was checking in back at the station when they said there's a lady wandering around over on this street and she says her boyfriend has a gun and he's threatening her and he's drunk. So we drove over there — I was with this military policeman — and there was the lady. She said her boyfriend was upstairs in the apartment and that he had a gun. But the lady was smelling very heavily of liquor, which should have warned me. So I said, "All right." My fellow cop pulled his gun and I looked at it and I thought, "Well, yeah." I should have told him to put it back. I drew my own gun, too. So we went in and the guy's fast asleep. So there we were, with both our guns pointed at the floor and not cocked and not charged, at least mine wasn't, and I hope his wasn't either. So I tapped the guy on the shoulder and I said, "Sir, wake up, wake up." But he was too far gone. He tried to go back to sleep because he thought we were part of his dream. So I said, "No, no, we're not a dream. Wake up, wake up. You've got a gun, sir. Could we have the gun?" He said he didn't have one and then he said he didn't know where it was. I said, "Well, I'll find it." So just to get rid of us, he swept all the books off his shelf and completely ruined his arrangement and finally gave me the gun. It was a starter's pistol.

C: I like the policemen in your novels — Grijpstra and de Gier.

vdW: There are meanings to the names. *Grijpstra* means "to seize" and *Gier* is "vulture." They really have nasty names, but they're good Dutch names and they're fairly popular names. I didn't invent them, but they're good police names.

C: Vulture and Snatch, a mean team of police. That's funny. Did you learn a great deal from reading American police procedurals?

vdW: No, I only read Chandler, and I read Hammett because of his Pinkerton experience. But I was very taken by Chandler's style. When he had someone cross the street and it was raining, the guy gets wet and the reader gets wet. Marvelous description. And I read Edgar Allan Poe. I can't stand Ellery Queen.

C: Did you read McBain?

vdW: Yeah. I thought it got a little repetitious after a while. And Joseph Wambaugh, the guy who wrote *The New Centurions*. But I wouldn't like to write that way.

C: It's considered primitive by some. Others reckon him to be Dostoyevsky.

vdW: But he has had terrific success. I wouldn't mind his success. Although I don't want to imitate any of his ideas. But there's good stuff about how cops think. I read him with pleasure.

C: Did you read Sjöwall and Wahlöö?

vdW: Yeah, I read one of their books, *The Laughing Policeman*, and I thought that I shouldn't because it's built pretty close to the lines of mine and I thought that it would get into my stuff.

C: Was Chandler well known in Europe?

vdW: They're all very well known.

C: You know Chandler was resurrected here in 1970 when Ballantine brought out all his novels with those wonderful pseudothirties' covers. That was the first time my generation had heard of him. We'd seen *The Big Sleep* with Humphrey Bogart, but the screenplay was written by Faulkner, so who could tell what was Chandler and what was Faulkner?

vdW: I saw that. Good movie. And *The Maltese Falcon* was a good movie.

C: Were those movies seen in Europe?

vdW: All of them were very well known, but only by the sort of intellectual class. All those books are translated, but God knows what happens to the translations. I don't know if they're really read, but they sell very well in English.

C: So people in Scandinavia and Holland read them in English?

vdW: Oh yes, and I know that I am read in English in Holland. They get American or British paperbacks.

C: Are they cheaper than the Dutch ones?

vdW: Much cheaper and they stack them next to the cash register.

C: That's great. You're obviously a national hero.

vdW: But they were written in English, so they don't have that feel of having been translated.

C: But you wrote the nonfiction books in Dutch.

vdW: Yes, and they were done into English later, but the detective books I didn't think I had a chance to get published in Holland.

C: Because of the low repute of the form?

vdW: Yes, so I thought, "I'll get them published in America, because that's got to be much easier." *The Empty Mirror* had done so well over here. It was a book club selection and everything, so I thought Houghton Mifflin might want to look at it.

C: Why did you choose Houghton Mifflin?

vdW: They found me.

C: Through the first, nonfiction stuff?

vdW: They somehow got a copy of the Dutch version of *The Empty Mirror*.

C: Your English is more than passable, a tribute to your ability to motivate yourself. Let's go to the fiction: was *Outsider in Amsterdam* originally entitled *Papuan in Amsterdam*?

vdW: Yes, but they didn't like the title because that would give away the killer.

C: That's hard to say, too, probably.

vdW: I didn't think so. And it has a much better cover.

C: Why did you choose a Papuan?

vdW: That was given to me. It was some Indonesian guy from some impossible little island nobody's ever heard of. It wasn't New Guinea — New Guinea is very well known. He'd had that business. He'd been a constable first class over there and a power figure and come to Holland, but there he could only be a parking cop. And he was complaining about it. He was a whiny guy in reality, but I suddenly saw a possibility in that character.

C: You could make him better than he was. And I believe that in the *Armchair Detective* interview you said that in the first version you had let him be caught. Justice had been served and so on. As it stands now, he gets away and we assume he's going to find his little island somewhere.

vdW: It was almost being set by Houghton Mifflin when I changed it. I rushed the different ending to them.

C: I bet they loved that. I enjoyed all your novels, but it seemed to me that *The Japanese Corpse* had more of you in it. But, of course, I could compare that to your nonfiction about life in Japan.

vdW: This woman who almost croaks because of a mushroom — that happened literally to me, after I left the monastery.

C: No one was trying to eliminate you, were they?

vdW: No, it was just bad food and the girl got sick. I saved the girl and then the gangster who owned the brothel gave me free entry there, but I didn't want free entry, so I had to buy presents to offset the typical Japanese thing of all this politeness. And the business where he goes into a little theater and sees himself on the stage being killed — that happened to me only I wasn't killed; they just made fun of me on stage. But they did it very well. They imitated me beautifully.

C: Damn, I thought it was all Shakespearean.

vdW: No, no. That all happened. And the meals in the various restaurants, dealing with the various characters — all inspired by real stuff.

C: What about the *yakusa*? Surely you made that up, where they're all dancing around.

vdW: I made that up, but I had a translation of a Japanese study of the *yakusa* in front of me, too.

C: There was an American movie made about the *yakusa*, starring a well-known Japanese actor, Robert Mitchum, and Robert Jordan. Did you see the movie?

vdW: Yeah, I saw it.

C: Was it true to life or romanticized?

vdW: It was pretty close.

C: The honor that had to be upheld and so forth.

vdW: Well, that was the key to my whole book — the honor. Once you know the honor code, you beat them every time.

C: There's a person in the book about the monastery in Japan, a master or a teacher, who wrote out a character for you and you apparently carried it around with you for a time after that. Was that the same character on page 240 of the paperback edition of *The Japanese Corpse*?

vdW: Actually, I got that one here, up the road. There's a Japanese who summers here who's a cello player from New York. He used to be a lawyer in Kyoto. He says he speaks English, but he really can't speak English at all. But he understands it, so I told him the idea of the book I was writing, *The Japanese Corpse*, and he got all excited and tried to tell me about the honor code, but I couldn't make head or tails of it. So finally he wrote a character down, but I misspelled it and it looked like "rabbit" to him, and that got him all excited. Then he said, "You must be careful because if they come after you, they'll kill you." So yeah, that's it on page 240, but messed up slightly, drawn like a European would draw it.

C: So that's not the character the master wrote for you when you left Japan.

vdW: No. That's a different one.

C: The *yakusa*'s a kind of Zen society too, isn't it? I mean, they have a sort of Zen viewpoint.

vdW: Yeah, sure. Zen is really into every Japanese creation.

C: It really stands behind everything?

vdW: It's been absorbed completely.

C: There are a lot of good touches in the book, the Commissaris' seeing his own face as a mask and so on, and it's also a wonderfully constructed book, but I thought that play-within-the-play was Shakespearean.

vdW: Oh no, they do that. Some strange-looking guy — to them — comes in and immediately he's on stage. It's a way for them to show off their acting ability. They can immediately imitate anybody.

C: What about that strange little No play they see just before the Snow Monkeys show up to take things in hand?

vdW: Well, that was my fantasy. I saw a lot of No plays and I liked the music. Black women I find very turning-on, so I just threw the whole lot together.

C: Miss Ah Boom Bah.

vdW: Yeah. Houghton Mifflin went crazy.

C: Your recent book for them, *The Mind-Murders*, has an interesting structure.

vdW: I wrote part one of *The Mind-Murders* at the request of the Dutch government. Every year a book is published by the Dutch government, but it can't be more than a hundred pages. They print more and more copies of this book every year (my year it was 400,000 copies), and they give it away at bookstores during the first week of April to anyone who spends more than ten dollars. On the one hand it's to stimulate reading and on the other hand it's to push some Dutch writer. So they asked me to do that, but I had to write a thriller in a hundred pages. And then I couldn't republish it in Holland for three years. Houghton Mifflin was after me to write another book and I'd been doing translations and articles, essays and this and that, editing collections of stories on the Far East, but they wanted a book, so I translated the first part and wrote a sequel to it to make it book size but using the same characters.

C: It's an interesting experiment. First you have the theme, and then the countertheme, and it turns out the countertheme is more important. It becomes apparent after a while that witnesses are unreliable in some instances, that the aunt and uncle are mad, and pretty soon the police suspect that everyone is. Finally, they work it out kind of mechanically at the end, where it all comes together. That's almost the first experimenting you've done with the form, isn't it?

vdW: Yeah. I always wanted to show the bumbling aspect of the police, too, because you don't have super detectives and there are so many factors, how can they get them all together? The Commissaris says that there are all these little events we know about, all of these facts, and if we just keep connecting them and continue the lines, the lines will meet somewhere. Of course, you can't draw an endless number of lines, but they do have some facts and they do connect. And he tells a little story.

C: Yes, here it is.

> "A jack rabbit runs through a field. He doesn't pay attention. He runs into a fence. The impact stuns him for a moment. He staggers about for a bit. A few cows are around. The jack rabbit bumps into a cow. The second mishap is too much for him. The jack rabbit faints. He's under the cow. 'Look,' the cow says to the other cows, 'I actually managed to catch a jack rabbit.' "
> "That's about the way it was," de Gier said.

Is that your metaphor for police work?

vdW: Yeah, that's how they work.

C: Cops of the world are biting their toenails as they read this.

vdW: Oh, of course you can torture them and they'll tell you the truth.

C: Well, they'll tell you something. It won't be the truth.

vdW: It'll be their interpretation of it.

C: In almost all the novels I've mentioned, there's some sort of dream sequence.

vdW: Yeah, of course.

C: Look at the trees, said the woodcutter. In *Outsider in Amsterdam* Grijpstra wanders upstairs into a cloud of feathers and is terrified and draws his weapon. In *The Mind-Murders* there's a vision of Asta that may or may not be true, we don't really know: was she doing the dirty bop on a table top with another girl while this crazy old cop was watching? Maybe? There's a surrealistic but not a dream sequence in *The Maine Massacre* when he sits down and plays his flute while a motorcycle gang blocks the door.

vdW: There are dreams in every book. I think dreams are tremendously important. Whether a guy realizes it or not, they are a big part of thinking.

C: Dreams and visions . . .

vdW: The complete dream you have at night that you remember a little bit of, but especially that state between waking and sleeping you go through in the morning. I go through it in the morning when I wake up. I keep on getting into consciousness and slipping back again into this very mysterious, almost fourth dimensional world, which probably is fourth dimensional. It gives you tremendous clues.

C: That's the Freudian interpretation, isn't it, that the mind works out its problems that way?

vdW: Yes, Jungian too. I hadn't read Jung when I wrote this. I write it now with Jung's support, but I wasn't doing that at the time.

C: I think writers always know these things before psychologists do. I find any number of adumbrations of Freudian discoveries in Victorian novels written while Freud was a child.

vdW: I have a scene in a book I'm writing — I was just reading it to my wife this morning — where the Commissaris realizes that he's up against the police, and against a very well known policeman, a sympathetic policeman and an excellent policeman, and he's shot the biggest bastard you can imagine. But I haven't written that out in the book; I'm leaving it mysterious. But the Commissaris realizes it, so then he falls asleep. The man who got shot is a Negro from Surinam, our ex-colony, so in this dream the Commissaris is in Surinam and he is in a corial — a kind of dugout canoe. There is a black cat in the boat with him and there's a vulture flying over, and he's having a marvelous time in this sort of landscape and suddenly he notices there's somebody with him in the boat. It's this little Dutch farmer about this high [indicating a midget] and he's wearing a black farmer's costume like I have, this corduroy stuff and little green buttons, and the farmer says, "Back to work." The Commissaris says, "What are you doing in this boat? Who needs you? Go away." He says, "How can I go back to work? The current is pushing the canoe. How can I row against it?" So next the corial is changing into one of those typical little flat rowboats we have in Holland, and the Commissaris is going through the canal and the farmer has become a smile and the smile fills the sky. The Commissaris says, "O.K., O.K." He wakes up and he knows he really has to do this: he's in Holland and that's his country. Exotic climes are very nice, but this is where he has to work and he really has to get at the police if necessary.

C: Do the Dutch take the monarchy seriously? As seriously as the British?

vdW: The country does, the country does. It's the mysticism of the Crown that's also very important. The Queen is tolerated in the cities and she's tolerated by the intellectuals, but there is tremendous force in the Crown. The Crown is the representative of God and you can't touch her and you can never charge her with anything and she has no power. She has veto right, but she's never used it. She is just this funny old lady who lives in a palace and hardly ever shows her face, but she's *there*. In the law they call it the Mysticism of the Crown, the mystic power of the Crown, and everything is done in her name. You wear the Queen's uniform and you're very conscious of it. I once embraced the Queen. It was a great moment in my life. I was in charge of the royal gate at a big football stadium and I had three military cops under me. I was a sergeant and the Queen arrived in her big American car with a military police escort. She's just a nice old lady in a fur coat, the mother of the present Queen. So she went in, but by that time everybody knew it was the royal gate, so when she came out, there was this enormous crowd. And they were squashing, squashing, squashing, getting closer and closer, and the corridor left to her car was just too narrow. She'd get mashed in there. So I embraced her and pushed her to her car. And I smelled her perfume. She smelled very nice. And she said, "Thank you, officer." But I actually embraced the Queen.

C: In England, you'd be taken to the Tower for doing that.

vdW: In England, I would get a decoration because I saved her. Then afterward I went home and for a week I told people I had embraced the Queen. My father was once asked to go to the palace with some other businessman. He'd just broken his leg, so he was swaddled with plaster. He came in as an invalid, put in a special chair. The Queen came over and said, "Did you break your leg?" Very obviously he had and she touched his leg. He came home and said, "I'll never take this plaster off. She touched it right here." I thought, "Silly old idiot." But when it happened to me, I felt the same thing.

C: What's next? What are you working on now?

vdW: That book — it's called *Street Bird*. Street Bird is the name of a vulture in Surinam, where this Negro guy comes from; it's always in the street because of all the crap lying in the street, and the people are very fond of it because it keeps the place clean. This black magician lives in Holland and has this vulture, so that's where I got the name for the book.

C: Are you ever going to write what's politely referred to as straight fiction?

vdW: I did. I wrote a book called *The Butterfly Hunter*. It's number two thousand in the paperback line of my Dutch publisher, and they're convinced I'll do very well with it. It's very different from the regular thrillers.

C: What's coming out next?

vdW: Well, we're trying to make a movie here in Dutch of *The Maine Massacre*, with American actors in some of the roles. *Outsider in Amsterdam* was a Dutch movie and was second only behind *Star Wars*. I have a book of short stories in Dutch that's sold fifteen thousand copies and I'm working on a very visual book called *Bliss and Bluster*. It's *very* weird.

MARK SMITH

Mark Smith, who was nominated for the National Book Award in 1973, was the recipient of a Rockefeller Foundation grant, and has written three masterpieces of characterization, all dealing with the psychopathology of both crime and goodness, redemption and damnation. He is one of the best-kept secrets of American letters. The "straight" fiction world took some notice, and deservedly so, of his novel *The Delphinium Girl*, but his three crime novels remain hidden from the average reader.

Toyland is about a college-educated assassin, Pehr, who claims at the beginning of the book that he hasn't forgotten his murders but "refuses to remember." His buddy, Jensen, and he have accepted a contract to kill two little kids, a girl named Iselin and a boy nicknamed Poor because his other nickname was Poor William. Their uncle wants them killed. All of Smith's crime novels are first of all exercises in the ability of the English language to describe, inflame, disorient, create a constant dissociative effect by metaphor and image piled upon metaphor and image, and explore all the dimensions of thought. Second of all, these three novels are built around philosophical and ethical problems that are heightened and given many more layers of subtlety by the rich, luxurious language that is their medium. They are not as accessible as other novels dealing with the themes of murder-for-hire, infanticide, and killing of other people for revenge. Thirdly, the novels are rich in the symbols that have come down to us from the classical, rabbinical, and patristic as well as apostolic writers. "Don't look back," Jensen says to Pehr after the first murder, warning him he'll turn into salt. Like Lot's wife. Smith is one of our most self-conscious, writerly writers, whose rich and varied style, while demanding, offers unusual rewards. Fourthly, the novels, especially *The Death of the Detective* and *Toyland*, owe much to Smith's love of the structure of opera and No plays, respectively.

The young writer has much to learn from *Toyland*: Smith's narrative strategy, his use of the situation for a meditation on guilt and redemption that is never, never boring, and his careful, meticulous characterizations. And if the beginning writer doesn't know now that novel-length exercise in characterization is a confrontation of the most desperate, brutal kind with one's own soul, then a careful reading of *Toyland* should have a wholly salutary effect.

The Middleman is the "first" of the novels (although published in 1967, two years after *Toyland*), because it is here we meet Uncle Walter, who wants the children murdered. Uncle Walter lives in the basement and plays with his electric train set. The kids, being kids, would like to play with it, too. So Uncle Walter decides to bump them off. Now, Uncle Walter has problems, but Smith does not take the easy way out and make him a figure of black humor. Smith makes him evil, and then deals brilliantly and creatively with the problems of his evil. One of the many remarkable things about *The Middleman*, which is more an exercise in words and word play than is *Toyland*, is the wonderfully rendered scene in which Uncle Walter leaves his body and becomes a citizen of the village, full of small lead figures, of course, through which his toy trains rumble and clack.

The Death of the Detective has been compared to the writings of Dickens. It bears up well under the comparison. The pure, joyous invention of character and incident is marvelous. But it is, more to the point, just as frightening, just as purely a creation of operatic melodrama, and just as much a game of art as is *Creature from the Black Lagoon*: the black lagoon in this case being the murky depths of modern life in Chicago, in which a retired cop, now head of a security agency, must find a crazed murderer. The story is interrupted from time to time by a variety of digressions Smith makes for multiple purposes. Every page seems as desperate a contest between the novelist and his vast sprawl of material as could be imagined; still, Smith does harness this raw power. There is not another American novel like it.

Smith now lives in York Harbor, Maine, in a wonderful old Victorian wooden mansion of the type used in the nineties as a summer home for a twenty-member family. When this interview was conducted, the place was full of kids, Smith's impressive collection of European and American impressionist paintings, and papers from the classes he teaches at the University of New Hampshire, where he heads the creative writing program.

CARR: Let's get your biography straight first. I couldn't find a satisfactory reference work for you. You were born in Michigan, though.

SMITH: Yeah, in 1935 in a town called Charlevoix, which is in Hemingway country. It's right across Lake Charlevoix from where Hemingway spent the summers. It's a resort town, something like a nice Maine resort town, right on the lake, a wealthy resort town. It's the setting of *The Middleman*. I went to six different colleges as an undergraduate. I started out at Western Michigan in Kalamazoo and then moved back to Chicago and took courses at Wright Junior College and the University of Chicago and Northwestern University. In fact, I went to both campuses of the University of Chicago, and both campuses of Northwestern, which totals up to six, and then I graduated from Northwestern in 1960. I was twenty-four or twenty-five years old. I'd been in the merchant marine briefly, on Lake Michigan, and gotten hurt, broken my pelvis in an accident, so I was laid off for a couple of years. That's when I did all my reading.

C: Had you always wanted to be a writer?

S: Well, I was interested in being an artist of some kind when I was very young. My first love, I guess, was either music or writing, and then I got sidetracked in later years in grammar school, when it was no longer fashionable to be a good student or interested in art. But I don't regret having gone through that course of my life at all. And then when I got to college I became much more interested in the life of the mind, eventually. But I think I went through what a lot of fellows went through back then. Originally I wanted to be an anthropologist and then in the humanities in some way. And then I wanted to be a professor, a poet-critic, and by the time I was a senior in college I decided this was not for me. I had to get out of there. And if I'd been an honest man, I would have probably quit my senior year and not finished, but I'm very grateful that I did because I never would have gotten a job.

C: That little union card never hurts.

S: That's right, and now you need an M.F.A. or even a Ph.D., but back then you at least had to have a B.A. Then I went off to write — to be a poet. And then I attempted short stories. I gave up on the poetry and wrote a number of short stories.

C: In the early sixties?

S: Yes. In a very fertile period of my life; for a year or two there I wrote every day. I wrote about thirty novels, novellas, beginnings of novels, and finally came to the conclusion that the novel was a more comfortable form for me. I wrote *Toyland*, which at the time was two novels — the first half was *Toyland* and the other *The Middleman* — and I've been writing novels ever since.

C: Are there people who for various reasons are more comfortable in the longer forms than in the short forms and vice versa?

S: I would think so. If you don't know how to end a scene or drop a character . . . I think the more interested you are in character, the more you're driven to the novel. Or if you're more interested in a number of characters or complicated actions and plots, or what you hope is a larger vision of life.

C: There's some confusion now, though, isn't there? Because I see short stories that are the equivalent of someone being ordered to do the minuet when he'd rather be running the 440. I guess young writers, now that the short story outlets are gone, are turning en masse to the form but without the benefit of many actually published examples, which results in the abandonment of the form, although they don't realize it. Isn't it true that if you have a good novel, you'd get it published a lot quicker than you would a story in *Antaeus*?

S: Well, you'd make more money.

C: Right. But isn't it probably true that you could probably get a decent novel published at least as quickly as you could a short story?

S: Well, probably sooner than in a commercial magazine where they really pay you some money, that's true. There are any number of small press publications that print short stories. In fact, yes, short stories have suffered the same fate as poetry — publishing a short story in a little magazine is like publishing a poem: there's really no commercial market for them. That may be one of the reasons I didn't go into short story writing. When I first started writing, you sold your first novel and your advance was $1,500, I think, on the average.

C: That's in '63, '64?

S: Yeah. And you weren't going to get any more money than that. That was it.

C: And at that, they'd probably exceeded themselves.

S: And they'd probably lose money. But there were a

number of magazines back then, maybe half a dozen or so, who, if they bought your short story, would pay you $2,000 or $2,500. When I started out, you only needed about $5,000 a year to live on, and you could make that if you'd written a story for the *Post* and a story for *Esquire*. Or *Collier's*. Or the *New Yorker*.

C: There was a lot of market.

S: There was a lot of market back then and they paid fairly well, and now those magazines — there are fewer of them — are still paying the same wages they paid twenty years ago.

C: Some people have decided, in the years since that scene vanished into the mist, that short stories have gotten better because they're now published in the little mags. Do you think they've gotten better for being less commercially intended? Do you think the quality has improved by their having been virtually driven underground?

S: I don't think the quality of anything has ever been improved by being driven underground. I think probably work is at its best — I mean good work — when it has a fairly large audience. I think the best American short stories I've read are by Faulkner, and Faulkner's not really considered a short story writer. I really like "That Evening Sun."

C: Did you later turn to his novels?

S: Well, no, I read the novels first, most of the novels, with a few exceptions. There are a couple of Faulkner novels I've never been able to read. I won't tell you what they are.

C: I bet one of them's *Absalom, Absalom!*

S: You're darn right it is. I don't know how many times I've read the first forty pages. But about short stories: I really don't know about short stories. I teach them. All my students write short stories but they're quite good and they have a very high level of competence. Well, we had three students in this last year who published novels. And we only admit about six students a year to the program. We are very selective, so I see good student work, but I really don't keep up with the literary journals, where the stories are by people in writing programs and professors. I just don't have the time.

C: I often wondered how you get a handle on it. It seems to me you could probably give away half your year's salary subscribing to them and then half your year reading them.

S: Some people do that. I know poets who do that and short story writers who publish pretty much only in the literary magazines, and that is their life, that's where their action is. They know who's publishing what and what magazines are out and they sit in the library and read them if they don't subscribe to them themselves, but I don't.

C: Let me ask you about the sequence of your novels.

S: Actually, before I published *Toyland*, I wrote *The Death of the Detective* as a kind of novella. It was simply the plot of the detective who was called out on the case and found this quiet murder, which led only to . . . and so on. It was an abstraction, the bare bones of the plot, or at least Magnuson's plot. I wrote that as kind of an existential novella and perhaps something of a satire on detective novels. Especially the plots. Not much, though. I set that aside and decided to make a novel of this idea, of this character, of this plot after I wrote *Toyland*. I began *The Death of the Detective*, maybe fifty or sixty pages of it, and it was just awful. I put it away and decided, I'd go back and write a final draft of *The Middleman*. I figured if I didn't do it now, while I was still a young man, when I was dumb enough to do it, I'd never do it. *The Middleman* is not really a mystery. It's written from the point of view of the man the murderers get the children from in *Toyland*, which was first. Actually, I wrote them both at the same time and then split them up. I wrote them as one novel, then split them up into two.

C: That's a great ending to *Toyland*. The guy was just wandering around, numb, unable to assume any responsibility for the kids, and you say the kids are going to "regelate together" — refreeze together. One of the most macabre, and funny, scenes is the moment when the two murderers have to kill a man and the rifle is flawed. The guy's able to elude their bad marksmanship and then the gunman smashes the rifle against the tree and has to go in and clobber him with his pistol. The only thing I had some misgivings about was the level of diction maintained by the bad guys.

S: Well, I think in those early books I was exaggerating naturalism a little more, especially in *Toyland*. I think the older I get, the more naturalistic I become, the fewer freedoms I take with that kind of exaggeration, with reality. But in *Toyland* I wanted to have intelligent murderers; therefore, I had them speak perhaps more intelligently than they could naturalistically.

C: And they know their opera pretty well.

S: Exactly. But I tried to set it up originally, as I recall, from the first page, because it's written from Pehr's point of view: first person, his language, his perceptions. He sees Jensen as making gestures as if they were in Kabuki — stylized. His whole vision is stylized.

C: There's this horrible thing: a white marble figure of a man is lying beside him when he wakes up from a dream. He puts his hand out and hits this thing and thinks it's a man, an enemy, but it is a statue and falls through all the floors of this rotten house down to the basement, where it breaks into pieces, and that's a kind of surrealistic stylization of his own body.

S: Certainly an image of himself. It was much more surrealistic than anything I've done since. I think in all my novels I have a tendency to begin them exaggerating naturalism, and I also have a tendency to begin them much more comically than eventually they turn out to be. I've always thought of myself as a comic writer. I think I'm never far from being comic at the moments when I'm most serious, but I don't know whether this comes off or not.

C: Oh, it does, yes.

S: But it is hard to pull off. It either happens naturally, I think, or it doesn't make it, but I have started off thinking a novel is going to be a little bit more fantastic and comic than eventually it turns out to be.

C: Is it just that a full-fledged novel with a certain density and length defeats the comedy? I'm not saying it defeats it in your work, as *The Death of the Detective* proves, but that novel is not exactly a zany novelette — I love that word "zany" — like the little novel that *M*A*S*H* was based on.

S: No, it wasn't meant to be that at all. I think when you start off with a novel, you're making something out of it; it's fiction and you haven't really established the ground rules yet of how your story is going to work as it relates to naturalism, and I think that if you're making things up, you tend to pump things up. For example, I have noticed that when I begin a novel, I'll use a lot of metaphors. I'll overdescribe scenes. I could spend three pages describing the setting.

C: I like that.

S: But eventually I have to go back and cut that down a bit.

C: Are you saying that your rhetorical devices — metaphors, images, similes — thin out toward the end? As they well might, because the action has to take over at that point, I presume.

S: Probably, but take those out of, say, Raymond Chandler, and you've got nothing.

C: Yes. When Marlowe says, "I felt like an amputated leg," that's much better than describing it à la Spillane, and there's that wonderful description of Moose Molloy looking as out of place "as a tarantula on a piece of angel food cake."

S: Or the description of that black man's fist as being the size and color of an eggplant. It would have been simpler just to say he raised his fist.

C: If you were just interested in all dialogue.

S: I think one of the great pleasures of my life was reading through Raymond Chandler's works.

C: When did you discover Chandler?

S: Well, I actually read several of his books when I was

younger, I think in my teens, and then it must have been about fifteen years ago that I rediscovered him and then I read right through everything. I wish he'd written more novels. I can't believe he wrote so few. And with somebody like Chandler, the great attraction is this picture of the thirties and of California, those streets and the little bungalows and villas and the gardens that the people have: it creates a whole world. He's showing Americans in California who have been influenced by movies and who are imitating the cinema in the way they talk and the way they act: the tough guy image they try to present. But speaking of images and description, I've always had a strong sense of locality. Like Chandler. But I don't think Chandler is a very successful detective story writer. I wouldn't look at Chandler for that reason. I think Chandler's great strength is his style, which is original, but very American, and is flawed. It isn't terribly good, but it's what is important in reading him. If he wrote flat sentences, you wouldn't read him. And his style is part of his vision. He's completely tied up with his vision of California and life at that time in America and Hollywood. But as for the mystery, that's always at war with his mystery plot. It's incidental, I think, with Chandler. Chandler is one of those writers who was caught with the formula and I think he did quite well with it, but could he have done otherwise? I doubt it.

But back to this sense of place. You have to make this come alive for yourself, whether it's Chicago or the Michigan woods, in order for your story to exist, for your people to breathe. I couldn't set it in such a rarefied atmosphere that only called for my saying "the street."

C: Yes, fiction has resisted the rarefied atmosphere throughout most of its history, hasn't it? Fiction should be set in some kind of world that has angles and edges to it.

S: I believe in a very particular world, even though eventually you make your own world. Dickens's London is not really London, but it's Dickens's London.

C: Let's get back to the order of your novels for a second.

S: I wrote *The Middleman* in about six months, which made me think I could turn out a novel at least every year. I was greatly misled by that. *The Death of the Detective* came out seven years after that. Then after *The Middleman* was finished, I began the novel that was to become *The Moon Lamp.*

C: Which is something of a ghost novel.

S: It has a supernatural element or pretends to — I'm not certain what. I'm not sure myself about it. I worked on that for a while, almost a year, and it was the only time I really got bogged down in a novel. Really stuck. What I was writing wasn't really good; I was going nowhere. One of the main problems was that what I really have to do when I write is run through a draft and get everything down in black and white, then I can go over it and revise it at my leisure. At least I know it's done. There it is. I've got something to work with. The writing of *The Moon Lamp* stemmed from my beginning to teach for the first time, to actually teach writing, to be conscious of what writing was all about.

C: In '68 and '69 at the University of New Hampshire?

S: Yes. So I was revising it as I went along. I was polishing each page. And it didn't work. So I abandoned that novel, set it aside to pick up later, and then went back to *The Death of the Detective* and that became five years' work, writing that novel.

C: It looks like fifty years' work. It's incredible.

S: And the vision then became much broader.

C: You mentioned in your letter that the Crime Writers' Association asked you to join. Was that after *Toyland*?

S: No, after *The Death of the Detective.*

C: I wonder if they knew about *Toyland* and *The Middleman*?

S: Probably not. The books were not very successful and they didn't go into paperback. They only sold a couple of thousand copies each. Of course, they're out in paperback now. Because Avon had been quite successful with the paperback of *The Death of the Detective*, they bought my other two books, my first two novels, and gave them kind of thriller covers.

C: One of the copyrights cited for *The Death of the Detective* is 1973.

S: That was for a section of it that was published in *Audience*, a now defunct hardback magazine.

C: *The Death of the Detective* is a real Chicago novel, too. The essence of Chicago, as I believe *Absalom, Absalom!* is the essence of the ante-bellum South.

S: I hope it is.

C: One of the things that convinces me of your immersion in the place is that you've figured out, recorded, whatever, aspects of that city's social psychology. At one point Magnuson comments on Chicago men. He says they'll get into little groups and ridicule someone.

S: Well, it was true for those characters in the novel. Certainly it was true to my observations and experiences in Chicago. Whether it would correspond with everyone's observation I don't know, but I think in the Midwest, and in the South and Southwest, there's much more macho pressure on a man than I think there is in the East. That's very true in Chicago. If you want to put a man down, you get at his manhood somehow.

C: Especially in bars.

S: Especially in bars.

C: But *The Death of the Detective* is a detective story, and a good one, and it fulfills those expectations: there's a resolution at the end and there are murders, some of them really gruesome. But there are scenes in there that are absolutely surrealistic; for instance, the scene in which Magnuson goes to the mansion to talk to the old man's nurse, who's so doped up she almost has steam coming out of her ears, and that's just the beginning of one of the most bizarre scenes I've ever read. There are other passages like that. It's almost Gothic in its affect. Was that conscious on your part? Did you determine that this was going to have a mood and a tone radically different from other detective stories?

S: Well, I must have. I don't think I consciously made it Gothic, although I suspect there are several metaphors that even use the word "Gothic."

C: We were talking about tone, mood, and so on. When you decided to write what almost became the detective novel to end all detective novels, did you think about using somewhat more involved and High Style language than 90 percent of the detective novels in print, some of which are written to the eighth-grade level, unfortunately?

S: In any of my writing I'm more concerned, I think, with creating mood than tone. Mood . . . I know it's out there. I can imagine it and I've got to get it. The sentences are put together in such a way, and words are chosen, to create a kind of palpable atmosphere. Tone is the author's attitude toward his material, I would assume, and not a certain quality, as in music or in a tone poem. What I wanted to do in *The Death of the Detective* was to use a great range of moods, styles, techniques, points of view. I knew it was going to be a big novel and I wanted to be able at any time to have certain freedoms to do what I wanted to do. I think this came as a consequence of having written two novels in the first person, which is extremely limiting. And I find it very frustrating, at least after two novels. So I'm back to writing an eight-hundred-page, first-person novel, but, again, I've chosen a narrator who's intelligent enough and articulate enough so that he can adopt a great many styles. He's not limited to one very confining voice and he can also see himself in the third person and the second person.

C: That's great.

S: You get smarter as you go along, but of course you lose the passion. You don't have the old fire. You have better taste and better discretion and, I think, more skills, but I'm not certain you have the passion you once had.

C: Let's talk about *The Death of the Detective* again, speaking of passion. Magnuson is a creep character, frightening in many ways.

S: In what way do you mean?

C: Well, first of all, he's alienated even from the men you'd think he'd have something in common with, like all those guys you see in the scene that opens up his section of the novel. And while they're in the living room, playing cards, he's stretched out on the bed, thinking woeful thoughts. *The Death of the Detective* is a very naturalistic novel, and what goes with naturalism, whether it's dictated by that vision of the world or not we won't get into, is the attitude of being spoiled, soured, ravaged by the world. Do you agree? Disagree?

S: You force me to think of a great many novels, but I think if we identify naturalism with Zola, or say "Naturalism," in caps, that would be true. It would also be true to a certain extent with Dreiser, who would write "naturalism," in lower case.

C: Right, and James Jones, the last American naturalist.

S: James Jones, perhaps, but I think *The Death of the Detective* is basically naturalistic with its surrealistic or operatic elements.

C: Operatic. I'm glad you brought that up.

S: And I hope all those elements blend into one vision so that I can get from one to the other and back again without leaving one sticking out of place.

C: It's a really unique vision of the world and its inhabitants because there really isn't any clear-cut, clean ending. They bury him and O'Bannon has to take care of some of the details. He has to hire these poor guys as mourners, really, and pallbearers, which is their function, and these mourner-pallbearers are not too happy about pulling this duty and half of them are boozed up. You make a great scene, incidentally, out of a small action that many another writer would dismiss in a couple of sentences. It is the perfect ending to a life that has been futile in some respects, tragic in others, comic in others, heroic in yet other respects, much like the lives of most of us.

S: I saw him very much as a kind of Chicago character and, I hoped, as ultimately a very American character, and I simply wanted to catalogue his experiences in this adventure — his awakening, his discoveries, as he went along in life.

C: Let's pick up one thing: the operatic quality. It is kind of an operatic novel and apparently you're quite a fan of opera: Jensen in *Toyland* even remarks to the other murderer that you're either a character in this opera or another one; make up your mind. Then in *The Death of the Detective*, Fiorio is the one person you use to articulate this aspect of giving directions to the audience from one of the characters. Did you write it as an opera without a score?

S: No, not deliberately. A friend of mine, after he read it, said it was very operatic and I said, "Well, you're right." I think what he meant by that and what I meant is that opera is life very much exaggerated, stylized, and I think there is that element in *The Death of the Detective*. Maybe it's the dominant element, but, as I say, there's that element, along with the more naturalistic stories; for example, the gangster plots — the gangster subplot is all done pretty naturalistically.

S: Some of the chapters that concern Magnuson, especially when he's investigating the murder, become a little more surrealistic or operatic or exaggerated.

C: The slaughter of the sheep is a terrific scene, but it left me almost physically ill. That's a real blood-and-guts novel: first they slaughter the sheep and then they slaughter Fiorio, literally, as if he too were a sheep. To go from pathos to bathos, do you know anything about slaughtering? You must if you're an aficionado of Chicago institutions.

S: Well, actually, what I know about butchering didn't come from Chicago but from living on something of a small farm in New Hampshire. We had our own sheep and pigs that were slaughtered constantly.

C: They're butchering Fiorio and someone says to break up the offal. I began to see how you work with metaphors.

S: I like that chapter very much. I haven't read it in years but maybe my two favorite chapters of that book are the killing of Tanker and then the killing of Fiorio. It seemed to me the chapters were very well written.

C: I liked that chapter early in the book about the old couple who are advanced alcoholics, who love to drink beer and for a long time have gone to exquisite lengths to hide their beer from each other. The husband's method for discovering hidden caches of suds is to bang away at the sofa and chairs until something dribbles out that looks like beer. You really get into what you're doing!

S: Well, when I first wrote a number of short stories, I thought of myself as a very literary writer. *I* would never publish in anything as distasteful as a commercial magazine. So I sent out a batch of these stories to the little magazines. And of course they abused me, lost my manuscripts, sent me standard rejection slips ten months later, wrote me insulting letters. I remember the only commercial magazine I sent a story to was *Esquire*. I got a letter back in ten days, saying nice things about the story and saying if I could rewrite it, they'd want to see it again. So I did. They still didn't like it, but I remember the fellow in his letter said that the one thing he'd liked about the opening scene was that it was fully realized.

And that somehow clicked in me: this is what you have to do. If you're going to have something in your novel or your story, then it ought to be fully realized; you ought to know what *can* be gotten out of it and *how much* you should get out of it.

C: Right. That's what I love about *The Death of the Detective*. Everything, every action, every gesture, every thought, is fully realized. You've gotten every ounce out of the situation.

S: Maybe you're saying I'm not a good editor.

C: No, the hell with that. I hate attenuated writing without even description or limited exposition.

S: I think if it's done well — attenuation — I like it very much. It's a quality I don't seem to really possess, but I do admire it. *Child of God* by Cormack McCarthy is a beautifully edited book.

C: That's what Hemingway wanted all of us to do, wasn't it? Leave out and leave out and leave out. Unfortunately, some of his latter-day disciples are leaving out everything but dialogue, most of it in simple sentences brightened here and there by a compound sentence. Do you really think that Hemingway's advice is all that perfect now; that the real writer leaves everything out, or at least as much as he can except that one telling detail? Isn't that more for writers of short stories? Maybe even writers of short shorts?

S: It's certainly very true for short story writers. I tend to write even longer novels than the final product.

C: Was there a longer version of *The Death of the Detective*?

S: Yes. I think I cut out about two hundred pages. And not two hundred pages in any one section or several sections: just knocking out a paragraph here and there. I think there is a quality of editing to writing. For example, in the novel I'm working on now I notice I have a tendency to write one sentence more than I need to write in a paragraph. Instead of ending it where I should have, I tack on another sentence. I think that the ability to edit is very necessary, but Hemingway's advice wouldn't really be pertinent to any writer. When you write a sentence or a scene, something in you says that's what I want, that's how to do it, that's me. And you simply keep working at it until it is you. I can't write leanly. I started out as a devotee of Hemingway's. In fact, the first story I published was a shameful Hemingway imitation: lean and spare and with a thirty-word vocabulary. But it wasn't me. It took a long time before I realized that what I had to write was something a little richer than that.

C: Did your editor try to steer you away from what he or she must have seen as genre writing? Did they say that you were going to have trouble with *The Death of the Detective* because you were falling between two stools?

S: No one has ever mentioned that to me and I've had a number of editors and publishers. I've thought about that myself. When you write something like *The Death of the Detective* or *The Moon Lamp,* which —

C: That's sort of genre, too.

S: It's sort of genre, too. Certainly it was promoted as a kind of genre novel. My ghost novel . . . "Smith does for the ghost novel what he did for the detective novel." I thought that's how they might promote it and I kind of wish they had promoted it that way, but they didn't because the two novels are so different from each other that the publishers were very much afraid people would be disappointed. They wanted *Son of Death of the Detective, Death of the Detective Redux.*

C: *Death of the Detective Gets Rich.*

S: That's right. And I was giving them something altogether different. But even so, I had rather hoped that the publishers would rather dishonestly promote it by saying, "What Smith did for the detective novel he now does for the ghost novel." That didn't happen. But I think when you're writing these particular kinds of books, the illusion is that you're going to hit both markets. That's the illusion from the writer's point of view — that the general market's going to like it because it's just generally good fiction.

C: And a good book.

S: Good book, right. And the detective story buffs are going to buy it; in the case of *The Moon Lamp,* the ghost story buffs are going to buy it. I think that worked probably for *The Death of the Detective*; it didn't work for *The Moon Lamp.* The danger is that the general reading public is turned off because it's got too much of the genre element in it and the genre enthusiasts are turned off because it isn't *their* kind of genre book. It's got more in it than they want.

C: Better writing, too.

S: And it's more interested in character and incident.

C: That leads me into something I've asked everybody. Do you think there is a difference between genre writing, especially in our case detective writing, and so-called straight literature?

S: Oh of course. I think good genre does follow the formula and is successful within that formula, not that it has to obey its clichés. It shouldn't follow the clichés. For example, if you're writing a detective novel, you don't necessarily have to have a detective in a trench coat whose sidekick, the police sergeant, is a dummy. Or if you're writing the English detective novel, your detective doesn't necessarily have to be an amateur, an effete aristocrat, like Lord Peter or any of the others. The convention by definition is not naturalistic; it does not reflect life, except in the most incidental way. When you try to go beyond that, when you try to impose real life on this unreal form, it doesn't work. I think in reading a whodunit, you read simply to find out how the plot works out. Who did it? You play that game. And you look for a writer who knows how to play that game well and reasonably originally within the genre. I also happen to like the pictures of Old World villages, the country houses and the gardens that you get in the English novels of the twenties and thirties, but you don't really read that novel for that reason — to see what it's like to be alive on a farm in Shropshire, to grow up with a mother who's an alcoholic, what it feels like to abort your child and be arrested for the crime. You don't read the novels for those experiences. Now there are attempts on the part of, I think, a lot of American contemporary writers to combine the two. Chandler is a good example of that. Another example among English mystery writers — whom I'm more familiar with — was Dorothy Sayers, especially when in a novel like *Gaudy Night* she attempts to write a serious novel. It doesn't work. I think she was more successful in a novel like *Murder Must Advertise*, where there is the metaphor that selling cigarettes to the public through advertising is like selling dope. But I think Sayers's best novels are those that don't attempt to go beyond the genre except to teach you how to ring bells in

England or play cricket. Another English writer who wrote very well was Margery Allingham, and she was always attempting to make her novels carry more weight than they possibly could with her implausible detective and her implausible plots. So I think that's essentially the difference between writing what we call straight fiction and genre fiction. I think genre fiction is by nature unreal and can be very successful.

C: But people are turning to it, even writers who wouldn't have had this thought twenty years ago, or before Ross Macdonald appeared on the cover of *Newsweek* magazine in 1970. A lot of people are turning to it and readers are turning to it. What does that say about America, if anything?

S: I think every novel Thomas Berger has written has been a play on some kind of genre, hasn't it? He did a detective novel —

C: *Who Killed Teddy Villanova.*

S: Right, and he did a wonderful Western. I don't know whether it's part of the American scene right now to be interested in that sort of thing. There is a tendency on the part of critics and writers to glorify the genre form and to consider it as serious fiction, as was the case with Eudora Welty's admiration for Ross Macdonald, and a lot of people's for Chandler. I don't feel they are writing serious fiction. I think you've got to accept them for the kinds of writers they are within the genre.

C: There's another thing I've wondered about. And I'm not sure there's an answer. Why do many writers, even writers who've done something else literary before, turn to detective fiction rather late in life? Relatively late. Say when they're forty. I asked the two women who write as Emma Lathen why that may be so and they said they hadn't really wanted to write about their emotional development and their childhoods or about the towns they came from, and that they began to write when they had a solid grasp of how business works. To cite someone else, Dick Francis, of course, was a jockey. Janwillem van de Wetering was a cop in the Netherlands, and had also been in business. He began writing in his late thirties. And you wrote this novel, which certainly fulfills genre expectations, at about the same age. Why?

S: Well, I think most detective novel writers — and I'm not one of them — have another career. In England usually they're Oxford dons or Dante scholars or poets laureate who turn to mystery writing as a sideline, and to make some money. I don't know why — I've always been interested in detective novels. I read them when I was a kid and I think there's always a mystery and a detective element in any book I've written and probably will write. I can't seem to get away from it. It's like a smoking pistol — what did some critic keep telling Chekhov — get rid of the pistol? And he never could. I can't either. Maybe someday I'll write something where I don't have to have a pistol. It could just be mentioned [*laughs*].

C: Well, even *The Delphinium Girl*, which is a beautiful book, ends in a death, really. And the mystery is an eschatological, or existential, mystery. Why do we have to die? Why do I have to die? Why now? Did you feel that was a major burden of the novel, that kind of theological mystery in a book that was not otherwise heavily plotted?

S: *The Delphinium Girl* was not plotted at all. In fact, there was a deliberate attempt on my part to write a novel that did not have a strong narrative. All my other novels have had strong narratives. Some people have even said that's my greatest strength, or my only strength — pure narrative power. So whether out of stupidity or not, I decided to write a novel that would *not* have so much pure narrative power. I wanted to see if the writing and the reader's interest in the characters themselves could carry the novel. I didn't want to write a heavily plotted novel, and maybe in a way it was a reaction against creating a mystery with a strong plot. Or a mystery plot that has a strong mystery element; mystery is something much more subtle and doesn't really rely upon the incidence of plot. Nothing really happens in *The Delphinium Girl* except that she gets sick. And dies, eventually.

C: Perhaps that's action enough. How much action is there in "The Lady with the Dog"? How was Russia, Dr. Chekhov? We're not told and there is no melodrama, no images, really, very little whippy dialogue. But it's masterful in the way *The Delphinium Girl* is.

S: But I hope the reader will become interested in the milieu, in the problems presented in a novel of contemporary life in America, and in the characters and how they're all going to work this out, or respond to her illness, her death. But, anyway, I'm now back to my strong narrative.

C: What are you working on now?

S: I'm working on a long novel called *Dr. Blues*. It's a first-person narrative. It does have something of a mystery element in it, or two mystery elements. One has to do with a murder that takes place on Mystery Hill, which is the site of what may be European prehistoric ruins — stone ruins — in New Hampshire. The narrator is an academic, a prehistorian, at the university and he's called into the case to help out the police. This isn't the main part of the novel; it's part of the plot, and eventually he is suspected by the police, too.

C: That's a good old turn that honors the conventions.

S: So there is that twist.

C: And this is a fairly long novel?

S: Yes, not as long as *The Death of the Detective*, but it'll probably be six hundred pages — about seven hundred typewritten pages.

C: What's the main plot?

S: Well, it's so amorphous, it's so sloppy, that it's hard for me to articulate. I suppose though if I could articulate the plot of something as messy and complicated as this, it wouldn't be messy and complicated, and it wouldn't exist, either. It's a kind of quest novel. A character finds himself rather isolated late in life and is wondering how his life worked out this way. The opening sentence is "Lately I have had the feeling that I have lived my life the only way I could have lived it while managing at the same time to live my life all wrong." The whole novel is predicated on that sentence, so we have to find out not only what his life has been and what it's like but what he imagines it should have been.

C: That's great. That's a mystery. It's the same mystery we all face.

S: Plus, he's grown up with his mother, who's a lawyer and a great storyteller, who's told him over the years as a kind of joke (you don't know but maybe it is) that he came from the sea, that he was a kind of gift from the sea. It's the story of having been left on the doorstep, which I was told as a child, and it used to terrify me. They used to say, "Well, you know, I'm not your mother; you were left on the doorstep."

C: That's very interesting. That happens to a character in *The Death of the Detective*, and there's a family betrayal in *Toyland* and *The Middleman*. Is that family thing buried in your own past?

S: It may well be. I suppose this is one of the elements that's fair play for the critics: something that the writer reveals of himself.

C: No. I'm saying that when you see a theme developed over and over and over again, you begin to believe it's probably part of the writer's soul.

S: I don't blame you, and it's a bit scary to discover that you are repeating themes. Or now and then you seem to be doing a scene or a character in a way that you've done before. You say, "Why am I doing this again?" But then you don't want to think about those things. A writer, if he's writing honestly, is going to reveal himself, even in genre fiction. And you can't help but do it. I think if you ever stopped and were able to psychoanalyze yourself and articulate your deepest fears and motivations, I don't think that I, anyway, would write anymore. It's something I really don't want to know too much about. I know it's there, but it's not for me to discover or to concern myself with. I think writing fiction is an unnatural and probably unhealthy exercise. That's why it amazes me that·so many people, especially housewives, want to become fiction writers in their spare time.

C: Oh yes. In their spare time.

S: If I had my druthers, I think, looking back on what I've done, I would probably prefer to have been a shepherd or a gardener, not to sit down every day and deny the real world, which is what you do. Why am I not out there sailing today? I sit here every day and say, "Gee, I wish I were out there." Why am I making up this story with these make-believe people and this make-believe world that I'm trying to make true, that I'm devoting all my effort to to make real?

C: Your world doesn't suit you?

S: Must not.

C: Or maybe there is no book in your library you enjoy reading better than your own and that's why you write a lot of your own.

S: Well, why should I even be driven to write books? Why shouldn't I go out and garden?

C: Or read?

S: But I do think that somewhere along the line something has to be a little wrong with you to devote yourself to spending so much time to writing fiction. I don't think it's the way life was meant to be lived.

C: Plumbers probably think that too after ten years of crawling around under houses. But I know what you mean: it's like that belief of the German romantics that artists are society's sickness.

S: I'm not familiar with that theory, but I think I could very quickly accept it. And the way we become the spokesmen or voices of society. In *The Delphinium Girl*, the writer, Stargaard, poses this problem again and again. What am I doing sitting down? Of course he's an autobiographical writer and he's writing about his own life, things that have already happened. He's dredging it all up, sitting in his study, regretting he can't be out living his life.

C: What about that guy in *The Death of the Detective* who

goes to see his mother? This weird old poet resembles Roethke staggering around the insane asylum. He's a writer, or we think he's a writer — a poet. And that figure occurs again and again in your fiction.

S: I think so. Again, that's a theme that keeps cropping up, and when you're aware it's making a reappearance, you say, "Well, what does this mean?" But you try not to answer the question.

C: And obviously you haven't edited it out.

S: Haven't edited it out. I think it belongs there if it fits in somehow. Every time Charlie Simic, a colleague of mine at U.N.H., reads one of my books he says, "You really do a job on poets."

C: That's true.

S: Poets always come off very badly. Maybe that goes back to my being a frustrated poet, wanting to be a poet at first and failing at it.

C: Faulkner said novelists were ruined poets. That was his case anyhow.

S: Well, that was mine, too. My problem with my poetry was that I couldn't find my own voice. I think the university was in good measure responsible for this, along with T. S. Eliot. My poems tend to be very academic and I always disguise my voice. How can you be a poet if you don't find your own voice and present it? I mean, a poet *is* his voice, and becomes the voice of the race; that's what makes poetry successful, and here I was — am — hiding my voice behind a mask. I read the book *Yeats: The Man Behind the Mask* and I subscribe to the theory that a poem was a kind of mask.

C: Have you thought about going back to poetry, now that it's changed?

S: For years I did. For years I had the notion that I'd be like Thomas Hardy: I would write half a dozen novels and make all kinds of money, then I would return to my first love, poetry.

C: And look at nice little thrushes.

S: Thrushes in the hedgerow, sorrowful little yew trees. But somewhere along the line, half a dozen or ten years ago, I realized this was not to be the case. I would never write poetry again and should not write poetry again. For better *and* worse, I was going to write fiction. I think the same is true of writing screenplays. When you're a younger writer, you realize that's where the action is. You're not yet committed to teaching in a university for the rest of your life. Maybe you've had a couple of film offers; people are asking whether you want to do a screenplay. And you say, "Well, that's a possibility. I could be a screenwriter *and* a fiction writer." But I've given up on that, too. I'll never write a screenplay. I'll never write poetry.

C: What do you tell young writers about writing? Their lives? Girls? Boys?

S: Well, I don't interfere in their personal lives at all or give them any advice. And I just hope they don't ask. My idea in teaching young writers — especially the students in the graduate writing program and the good undergraduate writers — is that it's my job to find out who *they* are as writers, to let *them* find out who they are as writers, to adapt myself to them and give them my criticism.

C: There's another level after you teach them to write decent, workmanlike English, which I think can be taught just as an artist can teach a tyro perspective and a ballerina can teach a little girl a way to dance on her toes, that gets into helping them tap into the unconscious.

S: Well, that would be off-the-page criticism. I like to confine myself pretty much to the page.

C: There are people who teach mental loosening-up exercises. What do you want most in the world right now? What do you hate about your life right now? Mix that up and you've got theme and plot. Imagine yourself in a brownstone in the Village and what animal you like best and remember something you never had as a child. Improvisations, like those in acting classes.

S: Well, I would never do that. To me it would be artificial and an imposition. But I would say that my criticism is not textual. I don't go sentence by sentence with a student. I think that can be beneficial, but you easily become a proofreader and copy editor, and you don't want to do that. That's not my business. I would ask a student, "Would your character really have done that?"

C: Logic problems.

S: Yes, and being true to your character. "Would this have really happened at the end? Is this the way to end this story? Do you have to end a story with your character shooting himself? Would he shoot himself?" You say, "Isn't it possible he might think about shooting himself and not do it, and wouldn't that make a more believable story? And more real?" It's more questions like that. Or you ask them whether this somehow really is a story. What *is* the story here?

C: Has anyone ever, since they've all probably read your books —

S: You're assuming too much.

C: Has anyone ever come to you and said, "Gee, Mr. Smith, help me write a detective novel"?

S: Yes. Someone asked me that the other day. I was coming down the main street of Durham. This happens very rarely, but he said he'd had a dream the night before about a body being discovered somewhere and thought it would be a wonderful detective story. I said, "Why don't you write it up?" He said, "I prefer to tell it to you because you write so well and you should write it for me." But that's the only time I can remember.

C: Are your students doing more or less "straight" fiction?

S: Yes. There's not much interest among students in detective story writing. They're interested in science fiction and fantasy and that's what's been in for ten or twelve years. So I usually require my students when they apply to take my course — they have to get my permission, anyway — to tell me if they want to write fantasy or science fiction. Then I say I really can't help them. If they did by chance want to write detective stories, I could help them, and I'd tell them I could, because I'm familiar with the genre.

C: Where are the writers coming from?

S: Most writers are going to come out of places like the University of Tennessee or the University of North Dakota, or they'll be dropouts from Ole Miss.

C: People used to say, "You're from *Ole Miss*?" and I'd remind them that it took us one year to produce a Nobel Prize winner in literature and it took Harvard four, and then he became British. What do you tell kids about the odds of becoming even moderately successful as a writer and making a modest sort of income from it?

S: I'm very honest. I don't encourage anybody to go into writing, largely because, as I said earlier, I think it's not really a healthy enterprise. I've just seen so much failure in writing: people who wanted to write, and have written books for years and never gotten them published, stick with it to no avail, and they were reasonably talented people, too.

C: Yes, I know some.

S: I certainly have read a number of books that could have been published and were better than 95 percent of the books that are published. And there's no money to be made from writing, unless . . . How many John Irvings are there? One in three thousand? I don't know what the odds are, but most of my students are going to end up teaching, and they realize they're going to have to teach if they're going to write; there are no illusions.

C: They don't aspire to do anything else for a living?

S: Most of them don't. They realize they're going to have to teach writing and therefore part of their battle is to get a job teaching writing, along with being able to write, because the two go hand in hand for them.

It didn't with me. My idea when I set out to write was to get as far away from the university as I could and never see the place again, but here I am a professor of English, and glad to be one.